FINANCIAL MARKETS AND THE BANKING SECTOR: ROLES AND RESPONSIBILITIES IN A GLOBAL WORLD

FINANCIAL HISTORY

Series Editor: Robert E. Wright

FINANCIAL MARKETS AND THE BANKING SECTOR: ROLES AND RESPONSIBILITIES IN A GLOBAL WORLD

EDITED BY
Elisabeth Paulet

LONDON AND NEW YORK

First published 2009 by Pickering & Chatto (Publishers) Limited

Published 2016 by Routledge
2 Park Square, Milton Park, Abingdon, Oxfordshire OX14 4RN
711 Third Avenue, New York, NY 10017, USA

First issued in paperback 2015

Routledge is an imprint of the Taylor & Francis Group, an informa business

© Taylor & Francis 2009
© Elisabeth Paulet 2009

BRITISH LIBRARY CATALOGUING IN PUBLICATION DATA
Financial markets and the banking sector : roles and responsibilities in a global world. -- (Financial history) 1. Financial institutions. 2. Banks and banking. 3. International finance. 4. Social responsibility of business. I. Series II. Paulet, Elisabeth, 1962–
332'.042–dc22

ISBN-13: 978-1-138-66334-3 (pbk)
ISBN-13: 978-1-8519-6652-3 (hbk)

Typeset by Pickering & Chatto (Publishers) Limited

CONTENTS

LIST OF FIGURES AND TABLES

INTRODUCTION

At the time of writing, the subprime mortgage crisis, despite the rescue plan of American and European governments, is still creating profound turbulence in the financial and real economic world. The extreme fluctuations on financial markets, solvency problems of banking institutions, lack of confidence of economic agents, who refuse to lend on a long-term basis are the new parameters to consider. The first victims are middle-class people and small and medium-sized enterprises, for which obtaining credit is becoming a nightmare. Confronted by these new elements, regulators, economists, nations and politicians face a very challenging situation. First, to stop the ongoing situation. Second, to solve the structural problem at its origin. To do so, the responsibilities of each actor have to be taken into consideration. Two parts will constitute this book: the first will focus on financial markets and specifically their role as regards financial stability in a global word; the second will give an insight into the banking sector with a special emphasis on Europe. The final objective is to give a hint of the actual situation as regards the integrity and/or transparency of the international financial system.

Part 1: Globalization and Financial Markets: a Dialectic Dynamics

The financial part will essentially focus on the evolution of global finance and its efficiency as regards international context. A few months ago, the New York Stock Exchange faced the greatest collapse of its markets since 1929. The question of the salvage of banking institutions was at the core of debate. Two antonymic paradigms were discussed: should the government and the central banker intervene in order to restore the confidence on the financial markets? Would it be more efficient to let insolvent institutions to leave the markets? The adoption of the Paulson plan illustrates a situation where the Americans have chosen to inject liquidity into economic markets to avoid banking runs. On the other side of the Atlantic, Europeans have chosen to adopt the same attitudes. For the first time in our history, a common decision was taken to limit an international financial crisis. The following chapters intend to provide an insight on the global context, in which these facts have occurred. The analytic elements, they propose, will help the reader to build up a critical analysis as regards the actual situation.

In the first chapter Michel Aglietta argues that shareholder value is the core principle of global finance. It is an intrinsically unbalanced principle for both financial stability and stake-holding on value creation in the corporate sector. It embodies a contradiction that has long been recognized: the separation between ownership and control. This contradiction has given rise to the 2002 crisis in corporate governance, which has struck pension funds and other institutional investors hard.

Because shareholder value cannot live up to its contention of being the one best way, it has given rise to competing models of corporate governance. In the last few years the structure of finance has developed to overcome the dilemma between ownership and control in implementing the concept of shareholder activism. Two competing models that have surged are positioned differently vis-à-vis the stock market. One is the model of hedge funds and private equity funds as dominant intermediaries between institutional investors and the corporate sector. The other is the model of institutional investors as universal owners, asserting their prominence on other financial intermediaries, including hedge funds and private equity funds. The paper analyses the capacity of both models to ensure financial stability and to fulfil the concern of corporate governance for social and environmental responsibility. Empirical evidence is brought about to show that the type of aggressive capitalism deployed by hedge funds and private equity funds entails very high hidden risks that will wreak havoc in more stringent monetary conditions. Furthermore private equity funds are serious threats for established social contracts and for the integrity of public services.

In the same line of ideas, Tristan Boyer and Elena Chane Alune argue that the securitization movement of the economy has a strong impact on corporate governance. In this context, the IASB has set a new framework for accounting and auditing. This framework has been designed to fit analysts' concern and shareholders' interests. As a consequence, this framework should induce analysts to lessen their need for other information than those provided by the accounting reports. Meanwhile, the IASB has launched a survey about adding a compulsory report of 'management commentaries' to existing financial statements. Some evidence show that the adoption of IFRS increases the need for non-financial information, they conclude that the securitization of accounting tends to broaden the analysts' perspective, and paradoxically to lessen the strict shareholder perspective they could have had.

Beside the question of standardization in accounting, ethical considerations could be important to understanding the place of financial centres in the globalization context. Though the case of Luxembourg financial centre, Jérôme Turquey aims to demonstrate that the ethical frontage of the self-regulated small country is definitely cracked, which is a threat for the international finance and raises the question of a certification to ethics for financial centres.

Luxembourg is probably not the worst financial centre, but the size and the lack of responsibility of many actors allows identifying ethical weaknesses, and realizing the limits of current international assessments in business ethics.

Therefore an actual certification to ethics for financial centres should be implemented, to go beyond the existing assessments. Six criteria should be taken into account:

1. Credibility of the ethical statements
2. Means for detection of improper business conduct
3. Credibility of sanctions
4. Transparency on issues
5. Independence of auditors
6. Protection of the client

In a nutshell the experience of the Luxembourg financial centre demonstrates the need to reinforce ethics in financial institutions and markets and to go beyond the current assessments.

As discussed before, the global situation could give difficulties for enterprises. Nadine Levratto tries to explicit the rules to improve the management of firms. The evolution of bankruptcy law is designed to achieve a number of objectives: economic security, creation and expansion of firms in a capitalist economy, protection of the interests of the agents involved in transactions that goes far beyond creditors and debtors, and prolongation of the activity of viable firms. This contribution examines the French insolvency law and its transformations since the nineteenth century from a concrete, historical standpoint which makes it possible to view the modifications and the uses of the legal rules in an economic and institutional context. We show that far from being only one means of selection by which the market could be cleared of its failing agents, France's bankruptcy law opens up a non-commercial space for the resolution of failures of market which, by releasing the actors of their former constraints, authorizes them to re-enter the business world.

To complete the preceding analysis of the global world, some specific arguments will be given as regards the European context. Miia Parnaudeau will develop the role of credit market in the European context of the securitization movement with low enhanced inflation pressure. As a consequence, the inflation rate might no longer stand relevant to explain economic fluctuations. Economic agents are facing financial instability. Hence, an appropriate definition for their anticipations is needed.

In H. P. Minsky's analysis, individuals' investment decisions are generating financial instability. But the fact that commercial banks get to financial markets in order to create more credit worsens the situation. Even if the Central Bank is limiting the credit offer, when commercial banks are using financial markets, they induce additional uncertainty for individuals. Consequently, individuals develop herding behaviours. In this chapter, these behaviours are illustrated by auto-realized anticipations on real assets' prices. Using a BIS database (treated by V. Arthur, C. Borio and P. Lowe) the evolution of real asset's prices in *Wicksellian* interest rate gaps is considered. On the basis of four countries (Germany, Spain, France and Italy), the results show that, according to K. Wicksell's intuition, a fall of the money market rate constitutes a leading signal for long term economic fluctuations. However, in our highly securitized European economies, long-term growth cycles are then better explained by auto-realized anticipations on real assets' prices. Anticipations on inflation no longer stand relevant. As a consequence, should European Central Bank target asset prices? Asset prices targeting could help to protect European economies from the financial instabilities that conduct long term fluctuations. But beyond European Central Bank's credibility to intervene (*ex ante* or *ex post*) on assets' prices, the results obtained in this paper suggest more to challenge monetary and prudential policies' efficiency.

Part 2: Globalization and Banking Institutions: Evolution of Their Role and Institutional Aspects

The second part will emphasize the role of banking institutions in globalization. This question is crucial, especially as regards the actual financial context. Banks are closely linked to the production and exchange. The activities of banks in the real economy are listed below:

- Clear and settle payments to facilitate trade and commerce,
- Aggregate and disaggregate wealth and flows of funds so that both large-scale and small-scale projects can be financed,
- Transfer economic resources over time, space and industries,
- Accumulate, process, and disseminate information for decision-making purposes,
- Provide ways for managing uncertainty and controlling risk,
- Provide ways for dealing with incentive and asymmetric-information problems that arise in financial contracting.

Considered as the principal responsible actor of the current situation, they react by becoming extremely cautious as regards the level of risk, they accept to bear. Hence, lending and refinancing activities are becoming more and more complicated, both for individual agents and enterprises. However, their intermediary role to provide liquidity to the real sphere is essential to recreate the necessary forces to stimulate growth. On this point, Europe and the United States face the same difficulties. The following chapters intend to analyse the delicate situations of banking institutions. The arguments proposed will lead the contributors to redefine their core business and incite most of them to replace the research of maximum profit with the concept of an optimum profit.

To begin with, let us consider the European case with its profound transformations. Kurt von Mettenheim reviews banking and public policy toward banking and finance in Continental Europe to reassess development strategies in Brazil and Latin America. Given the shift away from the Washington Consensus favoring privatization and liberalization, continental European experiences provide new perspective for developing countries. This chapter reviews the literature on several major Continental European countries, trends in public and non-profit banking sectors and the impact of bank-centred financial system on distribution of income and sustainable development. Special attention is given to government banking, development banks, savings banks and the financial dimensions of more socially ethical, coordinated market economies.

Caroline Vincensini will then explore the challenges facing the policy mix in Central Europe (Hungary, Poland and the Czech Republic) since the beginning of the 2000s. In a context of disinflation via direct inflation targeting and of preparation for EMU entry and struggle to catch up with the UE 15, clashes were observed between independent central banks and governments, leading to several conflicts on the policy mix and on the status of the central bank. How can these conflicts be explained? Are they related to insufficient credibility of the central banks, as was already suggested in the case of the conflicts opposing the ECB and the national governments in the first years of EMU? Or are other factors involved, such as lack of credibility of fiscal policies and imperfections of the institutional framework? The first two parts of the chapter outline the institutional and economic framework of monetary and fiscal policies in Central Europe, to identify the constraints weighing on them and to show their objectives often diverge. The third part exposes the policy mix conflicts observed in each country, identifying in each case the precise chronology, the sources and themes of the disagreements and whether the conflict mainly concerned the policy mix or attempts by the government to modify the central bank's legal status. The fourth part of the chapter explores whether these conflicts may be explained by a lack of central bank credibility, and suggests that the problem also lies with fiscal policies. The fifth part argues first that these conflicts are fuelled by diverging policy objectives, political factors and by the often excessive fiscal policies of the governments, then by the institutional framework. These conflicts will therefore probably not disappear mechanically upon entry into EMU. This result opens up an interesting normative debate on the improvement of the institutional framework, which can only take place at the European level.

Ingrid Größl will focus on the credit market. It has become a widespread practice among banking institutions to charge higher loan interest rates from households with lower incomes. In this chapter it is shown that the 'lower-income-higher-risk' argument which characterizes the economic perspective is flawed, and may lead to discrimination. Proceeding to the ethical perspective and in doing so, distinguishing between teleological and discourse ethics, it is shown that according to both positions, charging higher interest rates from lower income borrowers constitutes discrimination. However, both positions differ regarding their normative consequences for the behaviour of lending banks. Whereas teleological approaches shift responsibilities to the institutional environment, discourse ethics does not release banks from an ethical responsibility, irrespective of competitive pressures.

Elisabeth Paulet and Francesc Relano will hence give an insight on 'ethical' and 'alternative' banks. Their objective is to comply with these new demands of society. At the same time, 'traditional' banks have also tried to attract these new clients. They have thus stressed their commitment to sustainable development, for instance by signing the Equator principles or by issuing SRI products. Either way, at first sight it is not easy to tell the difference between the ethical/alternative banking born in the 1980s and the traditional banks recently committed to a more social/environmental approach. And yet, they are not at all the same. This chapter will show that beyond the threshold of ethical or sustainable banking, still compliant to some degree with refined 'greenwash', or the superficial moralization of the economy, there are some few institutions which act as real alternative banks. We shall illustrate this point through an analysis of the WIR Bank and its specific counter-cyclical behaviour within the Swiss banking system as regards the credit policy.

This book intends then to inform the reader about the amplitude, effects and consequences of this new international crisis. Far from answering all remaining questions, it intends to alert professionals and researchers about incautious attitudes of investors in financial sphere, which induces lasting turbulence for the real economy.

PART 1: GLOBALIZATION AND FINANCIAL MARKETS: A DIALECTIC DYNAMIC

Since the 1980s, the global financial system has faced several crises which forced regulators to consider new conjectural and structural problems. After a period of expansion for the world economy, the cycle has gradually moved towards a smoothed rate of growth which has implied a revision of economic and financial objectives.

The emergence of new partners like China and India has increased the amount of liquidity necessary to support economic development. Pressures on primary goods have led to a general increase of prices and the return of inflation for most developed countries.

These fluctuations of prices have made speculative strategies more valuable. At the same time, investors have adopted more and more risky attitudes. Financial scandals (Enron, WorldCom, Parmalat, etc) and several crises (New Technologies Bubbles, the subprime crisis, etc) enable economists and financial analysts to the following conclusions. First systemic risk has increased during the last thirty years. To solve this problem, regulators have led rules to evaluate information more efficiently (for example, in the implementation of the IFRS). If necessary, the actual crisis illustrates that it far from sufficient. Auditing agencies, in charge of evaluating information and risk for both enterprises and banking institutions have failed to provide investors and regulators with adequate data regarding the value of their clients. More improvement towards their independence should be made to guarantee their efficiency.

Second, long-term strategy must prevail over short-term financial decisions. The recent collapses of exchange places despite rescue measures (both in the United States and in Europe) exhibit the importance of anticipation as a factor in reaching stability for financial markets. Actually, both governments and regulators deploy enormous effort to re-establish the proper conditions for an effective functioning of the real economic sphere. Therefore, recreating a confident atmosphere for our international world appears to be a difficult problem to solve.

Third, aggressive capitalism has exhibited its limits. The bankruptcies of several banks in Europe and over-indebtedness all around the world have led to an enormous amount of liquidity whose primary use was essentially speculative investment. The last crisis has shown the necessity of reconsidering this form of capitalism to re-establish the bases of new stable market forces for enterprises and economic agents. Hence, a more sustainable approach could be considered in order to reach not only economic efficiency but also global social welfare. In this first part, contributors intend to give an insight into the major factors which can support all the above arguments.

1 TOWARDS A NEW MODEL OF LONG-TERM FINANCE

Michel Aglietta

Introduction: The Teachings of the Credit Crisis for Long-Run Investors

The so-called subprime crisis started as a local disturbance in a particular segment of the US mortgage market. It quickly became a global credit crisis, harming the huge securitized credit markets. The acute contagion that enabled such a disruption reveals much more than a temporary market failure. The widespread and persistent distortions in market pricing and financial firms' incentives points to structural flaws in the global financial system.

Under lax monetary conditions and low inflation, the tremendous expansion of the financial system has not followed economic value creation. It has drained massive rents from the economy. To illustrate the point, in 1980 the share of profits captured by the US financial sector was 10% of total profit in the corporate sector. In 2007 it reached 40%. Meanwhile the financial sector makes up 5% of employment and 15% of value added of the corporate sector.

The way the expansion arose suggests that the process could not go on forever. In the quarter of a century from 1982, the stock market capitalization of the US corporate sector was multiplied by 6. Within this tremendous growth, the share of the financial sector jumped from 6% to 19%. The counterpart of this rush to asset accumulation was the explosion of leverage. The share of debt in the financial sector was 10% of debt of the corporate sector in 1980. It surged to 50% in 2007.

These amazing figures simultaneously highlight and hide a change in financial paradigm. Finance has mutated from a model of credit servicing the economy to quite a different one. From a micro-financial basis based upon the division of risk, endogamic transactions within the financial sector have proliferated under the pretext of risk transfer. They have created an endogenous force whereby market intermediaries have generated fat fees at each stage of the chain of risk transfer. Prodded by leverage, the process was an incentive to aggressive risk-taking that could last a long time thanks to hedging via derivatives. All types of credit were liable to the breakup of complex risk in elementary risk factors and repackaging in synthetic financial products: mortgage credit, LBO financing, leveraged share buybacks, the purchase of distressed securities and other transactions performed by hedge funds

An investment-bank model of credit rose to prominence to link the origination of loans and the channelling of risks to institutional investors. It entailed a paradox in financial organization. Long-run investors collecting the main share of savings and bearers of social liabilities have become passive holders of risks they did not understand. Their failure to discipline market intermediaries has supported the rise in credit expansion and an asset price bubble that has led to financial disaster. Nonetheless the hope of financial reorganization to a more robust system rests on those actors.

A reorganization in finance is something that cannot be taken for granted but cannot be dismissed. For many years after World War II the credit model was based upon commercial banks. They initiated credit and bore the risk. The model serviced the economy rather well, supporting sustained growth. It was highly regulated and very robust to financial crises. However, it was tolerant to inflation that eroded the value of debts. Because the trend of inflation rose from one cycle to another, the model was rejected with the dramatic turnaround of monetary policy at the turn of the 1980s.

Financial liberalization was an outcome of the disinflationary era. The investment banking model of credit *'originate and distribute'* was an offspring of deregulation. It has become paramount since the development of credit derivatives in the late 1990s. This model has facilitated an expansion of credit much larger than the former model in which credit remains in bank balance sheets. However, in the chain of risk transfer, information has deteriorated and incentives has been perverse, leading to severe undervaluation of risk. Because central banks hamper debt deflation, the ratio of debt to GDP rises from one cycle to another. The drift in indebtedness replaced the drift in inflation until the means to eschew debt deflation became ineffective. It is why the present financial crisis is the most serious in the latest half-century.

It is likely that the long upward trend of debt and liquidity relative to world GDP has reached its limits. Credit will become more expensive and profit of market intermediaries will be curbed by tighter regulation. Meanwhile the world economy will still need financing huge investments in emerging market countries. They are long-run investment in infrastructure, education and technology to boost growth potential, so that those countries catch up with developed countries. This growth regime will replace the pattern of growth driven by US over consumption. It will be financed less by credit and more by capital. This is the realm of long-run financial investors. They will get out of their passive dependence to financial market intermediaries to raise to prominence. Who are they and what will be their strategies?

Who are the Long-Run Investors?

Long-run investors are part of the larger bundle of institutional investors. They are distinguished by the nature of their liabilities. Four types of long-run investors can be distinguished: perennial funds without contractual liabilities to individuals, reserve funds created to smooth pay-as-you-go retirement systems, defined benefit pension funds, insurance companies.

According to IMF data, perennial funds and reserve funds held $2,800 billion in assets at 2006 yearend. Pension funds held $21,600 billion with 60% under defined benefit contracts. Insurance companies weighed $18,500 billion worldwide. All in all this means that about $34,260 billion are under the control of long-run investors and $30,240b are managed without liability commitment: $8,640 by defined contribution pension funds, $19,300 by mutual funds and $2,300 by absolute return seeking hedge funds and private equity).

Types and Objectives of Long-Run Investors

– Perennial funds and reserve funds

These are sovereign wealth funds, endowment funds and public development banks. Their goal is to accumulate long-run assets and preserve their long-run real value. It is also to contribute to an institutional budget fed by the income drawn from their investments. Some of them take capital participation to foster economic development. Their objectives are defined and overseen by a government or an academic authority.

The most important entities in this category are sovereign wealth funds (SWF), which have made the headlines lately. Their resources come either from foreign exchange reserves or from commodities (mostly oil). Table 1.1 gathers the characteristics of the most important SWFs created in emerging and some developed countries.

Table 1.1: Characteristics of the main sovereign wealth funds

Countries	Name	Assets ($b)	Date of origin	Management	Allocation
United Arab Emirates	Abu Dhabi Invest Authority	875	1976	ADIA et ADIC	Unknown
Norway	Govern Pension Fund Global	380	1996	Norges Bank	60%equity 40% fixed income
Saudi Arabia	Multiple	300	Nd	Saudi Arabia Mon. Agency	Unknown

Countries	Name	Assets ($b)	Date of origin	Management	Allocation
Kuwait	General reserve future genera-tion	250	1953	Kuwait Inv. Authority	Domestic, regional, inter.
Singapore	Gov Inv. Corp	330	1981	Temasek Hold-ings	38% dom.
	Temasek	160	1974		40% Asia, 20%Oecd
China	China Inv. Corp	300	2007	SAFE	To be defined
Russia	Oil Stabilization Fund	127	2007	Central Bank of Russia	Bonds : 44%$, 46%€, 20%£
Libya	Oil Reserve Fund	50	2005	Gov Agency	na
Qatar	Qatar Inv. Auth	50	2005	Gov Agency	na
Algeria	Regulation Fund	42	2000	Gov Agency	na
Australia	Australian Future Fund	42	2006	Gov Special Agency	100% domestic
Brunei	Brunei Inv.Auth	30	1983	Brunei Inv. Agency	Global diversified
Korea	Korea Inv Corp	20	2005	Bank of Korea	Global diversified

Source: IMF and Morgan Stanley

The total amount of assets registered on Table 1.1 reaches $2,936 billion. The funds are managed by central banks or by government agencies. Most funds nurtured by the sale of oil are dedicated to the financing of pensions. The funds that manage foreign exchange will diversify much more than the narrow asset range allowed to central banks.

Sovereign wealth funds have a high potential to grow. According to IMF projections they might reach $10,000 billion in assets in 2012 and $12,000 in 2015. The growth is embodied into the persistent trade surpluses of emerging market countries and into the foreseeable rise in real commodity prices.

The reserve funds are designed to smooth out future financial constraints on pay-as-you-go pension systems. They are not perennial since they are programmed to decumulate their assets in the 2020–40 period. They should optimize the return of investments under a constraint of risk limit. For instance the opportunity cost of the French FRR is the average cost on public borrowing. Whenever the portfolio of the fund oversteps this threshold it creates a surplus for future financing of pensions. Since it has started its investment in June 2004, the FRR has gotten a 9.9% return on its portfolio against an opportunity cost of 4.4%.

– Pension funds and Insurance Companies

Table 1.2 gathers some order of magnitude in total assets for pension funds and insurance companies compared to mutual funds in the main developed countries. They are the biggest institutional investors. Pension funds are well-developed in Anglo-Saxon countries and in the Netherlands. Insurance companies are paramount in the Euro zone, the Netherlands and in Japan.

Pension funds collect contractual savings from employers and employees to provide retirement income. They are entities legally separated from their sponsors. Corporations are committed to contribute to funding the underlying pension plans. Trustees have fiduciary responsibilities.

Defined-benefit pension funds must provide retirement income equal to a predefined replacement ratio upon the end-of-working-life wage. In the fat years of the 1990s stock markets, private pension funds sponsored by corporations were underfunded because company executives relied on the appreciation of the funds' assets to meet the liabilities. The stock market crisis of 2001–2 revealed the extent of underfunding and prompted the conversion to defined-contribution pension plans mainly in the US.

Defined-contribution pension funds commit employers to specified contributions only. They reject the risks on both human capital and financial returns on the individual wage earners. Since they offer no guarantee, the members of the plans might end up with income insufficient to live a decent retirement life. Therefore it is up to the government to insure the plans. Correlatively it must regulate the management of the defined-contribution funds, so that their asset allocation respects the same principles as defined-benefit funds.

Market-value accounting due to the adoption of IFRS accelerated the shift because it precluded the license given to the corporations to spread the losses of their funds on a long period of time. The new accounting rule (IFRS17) stipulates, on the contrary, that all surpluses and deficits on the balance sheets be acknowledged in real time. It is why the UK and the Netherlands with big defined-benefit pension funds have reformed the regulation of their pension funds significantly.

Table 1.2: Total financial assets of institutional investors

Billions of U$	Insurance Cies		Pension Funds		Mutual Funds	
	1995	2005	1995	2005	1995	2005
Australia	128	241	146	566	48	700
Canada	172	391	230	550	155	491
UK	798	1979	760	1487	201	547
US	2804	5601	4216	7305	3526	8905
Euro Zone	1871	4664	nd	1194	1378	4307
Of which:						
France	642	1614	0	32	534	1363
Germany	779	1573	140	283	138	
Italy	120	528	nd	29	130	297
Luxembourg	8	53	nd	nd	338	451
Netherlands	162	407	335	749	65	1636
						126
Japan	2999	3243	731	997	420	470

Source: Investment Company Institute

The UK Pensions Act of November 2004 spells out the discount rate to value liabilities. This is a moving average of inflation-indexed government bonds. The law creates a public regulator of pensions and the Protection Pension Fund (PPF) to guarantee the members of a pension plan whose sponsor has become insolvent or grossly underfunded. As an insurance scheme for DB pension funds, the PPF is financed by a levy on the sponsors, modulated on the risk of insolvency.

The UK reform is an advance of public regulation with significant effect on the asset allocation of DB pension funds. It makes liability commitment the benchmark of asset allocation and thus provides an incentive for an effective long-run asset management, conform to the horizon of those investors.

In contrast to the UK, where irresponsible trustees were commonplace, Dutch pension funds (97% DB) are supervised by committees including all social partners. They have kept sound finances so IFRS has had not much impact yet. Nonetheless, new legislation in January 2007 imposes a solvency constraint on pension funds based on the value-at-risk.

Insurance companies differ from pension funds in so far as they are subjected by law to the matching in duration between both sides of their balance sheets. The requirement induces multiple restraints that limit their freedom in managing their assets. The liability restraints are a minimum warranted return on life insurance contracts, the tacit renewal of contracts, the redemption of contracts at face value at the initiative of the customer without penalty, the respect of contractual commitment with a probability $\geq 95\%$, and the provisioning of unrealized losses.

Furthermore there is a crucial mismatch of valuation between assets and liabilities. The former must be marked-to-market; the latter must be valued at their amortized cost. The asymmetry leads to the volatility of net profits. The answer lies in asset liability management, which entails a substantial reduction of the share of equities in portfolios and the increase in the share of government bonds.

The Need of Long-Term Finance

In a global economy the sources of saving and the opportunities of investment depend on the world growth regime. Two fundamental trends dominate the first half of the twenty-first century. On the one hand, the differentiated world demographic transition entails major discrepancies in saving amongst regions of the world. On the other hand, world growth is going to slow down with the world labour force. But differences in growth between developed and emerging countries will pertain and might widen. Investment opportunities will arise more and more in non-OECD big continental economies. Both evolutions will have a large impact on financial investments.

– Demographic transition and life-cycle saving

The demographic transition encompasses a dual tendency of lower fertility and higher longevity. The process is sequential amongst regions and spans the very long run. In developed countries the process has reached a phase where countries are aging from the top of the age pyramid under the prevalence of rising longevity. In developing countries the decline in fertility is much more recent and less advanced. They are aging from the bottom of the age pyramid. These differences impact the weight of population that save the most in the life cycle to build up assets for retirement, e.g. the population aged 45–69 (Figure 1.1). It follows that the aggregate rate of saving in the world regions depends upon the evolution of demographic structures in the long run.

The sequential nature of the demographic transition provokes a propagation of the high savers ratio from region to region throughout the half century to 2050. Long before 2050 the ratio will have peaked in Japan, Europe and Russia, followed by North America and China. Other regions will be in their upward stage. In emerging regions of the world, compulsory funded pension systems will be established, spurred by progressive aging. Huge amounts of contractual saving will be gathered by public and private pension funds. In Asian countries, where saving is already high but captured by low-yield bank deposits, financial systems will be transformed by the rise of institutional investors, including sovereign wealth funds.

The financial crisis will rebalance growth toward emerging countries with gigantic needs of public investments.

Figure 1.1: Differences in demographic factors of saving

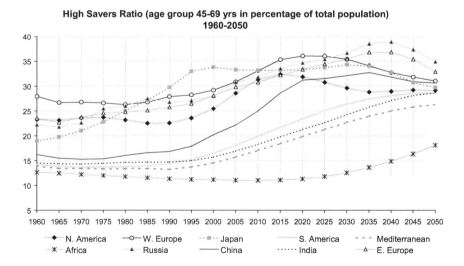

Investment Opportunities, Technological Catching up and Growth in Emerging Countries

Demographic trends are conducive to a potentially profitable intergenerational exchange between a dynamic labour-force-cum-scarce-capital in emerging countries and a declining labour-force-cum-intensive-capital in developed countries. It follows that a growth regime that transfers resources amongst world regions is formally possible (Figure 1.2).

Figure 1.2: A world growth regime

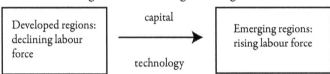

There are powerful impediments to such a grand prospect, however. The global financial system to channel saving and invest in growth-enhancing opportunities does not exist yet. The investment bank model of credit has financed US over-consumption with saving drained out of emerging countries, the exact opposite of Figure 1.2. The debacle of this model offers an opportunity to reorganize the financial system to seize the opportunity of boosting world growth. But it takes a long-run view on the opportunity of catching up to implement effectively the concept of a worldwide intergenerational exchange. Only long-run investors can do it. But it is not enough to correct the dysfunction in market finance, due to the confusion between investing and trading that has led to the demise of investment behaviour by institutional investors and to their passive surrender to asset managers for the sake of gambling. There is a more profound macroeconomic problem.

To transfer resources in the way highlighted on Figure 1.2, investment return must be higher in countries with abundant labour force and scarce capital. If this neo-classical assumption were true, higher savers in rich countries would transfer part of their saving through saving plans channelled by institutional investors. However the neo-classical assumption skips the social conditions of wealth accumulation. It has worth only in an economic universe without uncertainty, where perfect competition makes production factors perfectly substitutable.

The history of capitalism teaches quite another lesson. Capital and technology transfers must be assimilated by the host countries. This is a very hazardous process that triggers acute social tensions inimical to sustained growth. When social impediments to growth are not overcome, excess saving has the appearance of insufficiency in profitable investments. It means that growth is endogenous because it is conditional to political and social institutions. Mechanical neo-classical growth à la Solow must be replaced by an evolutionist model of Schumpeterian inspiration.

If growth is conditional to social processes that raise the social return of capital, it is path-dependent. Contrary to neoclassical growth, the social forces that make growth endogenous do so because they prevent the marginal return on capital to decrease with capital accumulation. Therefore growth depends on the saving rate contrary to the neo-classical model, on the proviso that saving be invested in specific investments that create the factors of growth impinging upon the marginal return on capital. Endogenous growth theory shows that these factors of growth are fostered by investments in education, infrastructure, networks, health care systems and R&D. These investments generate the social capital that is complementary to firms' assets and therefore sustains the profitability of all firms in the country, as much as they accumulate their own private capital.

Financing the production of such public goods in the long run is what distinguishes long-run investors on the asset side. They have the incentive to do so because enhancing the social return of capital matches their social responsibility on the liability side.

Mean Reverting Forces in Financial Markets

Long-run investors are patient investors. Their objectives are measured on long horizons, well over five years. They have, or should have, no incentive to play on the anomalies of financial markets to make elusive capital gains. Investing and trading are two quite different businesses. Conflicts of interests arise in delegated monitoring because of the disparities in timing. It follows that long-run investors have attitudes to market that differ from those of other participants. How do they interact with markets?

– Long-Run Investors and Market Prices

The standard mean variance model of asset allocation is time-invariant. There are strict conditions for the allocation to stay optimal, while time has entered the picture.[1] The returns on assets must be IID (independently and identically distributed). With IID returns, there is no innovation, no new opportunity of investment that can be exploited. Because time is deterministic under this assumption, it can be demonstrated that the optimal structure of the portfolio is constant over time.

Not only is an IID pattern of randomness a caricature of uncertainty that is irrelevant empirically, but it violates what long-run investors are all about. They are intermediaries whose very purpose is to invest beyond cyclical variations, to make allowance of time correlation between asset returns and to deal with non-Gaussian stochastic patterns over uncertain horizons.

The common explanation for the deviations from the standard approach is *the mean-reverting force in the long run.*[2] A long investment horizon can capture this process, while a short horizon cannot. Mean-reverting processes do not imply that the long-run values of bond and equity yields are stationary. They pinpoint that there are co-integration relations between the yields in the basic market securities and structural variables of the economy that are stationary in the long run.[3]

The mean-reverting force pinpointed in long-run analysis is shown on Figure 1.3. It arises for bonds and equities. The variability of their returns declines with the horizon. On the contrary, short-term bills are more and more volatile with the horizon because they must be reinvested at a more and more uncertain yield, which is linked to the random variations of the short-run interest rate.

Figure 1.3 shows also that the correlation between bond and stock return is not monotonous. Therefore with a long horizon the investor should increase its share of both bonds and stocks in her portfolio.

Because the volatility of equity returns is always higher than the volatility of government bond returns, bonds make the benchmark of asset in long-run portfolios. It can be either nominal bonds, inflation-indexed bonds or a mix of both types of securities, depending upon the inflation regime investors anticipate in their scenarios and the confidence they assign on their anticipations.

Figure 1.3: Variability of asset returns and correlation between bond and stock returns as a function of the horizon

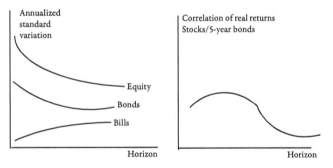

Source: C. Campbell and L. M. Viceira, 'The Term Structure of the Risk-Return Tradeoff', *Financial Analysts Journal*, 61:1, pp.34–44

– Possible Impact of Long-Run Investors on Bond and Equity Prices

Perennial funds and pension funds have quite different liabilities. Amongst perennial funds, sovereign wealth funds have the fastest growth. Their infinite horizon and their lack of contractual obligations to private agents make them eager to invest in equities. Conversely, pension funds and insurance companies face tougher regulation and accounting rules that make them more prone to invest in bonds. Therefore trends on the demand side are mixed. On the supply side large bond markets are sure to develop in emerging Asia.

The price effect of a rising demand for public bonds by institutional investors depends on the price elasticity of demand and on the supply of government bonds. Regulatory changes and the trauma of the credit crisis should induce an overhauling of portfolios towards government bonds and investment grade corporate bonds. According to an OECD study, the income drawn from the existing outstanding of long government bonds does not cover the obligations of investors because of future benefits to retirement plan members in the US and in the UK. Since tighter regulation compels pension funds to hedge their liabilities, an excess demand of ten years and over maturity should ensue. In the US alone the Treasury evaluates this excess demand at $300 billion. However, the demand pressure would be progressive enough and homogenous in required maturities. The supply of bonds would have enough time to adjust by issuing securities of longer maturities. Under a smooth portfolio adjustment, long-run interest rates would decline modestly by 10 to 15bp. Nonetheless in the UK, where regulatory changes have been more drastic and where DB pension funds have a much larger share of institutional saving than in the US and in Continental Europe (except in the Netherlands), real interest rates on very long maturities (30 years and over) are lower than in the US and in the Euro zone.

Conversely, sovereign wealth funds are more risk-taking. They are going to exert a growing demand for equities along with their expansion. Subsequently, capital flows will change: fewer loans and more equities. Corporations will be able to reverse the fashion to indebtedness and share buybacks. They will strengthen their capital structure and reduce leverage. In banking, sovereign funds inject capital directly. They stabilize the financial system in smoothing the absorption of bank losses by debt deflation. It can also be hoped that their mounting influence will reduce the incentive to unreasonably high financial returns that had fostered the drive to unsustainable indebtedness. Patient investors looking for yield close to the economic return on capital may promote a model of finance where investment banks and shadow banks adjust to the objectives of investors rather than the reverse.

The Strategic Behaviour of Long-Run Investors

Institutional investors are growing in size. Some have contractual obligations on their liabilities, others are financial vectors of the state. They must bear risks that financial markets cannot diversify away: risks embedded in the life-cycle of individuals and risks stemming from social and environmental issues. The conditions of their activity lead them to take a long-run view. They must be able to rest upon theoretical advances in finance dealing with inter-temporal asset allocation. However, this field of finance is rife with academic controversies and unable to recommend a clear articulation between strategic goals and tactical management.

Indeed, time alters the theoretical principles of portfolio diversification inherited from Markowitz and from Sharpe's capital asset pricing model (CAPM). However institutional investors with multi-period commitments must build dynamic asset allocations fed by prospective views. They are led to give up the dichotomy between strategy and tactic for an empirical, flexible and unified approach.

Another evolution that rebukes the traditional doctrine is delegated management. The problem of delegation has taken a crucial importance because investors have embodied alternative assets in their portfolios that require active management. Those new types of assets raise hard questions because they bear hidden risks with possible systemic implications. Being highly illiquid and not driven by mean-reverting processes, those asset classes entail risks that are not properly monitored by investors.

Principles of Strategic Asset Allocation

The optimal model of portfolio allocation is static. Theoreticians have searched the conditions enabling the multi-period optimal choice to be the same as it is on a single period. The conditions are drastically limited: the random returns on the assets must be IID and relative risk-aversion must be constant. The hypothesis that is untenable empirically is the IID distribution. With time-varying volatility and correlation, mean-reverting processes are the main characteristics that can help investors structure a dynamic allocation to suit their needs.

– Time-Varying Investment Opportunities, Mean-Reverting Returns and Dynamic Asset Allocation

Keeping the assumption of constant relative risk aversion, because, empirically, risk premia seem independent on the level of wealth, and making a log-linear approximation for wealth variation, it is possible to generalize the CAPM. The excess return of risky assets over riskless asset is a linear function of the covariance between the return of that particular asset and the return of the portfolio like in the CAPM. It depends also on the covariance between the return of the risky asset and the revision of expectations on future returns of the portfolio.[4]

It is why a long-run investor can take government bonds as the least risky asset, while short-term securities are riskier. If the market return on bonds is higher than the average long-run return, an investor that makes allowance for mean reversion will revise downwards its expectations of future returns. The correlation between these revisions and the present rise in the return of the bonds is negative. Therefore a forward-looking investor views the bonds as less risky than a myopic investor.

It follows that the optimal share of bonds in the portfolio of forward-looking investors compounds two parts. The first stems from a demand identical to the myopic investor. The second is the inter-temporal hedging against the prospect of lower returns in the future. The second part disappears only if future interest rates can be held constant. Conversely, the more risk averse the investor and the higher the volatility of interest rates, the higher the inter temporal hedging that leads to a larger share of government bonds in the portfolio. It ensues that the benchmark asset for a long-run investor is a long bond: a nominal bond if the future monetary regime is expected to be low and stable, an inflation-indexed bond if it is expected to be high and variable.

Then inter-temporal hedging applies to equities also, since it has been shown empirically that they exhibit mean-reverting returns (Figure 1.3). Figure 1.4 portrays the strategic allocation of a long-run investor, compared to the allocation of a tactical speculator and the buy-and-hold allocation of a naïve investor.[5] The tactical allocation has no consideration for inter temporal hedging since it focuses on short-term capital gains. If the expected excess return of equities over bonds is zero, the trader holds no shares. It is the reason that the upward-sloping line describing her allocation starts from the origin. It crosses the horizontal line that portrays the constant allocation of the naïve investor at the point where the expectation of the tactical investor is equal to the non-conditional average return (m). Strategic allocation is represented by a line that is both above the tactical allocation and more upward sloping because of the inter temporal hedging. The allocation contains equities even if the expected short-term return is zero, since a return much lower than m induces the investor to expect much higher returns in the future.

The strategic allocation is precisely determined if the average long-run mean of equity return is expected without uncertainty. Strategic asset allocation must be time-flexible, not only because it depends on mean-reversion but because the mean itself, e.g. the fundamental value of equities is uncertain. This is why a long-run investor must rely on value analysis.[6] She must be able to distinguish cyclical variations that impinge upon market price changes relative to the fundamental values of equities and structural factors that alter fundamental equilibrium values themselves. Cyclical factors are those which affect the relative supply of securities in the business cycle (variations in interest rates and companies' profits, changes in risk aversion of investors and in credit conditions).

Figure 1.4: Proportion of equities in portfolio as a function of investment
opportunities

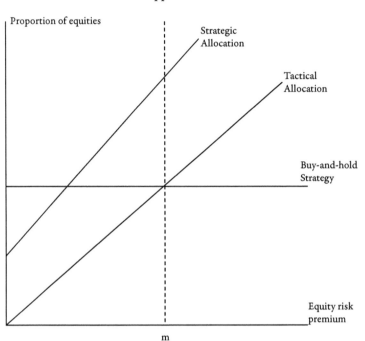

Source: Campbell and Viceira *Strategic Asset Allocation*, Figure 4.1

The structural factors that impinge upon fundamental values of equities are
threefold:

- Changes in the demographic structure, investment in human capital and
  enhancements in health systems that influence household saving in the
  life cycle
- Technological advances that boost total factor productivity and growth
  potential, thus increase the long-run real return on capital
- Changes in monetary regimes that make more likely that real risks or
  inflationary risks are preponderant.

Investors observe the market price of securities. However, the consequences
for strategic asset allocation are different depending on whether the source of
price variation is in structural changes, in cyclical fluctuations or in fuzziness in
market perception. Mean reversion can be expected and embedded in the algo-
rithm of portfolio optimization for the last two sources of change. If structural
changes are at stake, the underlying parameters of the model of allocation must

be revised. It is what value analysis is all about. It must help defining prospective macroeconomic scenarios that enable strategic managers to make basic assumptions on the fundamental equilibrium value of bonds and equities at definite horizons. It is why strategic allocations are dynamic according to two dimension of time: the cyclical reversible that is captured by mean reversion and the irreversible that shapes fundamental real returns.

– Making Allowance for Liability Commitments: Asset Liability Management (ALM)

Any pension fund must fulfill the objective of the underlying pension plan: delivering a desired consumption flow to its members throughout the retirement. The discounted value of anticipated consumption determines the value of the fund at retirement that should have been accumulated along the working life.

Random variables generated by the liability side must be accounted for to define a working strategy: date of retirement, human capital and real estate wealth of the members. Human capital is the most critical variable. At each point of time it is the discounted value of expected future salaries until retirement. Both human capital and real estate have bond-type risk profiles: finite maturities and flows of revenues less random than dividends. Therefore if income from human capital is reasonably steady, the pension fund portfolio should keep a high proportion of equities when the plan member is young (human capital high). The portfolio structure should shift toward a lower share of equities and a higher share of bonds as long as the individual gets nearer retirement age.

This is the basic tenet of asset liability management (ALM) the principle of which was established by Sharpe and Tint.[7] Any contractual liability that is the source of predefined future payment must be considered as a non-negotiable debt or as a negative asset by the pension fund. The optimal diversification of the portfolio must hedge the risks of the liabilities as a prerequisite and maximizes the surplus. Therefore the portfolio must contain assets that have a positive covariance with liabilities. Because the liability side is constraining (it embodies social commitments), the asset side must be managed to provide a hedge. It follows that the optimal portfolio is different from the strategic portfolio defined here above.

The surplus (S) is the difference between the value of the asset side (A) and the liability side (L) multiplied by the weight (k varying between 0 and 1) that the asset manager grants to the hedge of liabilities:

S=A-kL. For a DB pension fund, whose liabilities are legally binding, k=1. At the opposite end, a DC pension fund that rejects entirely the liability risks on the plan members behaves as if k=0. It is not distinguishable from a mutual fund. DC pension funds that recognize the correlation between asset and liabilities and that are subject to solvency and funding regulation without providing legal guarantees, have weights nearer to 1 the stricter their supervision is.

Pension fund managers meet the problems of dynamic optimization analyzed above: but they are applied to the surplus. The further problem comes from the measure of risks due to the random variables that shape liabilities and from the difficulty of making hypotheses on their long-run changes.

The variation of wages during the working life is the paramount variable. For the plan members, the flow of wage income over remaining working life is an implicit asset that must crowd out explicit assets of similar characteristics in her pension plan. If wage income is steady, the pension fund portfolio should be heavily biased toward equities while the plan member is young, the equity share declining progressively from age 35 or so to the age at retirement.[8] Figure 1.5 depicts a simulation that highlights the portfolio adjustment to the age of the contributor.

Figure 1.5: Optimal share of equities in pension funds at different ages of contributors with stable wage income

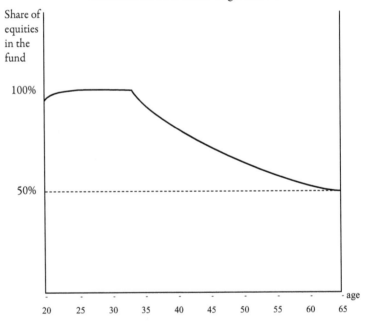

Source: D. Blake, A. Cairns and K. Dowd, 'Turning pension plans into pension planes : what investment strategy designers of defined contribution plans can learn from commercial aircraft designers', Pensions Institute Discussion Paper, PI-0806, April 2008

If wage income is uncertain, the optimal portfolio structure depends crucially on the degree of correlation of wages with the yield of risky financial assets in the fund portfolio. If the correlation is high, the relation with the age of the contributor should be reversed. The portfolio should favour bonds to offset the weight of risky human capital and the proportion of equities should rise with age as much as the weight of human capital declines.

Since the risks on the liability side are difficult to assess, there are pitfalls in optimal management. It is why ALM uses more empirical and less sophisticated methods. The method that eliminates completely the mismatch between the cash-in flows from the asset side and the cash-out flows from the liability side is cash-flow matching. The surplus is always zero. However the perfect hedge is rarely accessible. Liabilities are long. They reach maturities for which there are not enough liquid markets for the adequate hedging assets. Moreover liability commitments often include hidden options that have no counterparts in available financial options.

It is why empirical techniques often use straight immunization and contingent immunization. Straight immunization is a proxy for hedging that bears on durations. It fits very risk-averse investors. For those investors, minimizing risk is nearly equivalent to surplus maximization. Contingent immunization is an asymmetric technique that compromises between the riskless approach of cash-flow matching and a risky approach that does not consider liability restraints. It leads to the core satellite organization of pension fund management. The core is a standard portfolio that invests in plain vanilla marketable assets with low transaction cost. It tries to match duration in assets and liabilities. Satellite pockets look for high returns free of liability restraints. They are the realms of alternative assets, are actively managed and use delegation to professional asset managers. Introducing reasonably alternative assets in portfolios implies for investors a solid knowledge of their risk characteristics and a capacity to monitor the delegated managers. Investors have rushed into alternative assets in the early 2000s without the ability to satisfy these conditions. The results have been heavy losses in the mortgage credit crisis.

Problems with Alternative Assets and Delegated Management

Alternative assets comprise two categories: real estate and infrastructure on the one hand, absolute return assets (hedge funds and private equity) on the other. As much as those assets have a low covariance with equities they can be used to diversify risk.

Real estate and infrastructure are hybrid assets. Their streams of income are rents and leases that hedge against inflation. They can hedge against future inflation risks like indexed bonds. Their ownership value fluctuates like equities, but they are not strongly correlated with equities. Infrastructures are very long term. They stem from the privatization of the public domain (airports, ports, railway tracks, highways, telecom networks, etc...). Residential real estate is more cyclical, but its fluctuations may have low or negative correlation with equities. It is closer to a debt instrument. Only commercial real estate is closer to equities.

This type of assets is alternative because it is highly illiquid and because there is no reliable benchmark to anchor a passive management. It is necessary to resort to specialists of specific markets to detect investment opportunities.

The fancy of investors for absolute return assets is quite another matter. Directly or via funds of funds, pension funds have become large investors in hedge funds (HF) and in private equity funds (PE) (Figures 1.5a and 1.5b).

– Incentives to invest into absolute return funds

Hedge funds and private equity funds have created a form of ownership within the larger category of investment funds, which exert a profound influence on the whole economy. According to Hedge Fund Research (HFR), a data provider, there were 10,500 hedge funds in the world in 2006. Total assets under that alternative management class amounted to $1.4 trillion. It was less than $150 billion in 1997. Nowadays hedge funds manage about 8–10% of assets under management in the US mutual fund industry and 7% in Europe where the phenomenon is relatively recent. Their share has been growing rapidly until the financial crisis caught them unawares.

HF and PE funds are private investment vehicles, the management of which is quite opaque. There is a dearth of data, besides which are widely disparate amongst the four only providers.[9] The databases are plagued with severe biases. The *self-reporting bias* stems from voluntary reporting. When a fund has reached its optimal size, it is closed to new investors and thus has no interest in reporting. The same arises with funds whose performance is mediocre. The *database selection bias* refers to the variety of criteria used by the data providers to select funds. Therefore the databases cover a modest part of the universe of hedge funds and they are far from overlapping.[10] The *survivorship bias* is due to the withdrawal from the data of the funds which has ceased to provide information. Since they are the bankrupt funds and those with bad performance, indices based upon the data grossly overestimate the average performance.

The piling up of biases come up to hugely different estimates of performance for the same strategies.[11] It ensues that institutional investors devoting a portfolio segment to alternative assets have no reliable means to monitor the activity of the delegated managers. The shortcomings are all the more serious when institutional investors have become prominent investors in hedge funds (Figure 1.6a).

Figure 1.6a: Global hedge funds by sources of capital

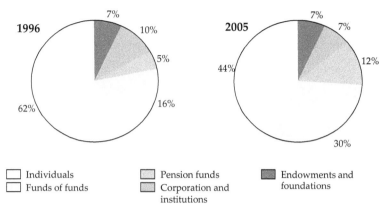

Source: Hennessee Group LLC.

In 1996 wealthy individuals, risking their own money and able to take care of themselves, made by far the largest share of total assets. In 2005 their share had shrunk dramatically. The share of pension funds and funds of funds, which channelled the saving, collected by mutual funds, had doubled. Whether corporations, insurance companies, endowments and foundations are included, public money make 56% of assets at stake. And this share is fast increasing. Therefore the lack of investor protection and of disclosure requirement becomes intolerable.

The surge in private equity funds has been as much spectacular in Europe as the one in hedge funds. A most recent report by the PSE group of the European Parliament highlights clearly the similarity and the differences between HFs and PE funds.[12] 'Private equity funds are similar to hedge funds in some respects. Both are lightly regulated, private pools of capital that invest in securities and pay their managers high fees as a share of a fund's profits. But there are also substantial differences. Most hedge funds invest in arbitrage between different securities of the class, either fixed income or equities. Private equity funds invest much more directly in relation to the 'real economy', i.e. directly in companies. These are very illiquid assets, such as early-stage companies and buy-outs of bigger, established companies. Consequently, investors are 'locked in' for the entire term of the fund. There are, however, examples of hedge funds investing in private equity companies' acquisition funds'.

Hedge funds and PE funds alike have benefited from the interest of pension funds that are the dominant investors (24%). Investment banks and large commercial banks follow them (18%). The third contributors are Funds of Funds, e.g. hedge funds themselves (13%). The share of wealthy individuals, dominant in the mid-1990s, has shrunk to 6% (Figure 1.6b).

Figure 1.6b: Sources of new funds raised in private equity (2005)

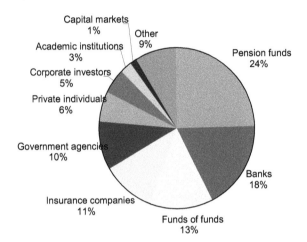

Source: EVCA/PWC/Thomson Financial

The fancy for private equity has made it a significant share of investment in US public pension funds, with 8% of asset under management. The assumptions that underline the drive of institutional investors for this 'alternative asset class' are a supposed higher net yield than tradable assets and low correlation with tradable assets. These assumptions are questionable.

The problem of risk assessment is acute because institutional investors' craze for hedge funds and private equity funds has been spurred on by shareholders' pressure for high yields in a benign financial environment of abundant liquidity and low long-term interest rates. Underestimates of risks might be conducive to disappointing outcomes for the ultimate savers.

– Hidden Risks in Absolute Return Funds

Hedge fund managers boast that they can achieve high returns and low volatility because they allocate to eschew the impact of stock market fluctuations. However hedge funds are hugely diverse according to their performance. They resort to very different strategies. Some of them are somewhat or plainly directional, meaning that they depend on bets on the future direction of change on certain market prices. Others are grounded on arbitrage, shunning them in principle from overall market price changes. Still others are bets on specific events being realized (event-driven) or are quite opaque about the manager's activity (multi strategy).

The probability distributions of returns in HF strategies are far from normal. To reach high absolute returns, hedge funds must sell option-like products whose risk profiles are highly non-linear. These strategies are vulnerable to extreme risks due to asymmetric biases toward losses (negative skewness) and to fat tails (high kurtosis).

Using the CSFB Tremont database which publishes statistical indicators by strategy, one can measure long-run performance on a monthly basis (Table 1.3). One can see that the performance for the average global index is far from being outstanding. The average return is 3.78% with a standard deviation of 7.50%. Moreover the index exhibits a skewed distribution tilted on the side of losses (skewness at −1.272) and fat tails meaning a likelihood of large unexpected losses much higher than the normal distribution (kurtosis well over 3). Moreover, as expected, higher-return strategies are much more risky. This is the case of emerging market, event-driven, distressed, long–short equity and multi strategy.

Furthermore, even the reality of high returns has been contested. For example, the investment bank Barclays Capital put the typical level of overstatement of returns at 1 to 6% a year, depending on the index.[13] A recent study by Berton Malkiel and Atanu Saha reached an even more pessimistic conclusion.[14] According to the authors, the chief reasons are the biases in data that has been identified here above in this paper. Using Tremont HF index and correcting for the biases, they arrived at dramatically lesser returns that the ones published in financial newspapers (Table 1.4).

Systematic biases come directly from the opacity that hedge funds enjoy in running their business. They have very loose requirement of disclosure. Because hedge funds can choose if they prefer to disclose information or not, there is a *self-reporting bias*. Only hedge funds with good performance and willing to attract new capital have an incentive to report. A second bias is due to partial and non compatible coverage in the different databases. This is the *selection bias* whose consequence is the disparity in performance measured by several indices. The third bias is the worst. It is the *survivorship bias* stemming from the withdrawal from the database of hedge funds that have stopped giving information, because they have poor performance, or they have been liquidated, or they are closed to new potential clients. When those funds disappear from the database, the index is biased toward a more flattering performance.

Table 1.3: Characteristics of hedge fund returns
(database CSFB Tremont, monthly data, period 01–1994 to 01–2008)

	Rendement	Volatilité	Skewness	Kurtosis
Stratégies HF				
Convertible Arbitrage	1.79%	4.59%	**-1.272**	5.929
Dedicated Short Bias	-1.60%	16.82%	0.822	4.936
Emerging Markets	6.36%	15.54%	-0.714	8.014
Equity Market Neutral	2.80%	2.81%	0.337	3.480
Event Driven	4.50%	5.57%	-3.159	24.687
Distressed	4.71%	6.16%	-2.798	21.452
Multi-Strategy	4.44%	6.07%	-2.267	17.191
Risk Arbitrage	2.46%	4.13%	-1.025	8.802
Fixed Income Arbitrage	1.79%	3.63%	-2.928	18.468
Global Macro	4.55%	10.43%	0.001	6.268
Long/Short Equity	4.24%	9.87%	0.194	6.868
Managed Futures	1.75%	11.92%	-0.007	3.161
Multi-Strategy	3.49%	4.36%	-1.084	5.656
Indice global CSFB	3.78%	7.50%	-1.272	5.929

Source: S. Khanniche, 'Measuring Hedge Fund Risk', *Groupama-am*, June 2008,

Table 1.4: Average annual return with and without adjustment

	1994–2003	1995–99	2000–02	2003
Tremont HF index: returns *without* Malkiel-Saha adjustment	11.11	18.16	4.09	15.47
Tremont HF index: returns *with* Malkiel-Saha adjustment	2.32	9.37	-4.66	6.72

Source: B. Malkiel and A. Saha, 'HFs: Risk and Return', *Financial Analysts Journal*, 61:6,
CFA institute from the TASS database.

Very high skewness and kurtosis also plague private equity funds. Buy-out funds are akin to event-driven hedge funds with large negative skewness (–2.6) and kurtosis (over 20). Along with the most risky hedge funds, standard measures of risk (Sharpe ratio) have no meanings and the CAPM does not hold to support portfolio allocation.

The multiple bias in the measure of performance, already noticed about hedge funds, are exacerbated with PE funds. Valuation is more infrequent and spurious auto-correlations in yields abound. Correcting this bias leads to the exhibit of high and variable correlation with equities. In Europe the correlation was 50% on average for the period 1994Q1–2004Q2. It increases markedly in stress conditions. In February 2007, the correlation between stock market indices and private equity yields was as high as 90% according to Merrill Lynch.

Private equity has the further handicap of being a highly illiquid asset class. This is a serious risk for institutional investors, the risk of not being able to rebalance that part of the portfolio because assets are stuck for several years. Such risk shall be compensated by a *liquidity premium*. Portfolio simulations have shown that the premium reaches about 3.5% to 4% on average. It means that out of the apparent high yield of PE funds, the liquidity premium should be deduced to compute the net yield for the institutions that invest in those funds.

Buyout strategies have also the characteristic of being extremely leveraged. It explains much of the higher performance and the hidden risks of PE funds. A recent City Group study has shown that, if one applies the same leverage to a basket of mid-cap quoted stocks and if one back-tests the performance over a ten-year period, the public market sample fares better.

The combination of high leverage and low liquidity is deleterious for investors in PE under adverse market conditions. While prohibitive fees that the managers of those funds are able to extract have been added up, the net return for institutional investors might not be that spectacular. Cumulating skewed and leptokurtic distribution of risks, illiquidity and variable correlation with other asset classes and high leverage make the portfolio allocation inadequate and potentially dangerous.

Figure 1.4 illustrates the problem facing institutional investors. Let us suppose that they invest in a portfolio of bonds, marketable shares and private equity and that they apply standard portfolio theory. They suppose that the efficiency frontier stays put, the introduction of the new more risky asset class changing the position of the optimal portfolio on an unchanged frontier. But the multiple biases, the non-Gaussian distribution of returns and the compensation for illiquidity shift the frontier to the right. Therefore applying standard theory gives a false sense of safety.

Investing in private equity requires specific skills and is essentially a business of picking up the right general manager in the beginning and negotiating fees. After the deal is struck, pension fund trustees and administrators have virtually no means of control.

– Impact of Hedge Fund Behaviour on Financial Stability

From the analysis in the above sub-section one can identify six factors interacting with one another that threaten financial stability. They are the following: risk-taking in the context of growing competition and high performance fees, short-selling, increasing correlation under market stress, shift to strategies operating on less liquid markets, high leverage and concentration in complex derivative products. Some of these factors apply to both hedge funds and private equity funds. Thus private equity funds may also pose threats to financial stability

Pursuing absolute returns, hedge funds have always tended to be risk takers in a number of markets. This is particularly the case in complex markets, where risks are difficult to quantify and hedge funds have a competitive edge because of their often-superior models. Two reasons are particularly important in explaining why hedge funds are prone to take risk. The first is the extensive use of performance fees in the remuneration packages of hedge fund managers and the other is the increasing competition in the hedge fund industry. Management fees in hedge funds are considerably higher than the fees paid to mutual fund managers. Normally, the hedge fund manager will receive both a management fee and a performance fee, with the latter playing the predominant role. The typical performance fee amounts to at least 20% of the gains above a specified benchmark over a comparatively short period of 3– 12 months. Performance fees tend to encourage investment strategies that increase the probability of exceeding comparatively high return benchmarks. Such strategies are most likely to entail greater risk that could spark a crisis in the advent of failure.

Figure 1.4: Impact of PE investment on portfolio allocation

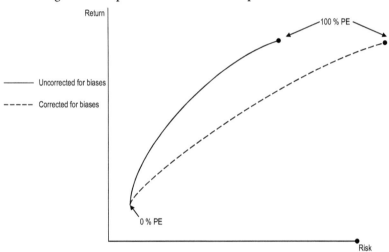

Due to increasing competition, hedge fund managers have engaged in a search for alternative ways to maintain or increase yields in a market where average yields seem to be sloping downwards. In this context, many hedge fund managers are likely to consider investment opportunities involving the risk of extreme losses. They are strategies entailing negative skewness and high kurtosis.

Historically, hedge funds are often associated with short-selling, i.e., the use of strategies allowing investors to gain from the decline in price of securities, as well as currencies or raw materials. It is only a limited segment of hedge funds that are actually practising short-selling. Yet those who do are often charged with being trendsetters, i.e. of causing price depreciation independent of the underlying market fundamentals.

There is a specific challenge in short-selling. Losses do not have the same impact on long and on short positions. A long position increases in value if it is winning. Losing on a long position stems from an unexpected price slump. But the very decline of the price diminishes the weight of the losing position in the global portfolio, thus abating the negative impact on the overall return. Conversely, a short position shrinks if it is winning. Short sellers benefit from price crashes, but their positions are vanishing. When price jumps unexpectedly the short position is both losing and increasing in size. Those losses magnify the negative impact on the overall return. Last but not least, short-sellers must borrow securities. If the seller of borrowed securities wants to recall the securities before the trade is completed, the short seller must replace the borrowing or lose the position.

In stressed times a squeeze can arise especially in less liquid markets. When a bunch of hedge funds, who have packed on the same strategies, rush for cover, liquidity evaporates suddenly in those market segments. Instead of bringing in liquidity, hedge funds generate liquidity risks. The mix of credit and liquidity risks in investment styles using short-selling with leverage can make hedge funds the weak links initiating a systemic event. When hedge funds are induced to withdraw together from the same markets under the constraint of a higher cost of financing or margin calls, the forced selling of assets triggers the same behaviour with more traditional investors applying portfolio insurance hedging. A market meltdown is to be feared in these circumstances.

The current empirical evidence as to whether hedge funds and institutional investors engage in such 'copy-cat' behavior is alarming. According to ECB calculations, the recent increasing competition in hedge fund markets has come along with increasing correlations among hedge fund strategies. In this connection, the ECB has stated that '... the correlations among hedge fund strategies tended to increase more or less continuously after mid-2003, reaching an all-time peak in 2005'. It is important to note the fact that correlations are rising not only within some strategies, but also among strategies, raising concerns that some triggering event could lead to highly correlated exits.

Despite the increasing correlations, the more recent default of the hedge fund before the global crisis, Amaranth did not appear to have threatened or even influenced financial market stability. Thus there has been an absolute absence of contagion spreads over the other financial markets: no volatility spikes were registered during September 2006, neither on the stock markets, nor on the bond markets. Nonetheless the absence of contagion spreads in the Amaranth case is no assurance that hedge funds have become any more robust. One of several important differences to the LTCM crisis of 1998 was the situation of global financial markets. In 1998 they were under extreme stress in the aftermath of the Russian crisis. In 2006 they were awash with cash after many years of loose monetary policy. The acute liquidity crisis had a devastating impact on thousands of hedge funds.

In addition to increasing correlations, the ECB has stressed that the liquidity of many hedge fund investments may be decreasing. More and more funds are turning to exotic strategies like event-driven, emerging markets or fixed income arbitrage involving high-spread low-rating securities. They are exposed to illiquid markets to boost their apparent return in earning the liquidity premium. Such exposures generate vulnerability to redemption risks in the advent of a crisis. Thus, in stressed times, a squeeze can arise especially in less liquid markets. When several hedge funds that are pursuing the same strategies, rush for cover, liquidity evaporates suddenly in those market segments. Instead of bringing in liquidity, hedge funds generate major liquidity risks. The mix of credit and liquidity risks in investment styles using short-selling with leverage can make hedge funds the weak links initiating a systemic event. If hedge funds are induced to withdraw together from the same markets under the constraint of a higher cost of financing or margin calls, the forced selling of assets could trigger the same behaviour among more traditional institutional investors. This could in turn spark a financial crisis.

A key characteristic of many hedge funds is a very high degree of leverage compared to mutual funds. Leverage (or gearing) can be defined as the use of given resources in such a way that the potential positive outcome of the use is magnified. Thus, leverage allows greater potential return to the investor than otherwise would have been available. However, the potential for loss is also greater because loans and other sources of leverage need to be repaid. Economic leverage from outright loans is not the preferred way of hedge funds, although they ensure credit lines from banks for liquidity purpose. They prefer financial leverage via the use of derivatives. They allow leverage without borrowing explicitly. However the risk of borrowing is implicit in the price of the derivative. An adverse change in market conditions could force hedge funds to sell their leveraged positions to meet margin calls, potentially leading to a domino effect across markets. Moreover, much lending is short-term, which in combination with high leverage, further decreases the ability to wait until a possible price recovery.

Asset Allocation of State Reserve Funds and Pension Funds

Optimizing surplus value according to the Sharpe and Tint model is the best way, while asset classes are not perfectly correlated with liabilities. It strikes the best arbitrage between liability risks stemming from not perfectly hedged liability constraints and excess return from profitable assets generating priced extra risks. This arbitrage depends on the future liability commitments, on the risk aversion of the funds and on national regulation (Table 1.5a)

Public pension funds, with defined obligations to make future payments, have strikingly different strategic allocations. The US funds are the ones which take more risks with a large proportion invested in equities, including private equities. Canadian and Dutch funds take a more prudent view. They invest much less in equities and diversify more in real estate, infrastructures and other asset classes, including hedge funds, short-term securities and cash.

Reserve funds set up by government to alleviate the future burden of pay-as-you-go systems and endowment funds owned by foundations of prestigious American universities do not have specifically defined liabilities. Those funds take more equity risk than non-US pension funds. Endowment funds have a structure much more heavily invested in other asset classes mainly in hedge funds (Table 1.5b)

To meet the challenge of optimizing a portfolio made of heterogeneous asset classes, institutional investors split the portfolio in two parts that make up a *core satellite* management. The core is benchmarked and resorts to contingent immunization. The satellites are specific asset classes (midcaps, private equity, real estate, commodities, and investment in hedge funds). They pertain to non-standard pockets in illiquid markets. To make profit with those pockets, a continuous dynamic asset liability management is of the essence. It raises hard questions that are not only technical but involve corporate governance.

Table 1.5a: Strategic asset allocation of pension funds (% of total)

Countries	Bonds		Equities		Mutual Funds		Claims		Others	
	1995	2005	1995	2005	1995	2005	1995	2005	1995	2005
Australia	41	30	41	53	-	-	13	11	4	6
Canada	53	51	13	26	-	-	29	15	5	7
France	59	52	14	18	12	23	11	5	4	3
Germany	15	10	14	20	11	18	54	46	6	6
Netherland	23	37	21	33	0	0	49	20	6	10
UK	30	41	53	33	8	10	8	11	2	6
US	62	56	16	24	1	2	14	12	7	6
Japan	32	52	21	24	1	2	40	20	7	3

Source: Committee on the Global Financial System, CGFS Papers, *27, Institutional Investors, Global Savings and Asset Allocation* (February 2007).

Table 1.5b: Strategic choices by government reserve funds and endowment funds (%)

Strategic portfolio allocation in 2005	Equities (incl. private)	Bonds (incl. inflation-linked)	Real estate and infrastructure	Other asset classes
API-AP4 (Sweden)	54–61	36–40	0–9	0–3
FRR (France)	56	44	0	0
NPRF (Ireland)	77	13	8	2
Canada Pension Plan	61	35	4	0
Government Pension fund (Norway)	60	40	0	0
NZ Super (New Zealand)	60	20	12	8
Harvard endowment	43	22	10	25
Yale Endowment	47	13	20	25

Source: Web sites of various funds

Conclusion: Ten Recommendations for Long-Run Investors

The first recommendation is a golden rule: *the business of the investor is totally different from the business of the trader.* It follows that market timing is the best way for an investor to lose money, all the more than performance fees of managers and advisors are asymmetric and exorbitant.

The second recommendation is a direct corollary. An investor must gather the intellectual expertise and the information resources to make the strategic asset allocation in-house in so far as the allocation is specific. It depends on political and social commitment for sovereign funds and on underlying pension plans for pension funds.

Third, the fulcrum for the structure of the portfolio is a government bond nominal, real or mixed depending on the monetary regime anticipated in the scenario and how much it is trusted. Asset classes in the diversified portfolio should be defined by the supervisory committee that oversees the allocation. The group of experts that makes the technical work should make hypotheses on the macroeconomic factors that impinge upon long-run returns. A scenario generator allows one to assess risks. Allocations must be time-flexible, e.g. they must be revised yearly and be applied on a moving long-run horizon.

Fourth, the most important dynamic relationship for a long-run investor is mean reversion in liquid bond and equity markets. They can be captured with sufficiently long horizons (five years and over).

Fifth and corollary from the above, the share of equities in the strategic allocation should make allowance for the inter-temporal hedging stemming from the serial correlation of returns associated with mean reversion.

Sixth, uncertainty in the hypotheses underlying the scenarios should make room for judgement. Quantitative modelling is much too unreliable to give any indication other than the direction of change at best, never the magnitude of change. Technical expertise should always be under the control of the collective body that should make the final choice.

The seventh recommendation is the second golden rule: *never investing in assets whose risks one is unable to assess on one's own.* Had this prescription be applied, investment banks and rating agencies would not have been able to fool investors to the extent that they did in selling toxic securitized real estate credit.

Eight and correlatively, institutional investors should add alternative assets only with extreme caution because the quest for absolute returns is trapped with hidden risks and perverse incentives. Investors must lobby to get regulators change disclosure rules for hedge funds and private equity in the direction of much more transparency.

Ninth, core satellite is the right organization to circumscribe risks in alternative asset management. The recourse to delegated asset managers is justified only after careful inspection and for specific types of asset whose presence in the portfolio has been approved in the definition of the strategic portfolio.

Tenth, asset liability management is standard method for all funds whose objectives are embodied in contractual liability commitments. Contingent immunization should be used to protect the interests of pension plan members in the life cycle.

2 IFRS AND THE NEED FOR NON-FINANCIAL INFORMATION

Tristan Boyer and Elena Chane-Alune

Since 1 January 2005, the introduction of the IAS/IFRS[1] standards has lead to understandable stirs in the community of financial analysts, who are rightfully challenged by the necessity of a correct apprehension of the annual accounts established according to a referential the interpretation of which remains complex. More basically, the issue here is about the soundness of an application of the IAS/IFRS standards – of Anglo-Saxon origin – to countries belonging to the continental European accounting trend. Indeed, the diffusion of these standards is not historically a hazard. Accounting always refers to a socio-economic 'ecology'.[2] The reason why the application of accounting standards reflects the power exerted by a dominant figure is because the actionnarial model has imposed itself in our economies. Consequently, the introduction of the international IAS/IFRS standards comes together with the use of a new accounting evaluation system focused on shareholder's provision of information. However, the IASB[3] published in October 2005 a discussion document about the quality of the management reports going with the financial states. This document aimed to delimitate the role that the IASB could play in the standardization and improvement of the management report. This initiative is linked with a demand for qualitative information to go with financial information. The discussion document thus reviews the legal duties linked with the management report at a national level, so that better practices are adopted in this field.

Firstly, we aim at giving a general view of the context in which the latest accounting evolutions appear, linked with the actual financialization of the financial market. Isn't there a risk that the new IFRS standards and their concern about transparency and comparability could impoverish the information by giving to accounting, with the application of the right value, the function of capital fundamental evaluation? Secondly, we show the importance of non-financial information able to supplement the provision of information, which is useful for the economic players when taking decisions, and described on the reworking of the financial information by the players led to use it.

1. IFRS and Financialization

1.1. The Microeconomic Consequences of Financialization: Introduction of the Account Standards IAS/IFRS

The financialization is nowadays very well known. However, we have very few elements about it, apart from the obvious changes, such as the noticeable increase of the dividend level, the development of the remuneration's outlines linked to the market rate, and the assertion of the shareholder's power.[4]

Aglietta[5], Boyer[6] and, from a slightly different angle, Orléan,[7] have focused on the transformations in the financial markets since the 80s, as a driver in the change of the accumulation system. In this way, the financialization is a macroeconomic mechanism marked by a change in the power relationships between the various economic agents. Indeed, the liberalization and globalization of the financial markets, beginning in the 80s have gone with the assertion of the power and the principles of creation of share value, through the actions of a particular type of player: Anglo-Saxon institutional investors. The appearance of the latter type has been made by more and more important takeover by in the capitalization. They detained more than 40% of the capitalization of the American firms and close to 70% of capitalization in Great Britain in 1998.[8] In the same way, about 40% of the social capital of the great companies composing the CAC 40 is today detained by foreign investors. This proportion is in constant progression: 12% in 1986, 23% in 1993 and 36% in 1998.[9]

The institutionalization of the transferable securities market means that the securities of public companies are now mainly concentrated in the hands of financial institutions who have an expertise and an economic scope greater than most of the individual investors.[10] This concentration and changes in the composition of the listed societies' shareholding have a significant influence on the corporate governance of these societies.[11] Rather than following Wall Street – that is, selling their actions when they don't agree with the business management – the institutional investors will adoopt a more and more interventionist attitude in order to protect their interests and improve company returns. They thus abandon the passive attitude they traditionally had, and have a growing influence on the corporations' governance by modifying the dynamic of internal relationships, as well as proposing changes to the structures of the corporate governance, through the elaboration of governance codes.[12]

However, this new activism of institutional investors can be put back in perspective, depending on the different perceptions of the investors towards the mandate they've been given. The investors can thus choose to be more or less active.

The reports of the first appearance of activism in the USA. outline the presence of activist initiatives during annual general assemblies, particularly through questions submitted in person or by propositions spread in information circulars.[13]

During the intense period of takeovers in the 80s, when the companies resorted to an array of defensive measures, the institutional investors became aware of the necessity of protecting their interests. They thus have opposed to the measures that permitted the leaders to protect their jobs inside the targeted companies, especially towards subscription rights systems (poison pills), freezing agreements, spreading out mandates inside the board meetings and creation of subordinate actions and privileged actions involving discretionary rights.[14] Institutional investors have also intervene to prevent any opportunist behaviour from the leaders, for example when transactions between linked people are made to the detriment of the minority shareholder's interests, or in the case of excessive remuneration system made for the leaders.[15]

Traditionally seen as passive shareholders, institutional investors have thus gradually become important figures in the corporate context, because of their efforts to maximize the return of the shareholders' holding[16] and to promote collateral of economic, politic and social aims, such as ethical fund management.

The explanation given by these investors to justify their relative passivity was to define their mandate in the opposite way to the normal leader function or to a long-term shareholder who has to show some loyalty towards the companies he supports. Coffee sums up as follows the attitude of many institutions: 'Structurally, historically and culturally, institutional investors are not natural monitors of management; rather, they are natural traders, inclined to rely more on exit than voice'.[17]

The implications attached to institutional investors depends on the percentage of shares they have in a company. For example, when an institution detains more than 5, 10 or 15% of a company's capital, the relationships between them will of course be tighter, resulting in particular to regular talks with the company. While admitting the larger implications of institutional investors at the time of significant investments, Crête & Rousseau[18] point out that they still don't become 'associates': their role is to keep an eye on the management, as would a principal towards his representative.

Within the context of their management mandate and underlying bonds, institutional investors sometimes have to exercise some rights linked with the property of shares. Shareholding implies a controlling role and in that context, exercising their right to vote is one of the main ways for institutions to protect their interests, by taking part in the election or dismissal of the directors, or approving important structural changes at the time of shareholders' meetings.

The concern of institutional investors about exercising their right to vote can also be seen with a changing intensity and from various angles. Some of them have adopted an internal policy concerning this side of the management mandate (instructions for internal vote), while others will rather use policies or recommendations from certain intermediate organizations (proxy voting).[19] For this reason, it is still difficult to know the intensity of the control exerted by institutional investors on companies. Stapeldon[20] puts into focus the fact that the very strict nature of vote instructions can sometimes be considered as window dressing. It is then possible to think that some investors could maintain a limited surveillance of these companies, as regards the important investments they have made in these.

The activism of institutional investors can also be influenced by the costs of control. A survey by Montgomery[21] shows that the main reason for passive behaviour from institutional investors could be the efforts (in costs and time) needed by the gathering, processing and analysis of the information.

Aware of the costs implied by different types of activism within the companies they have invested in, portfolio managers will intervene only if they are convinced of the success and renting of their action that will reflect in the value or the price of their shares. They will thus focus on the situations where the rights and interests of the shareholders are directly touched.[22] They will also intervene in a reactive and 'ad hoc' rather than proactive and continuous way.[23] This pragmatic attitude limits the institutional investors' interventions. The remuneration they get generally covers only the expenses needed for the minimal bonds linked with the exercise of their right to vote. Beyond this task, it becomes more difficult for the managers to spend some more energy, especially when they are not sure of the profitability of their shares. We remind here the words of an American institutional investor, interviewed by O'Barr and Conley.[24] 'external money managers rarely propose to do anything out of the ordinary. Their perception is that attention to corporate governance is unrelated to their incomes'.

Seeing the various appearances of activism through literature, we can see that the behaviour of institutional investors is characterized by a pragmatic approach, which takes into account the profits and costs resulting from the intervention. This approach brings them to intervene mainly when they are sure of net gains or avoided losses, in situations of abuse or iniquity and in cases of strategic decisions or important structural changes that could affect their portfolio. The institutional investors generally appears as peaceful shareholders who keep an eye open and appear at the right moment, mainly favouring the interventions which can have short and middle-term benefits. For companies, these institutions are important financing sources; they can't ignore them. Facing this latent power, the companies will rather proceed in a preventive way, doing informal consultings with the main investors, in order to ensure their support and pre-serve financing sources for the future.

Even though the activism of institutional investors is considered as one of the main reasons for the financialization's pressure on the companies, we can see here that the intervention of the fund managers does not necessarily imply a concrete role in day-to-day management. Only market return objectives expected by fund managers can constitute a demand for company leaders who will set themselves rending rates which will influence the whole management. While pension funds could be considered as an exogenous power for the company, the adhesion of leaders to the internalization of the pension funds' threat and the principles of value creation for the shareholders lead to a change in power relationships from which the shareholders can profit, and establish the financialization by the adhesion of new rules from all parts. This legitimacy helps to make a central evaluation authority with finance.

1.2. Why are IFRS Standards a Way to Financialization ?

In July 2002, the European Parliament and the EU Ministers Council approved the plan for the adoption from 2005 of IASB standards concerning consoli-dated accounts. This decision shows a fundamental change in the companies' life because it takes into account the consequences of globalization by increasing the protection of shareholders' interests and according the priority to the fair-value principle.

The history of accounting shows that it has always been intimately linked to the main economic and social changes, and that every accounting system is bound to change with the wants and needs of the players are their conflicts and agreements. An accounting system is therefore the result of constructions and evaluation choices that can lead to different figures. This depends on principles, standards, conventions, rules capable of infinite combinations and that can be modified to players and politics' liking, or with the needs of economic developments.[25]

Accounting conventions and principles, which used to change according to the countries and ages, have been turned upside down by the development by the IASC[26] of the international accounting standardization. The IASC aims to develop a unique set of high quality accounting standards, understandable and applicable concretely, requiring clear information, comparable in the different financial states, in order to help the players in taking economic decisions.

The transparency organized by the IASB standards is mainly aimed at the finan-cial investors. The IASB never hid the fact that his conceptual framework was to favour shareholders, because they have 'a reasonable knowledge of economic activities and accounting and the will of study information in a fairly diligent way'.[27] The needs of other users categories are not put aside, but should be reached if these users are satisfied. As a consequence, we may say that a gap exists between the traditional perspective of accounting standards and the explicit 'philosophy' of the IFRS standards: the latter is closely subordinated to the interests of investors who are directly concerned with a day to day valuation of financial assets.

Through this development of an international accounting standard, we can see the trend toward the adoption of the stockholders' perspective that characterizes both IFRS standards and the financialization phenomenon.

The IASC was created in 1973 through a process of federation from different countries, professional associations of accountants. Until the mid-80s, the IASC developed itself separately from the European government institution that worked on accounting standards harmonization. Nor the 1978 fourth European Union directive upon annual accounts, neither the 1985 seventh EU directive upon consolidated accounts referred in any way to the IASC works.

The development of the IASC relied on the new membership of large professional organizations, mainly from developing countries with an Anglo-Saxon approach to accounting[28] (which obviously had an influence on the kind of approach the IASC developed). During this first part of the IASC's life, IAS conventions could be amended by numerous options, allowing any accountant to retrieve its own national accounting philosophy and still use IAS norms. In other countries, the IASC had practically no influence, except in very specific cases (of consolidation, or concerning specific financial measures for example), where local legislation did not provide enough guidelines.

Since the beginning of the 80s, the IASC tried to attach itself to a supra-national institution. It finally succeeded when the IOSCO[29] chose the IAS norms as the framework for financial reports: since that decision, companies wanting to raise funds on these financial markets had to comply with IAS rules. In 1989, the IASC decided that comparability between financial statements had to be improved and considered as a priority ('benchmark treatment'). This same year, the IASC adopted the same conceptual framework chosen by the FASB:[30] the primary objective of accounting was explicitly described as giving accurate information to the investors because of the specific needs centred on the 'shareholder value' they have. The underlying justification of this position is that the shareholders (considered as the residual claimants of the company) by maximizing their return on equity, are also optimizing the situation of the other stakeholders. Moreover, the markets existence guarantees the possibility of varying contract forms. These theoretical contractual basis considers all contractors to be on a position of equality, and neglects the fact that the capacity of a co-contractor to operate without the exchange gives it superior negotiating power.

Another turning point gave birth to a true normalizing approach. This took place in 1995, when the IASC promised to establish a complete body of accounting norms before 2000, in exchange for an official acknowledgement of its work by the OICV. The IASC then developed ad-hoc structures (consultative normalization committees, interpretation committees, formalized procedure for the creation of accounting norms, etc.), before adopting in April 2001 the same structure as the FASB, changing its name to become the IASB. Instead of a council of spokespersons representing their countries and national accounting bodies, it adopted a body of fourteen full-time 'professionals', 'chosen for their expertise', and named by nineteen trustees attached to a foundation (IASC). The international accounting standards (IAS) became 'the' standards for financial reporting (IFRS). Following a normative approach founded on principles, as in the American accounting standards, forty-one IFRS standards were adopted.

IFRS allowed the EU to establish the unification of accounting principles – the European reflection on accounting having stopped with the fourth and seventh directives, stating that listed companies will have to publish their consolidated accounts using the IASB referential from 1 January, 2005. The European Commission imposed IASB as a normalizer, despite controversies about IFRS standards 32 and 39[31] (relative to financial instruments).

The IASB so went from encouraging international accounting harmonization (looking for equivalences between differing practices) to pushing for normalization, which supposes uniformity in rules. This accounting normalization is consistent with the idea of comparability of financial statements. It must be noted, however, that some options that were maintained (and could be seen as concessions) raise some questions about whether this objective has been attained. This is, among others, the case for the fair-value option. The IFRS referential is made of standards, themselves set on general principles and on objectives assigned to the financial information contained in the conceptual frame. As IFRS standards leave considerable room for interpretation, they give the interpreter a central role in the system's workings. Auditors and listeners must analyse, stand back, and ensure that the envisioned accounting treatment is coherent with the underlying principles. The professional's eye is central in the standards' application. It could be said that the interpretation is just as authoritative as the norm itself. This 'principle approach' is also less comfortable for auditors, less protected in this context than in the rule-based American referential. The growing use of IFRS standards will lead to numerous interpretation conflicts, and there is currently no interpretative authority outside of the IASB.

The IASC/IASB project, progressively built through the steps we previously covered, has brought answers to the needs for accounting harmonization of:

- Great groups: in the context of globalization, the multiplication of accounting standards for their separate branches generated numerous risks, as well as additional accounting and organizing costs,
- Financial markets, because of their interconnection and their drive for harmonization in the listed companies' presentation standards,

- Audit firms: global normalization lowers risk and allows a rationalization of auditing practices, reinforcing their roles as advisers.

Finally, the highly political process of acceptance of these norms allowed for an answer to the demands of financial globalization. As the generalization of American US GAAP accounting standards, seen as too close from the American financial power, was politically difficult, IASB appeared as an 'independent' and 'acceptable' alternative.

1.3. Risks of Applying IAS/IFRS Norms in Companies.

The IFRS referential has some significant structural limits. First, it offers opportunity to manipulate accounting data, because of the room for interpretation allowed by the standards' flexibility. It should prompt decision-makers to choose the documented treatment reflecting the operation's economic substance; however, they can just as well use their interpreting liberty to choose a treatment straying from the economic substance – as long as they can convince the interpreters of its soundness. The IFRS creates a different reasoning. The issue will be to determine whether the investment will pay off in the future, and the depreciation method will have to depend on how soon the asset's financial profits will be used. Moreover, the introduction of the component approach will force accountants to use different depreciation values between the components of one tangible asset, in order to account for their respective time of use. Depreciation costs will not be fixed, and fixed assets management will force managers to rethink every management tool. The whole management process must be rethought around the concept of 'de-clustering' (division into sectors and Cash-Flow Generating Units). Groups will have a certain amount of strategic choices, but each one will need to be documented. A good quality of exchanges with the auditors and the financial analyst will then become critical. Industrial Sector definition will bring companies to make choices taking into account potential competitive risks. This will be the case, for instance, with a listed company with unlisted competitors. The application of IFRS will cause the creation of an IFRS structure internal to the firm. This structure's architecture and management will have to be carefully thought over in order to allow conform functioning.

In addition to these difficulties, the standards' application could jeopardize the comparability and viability principles of financial statement. As this normative approach leaves a lot of room for interpretation, there is a risk of it being applied differently over time. This could lead to reduced comparability, when comparability is one of the major goals of the IASB and the financial community. IFRS application could then lead to new evaluation difficulties. For instance, the methods used to evaluate the value loss of goodwills (impairment test), as well as the use of a mixed system for the evaluation principles (historical cost versus fair value), will lead to greater difficulties in comparing the assets of two companies. Another limit of the IFRS referential is the risk of added volatility of results, through the use of fair-value for evaluating tangible and intangible assets. This kind of evaluation is pushed by the financial markets, more driven by cash-flow[32] than by evaluation – a phenomenon amplified by the 'opinion market'.[33] Orléan[34] puts this idea more formally: in radical uncertainty situations, anticipations and preferences of the actors have no objective basis, and behavior is polarized by mimesis. Financial markets may then be considered as a collective mechanism producing valuation – that is, a common opinion on the company's value, but not necessarily a 'true' one. This limit brings up a question: should accounting be responsible for fundamental or intrinsic capital evaluation, which is theoretically the financial market's role ? Moreover, the real functioning of these markets, and its limits (strong volatility and cash function's domination over stock-valuation function, among others) show that this fundamental evaluation space is often left to the financial statements.

More generally, there are two opposed functions of accounting: an evaluating function, dominant in the IFRS referential, where the substance of operations is more important than their form and where accounting must deliver pertinent information for stock-exchange investors, and an account presentation function privileging prudence over fair-value application and the viability principle over the pertinence principle, allowing easier comparisons. The account-presentation function has often been privileged, because it allowed creditors to make a prudent evaluation of a company's solvency.

At last, despite the accounting innovations introduced by the IFRS, these standards, even in their concrete applications, will always have difficulties in evaluating intangible assets – namely organizational intelligence and internally developed knowledge and competences.[35] The evaluations of these assets, which are often the most valuable, will have to be revised each year depending on their constitutive element's market value. These assets will then no longer aim to incorporate or consolidate an integrated industrial capability while taking into account competence building and the firm's capacity to innovate, create investment opportunities and modify its environmental perception. The implementation of IFRS will bring a potential separability of these elements, allowing the revelation of future products and of their value. This evaluation method sees a firm as a sum of saleable assets, with no added value in their combination or implementation.

2. Financialization and Needs for Non-Financial Information

Financialization is a macroeconomic phenomenon privileging the shareholders' role (especially the institutional investors') in global economy. Their activism and their weight in the companies' economical choices is seen as the main factor of instability in this new growth regime. The microeconomic consequence of this financialization phenomenon is the need for better financial information, that is supposed to guarantee more efficiency from the financial markets. As such, *Corporate Governance* is the framework traducing this pre-eminence of actionarial value in companies. The main exigence of *Corporate Governance* is transparency of financial information. This exigence originates in the agency theory; its main concrete manifestation is the striving for a larger diffusion of information, and a drive for its standardization in quantity (because it has to be diffused to all actors in the same way) as well as in quality (the IFRS aim to standardize this information to allow better comparability). According to W. Crist (1997), 'the pressure enforced by big pension funds on firm managements for more transparency in accounting standards, complete information, independent auditing, fluid communication with shareholders and others good-practice rules are nothing but a careful exercise of an owner's responsibilities'.

The IFRS are an answer to the paradigmatic need for efficiency of the financial markets. But in neglecting the intangible assets of the firm, and in largely introducing the market's fluctuations in its book-price, accounting modifies its evaluation, risking to lose information (intern valuation of debts and claims gives more information to the analysts than an external and public valuation). Indeed, analysts use the financial management indicators provided by the firms to judge of its economical performances (despite the possible manipulations of financial results).

To analyse the impact of IFRS norms on investors information (and therefore on their needs), we must understand the methods they use for buying and selling decisions. The investor's work is to sell a title when anticipating a drop in its value, and buy when expecting a rise. They use evaluation models to guide their choices. These models are used to make quick decisions while limiting losses. They are adapted by their users, but are set on the same underlying principles.

2.1. Decision-Making Tools on the Financial Markets

In deciding to buy or sell a title, investors use methods to anticipate the rise or drop of its rate. These methods are based on different principles. The 'fundamental's method' is based on the evaluation of the firm's 'real' value, and the 'chartist method' uses the rate's past evolutions. Each one of these decision-making tools can be used either alone or combined with the other.

The fundamentalist decision-making model is based on the economical hypothesis[36] that the actors of the financial markets, by buying and selling titles, ensure the coherence between the real and financial economical spheres; in other words, between the firm's value (called 'fundamental value') and its market value, which is the stock price. In this model, agents buy actions of firms they see as underestimated, and sell those they see as overestimated. To use this decision model, the agent must have an idea of the company's real value.[37] This real value is estimated on the basis internal or external data: accounting analysis and financial reports.

This evaluation can also be done by referring to past transactions: this model takes a market price and transposes it to the concerned firm. These methods will then try and find common characteristics between companies. For example, observing that a given firm has sold for x times its turnover, the same coefficient will be applied to the evaluated company's earnings. Other methods exist, based on the cost/benefit ratio (C/B, or Price Earning Ratio). The underlying hypothesis is that the rate measures the profit's capitalization: it expresses the 'theoretical' rate of the title as a multiple of by-title benefit. A last method of evaluation relies on the replacement value: the firm is evaluated by adding all its assets. In the 80s in the USA, this method has brought a wave of buying firms to sell them by 'apartment', that is by liquidating them by selling separately or not every possible asset when the rate was under the sum of the asset's value, rather than wait for the rate to go up again.

The comparative method's difficulties are caused by the firms' specific characteristics; the comparison changes with their times, places and activities. In consequence, they can be used in combination with other methods aiming to anticipate rate fluctuations. The patrimonial approach is not identical to strict accounting evaluation; it sees firms as sums of independent assets. To evaluate these assets, it must often use actuarial or comparative methods, or even empirical studies based on witnessed market prices.

The stock's ß is empirically deduced from observation made on the stock's price, its volatility and its rate variation. These models are widely used as decision-making tools.[38] They are used to measure a share's specific risk: the ß coefficient measures the risk taken by an investor when buying or selling a share. It is the base of the control exerted by the bank (back office) on the financial decisions taken by the traders (front office).

The main weakness of these models is their sensitivity to discontinuities resulting from an exogenous and unanticipated event. Their predictive ability is limited to an unchanging world. Their second weakness is that the ß coefficient is very difficult to determine for a given firm. This explains why this model is not used alone, but combined, for instance, with a fundamentalist model, allowing for better appreciation of each company's specificity, despite the difficulties and the weaknesses of such an exercise. However, as long as the economic environment is stable, and thanks partly to the auto-referential nature of financial markets,[39] the chartist decision-making method is profitable; whether the past prices of a title are a good indication of its future performances or not, if all investors follow this decision-making model, they will all anticipate the same evolution. For instance, if they anticipate the rise of a title, they will all buy it, which will provoke its rise, fulfilling their prevision.

These decision-helping tools are largely used by all investors, in combination with other means gathering information, such as surveys or notes, external information and market knowledge.

2.2. The Means of Non-Financial Evaluation

Outside the models used to anticipate the fluctuations of a title's price, investors, when making buying or selling decisions, use information from analysts, informal conversations, information about the global or sector-based economical context and information from the firms themselves.[40]

A company's evaluation by investors is not done exclusively 'distantly': the growing activity of stakeholders, linked with the long-term investments of pension funds, goes hand in hand with a growing control over the implementation of the firm's strategies. This control is based on information collecting, particularly through 'road shows', meetings allowing investors to collect financial and non-financial information from the company organizing it. These huge communication operations are consistent with the Corporate Governance principles. The reason for these more in-depth investigation about the company's middle- and long-term strategies is that pension funds usually invest in companies for between two and five years – not exactly a long-term investment, but not a short one either. Pension funds don't use speculative back-and-forths; they exert a classical financial management, investing important sums for long periods of time, making benefits in about three years in average. When a pension fund leaves an company's capital, it is generally replaced by another fund ; as a consequence, it doesn't destabilize the title.

These twice-yearly meetings are completed by face-to-face meetings, evaluating an company's strategy, usually led by the pension fund's analysts. From Morin:[41] 'Fidelity, the world's first tier manager, declared to have visited 24.500 companies in the USA and 6500 in Europe. This type of meeting is more than a classical evaluation and public information-research; it shows a deep interest of the fund managers for the firms' leaders. It seems that the investors have, in that way at least, a will to know the company well beyond what would be needed to implement a purely indicial method of asset management'.

The sources of this information are many, as shown in a study by Mavrinac and Siesfield.[42] The significance of non-financial information sources are shown here, rated from 1 to 7 (see Table 2.1).

Table 2.1: Significance of non-financial information sources

Source	Mean score
Management presentations	5.54
Company filings	5.34
Sell-side analysts	4.82
Competitors	4.77
Business press	4.56
Company investor relations personnel	4.56
Customers	4.55
Buy-side analysts	4.53
Trade press	4.51
Informal networks	4.27
Independent ranking agencies	3.99
Industry trade associations	3.93
Online services	3.77

The variety of sources shows that institutional investors are ready to spend time and money for pertinent and reliable information. To see beyond what's given by the firms themselves through their accounts and end-of-year statements, the investors question the firm leaders to know about their long-term engagements. They aim to invest in enter prizes whose durability and growth are ensured. 'The fund's main investment criterion is the affirmation of a middle- and long-term, believable strategic project (a CEO once told me with a smile that often, in road shows, representatives of Templeton or Fidelity could be mistaken for syndicalists, because of their questions).'[43] Investors try to determine whether the leaders can be trusted to implement a long-term strategy compatible with their interests, and they rely largely on non-financial information, which must be carefully weighed.

2.3. Non-financial Factors and their importance to the investors

Mavrinac and Siesfeld's investigation aimed to analyse the importance of non-financial factors in the decision-making process of the actors in financial markets, and to determine the more important sources of this type of information. This study relies on a panel of 275 American portfolio managers (14% of this profession), all types of financial institutions (pension funds, insurances, banks) and analysis of 300 independent analysts' reports.

The importance of non-financial information in decision-making brings interrogations about the information that are considered as having a significant importance in the final decision. This study lists them by order of importance:

Table 2.2: Non-financial factors

The 39 specific non-financial criteria used most by sell-side analysts grouped into eight factors.

FACTOR	Criterion	Rank
QUALITY OF MANAGE-MENT	Execution of Corporate Strategy	1
	Quality of Corporate Strategy	3
	Management Experience	7
	Quality of Organizational Vision	16
	CEO Leadership Style	24
EFFECTIVENESS OF NEW PRODUCT DEVELOPMENT	Research Leadership	9
	New Product Development Efficiency	14
	New Product Development Cycle Time	17
	Percentage of Revenues Derived from New Products	20
STRENGTH OF MARKET POSITION	Innovativeness	4
	Market Share	6
	Brand Image	13
	Strength of Marketing and Advertising	21
	Global Capability	22
STRENGTH OF CORPORATE CULTURE	Ability to Attract and Retain Talented People	5
	Quality of Workforce	18
	Quality of Incentive Performance Systems	23
	Quality of Employee Training	28
	Employee Turnover Rates	30
	Environmental and Social Policies	37
	Use of Employee Teams	38
EFFECTIVENESS OF EXECUTIVE COMPENSATION POLICIES	Alignment of Compensation with Shareholder Interests	8
	Performance-based Compensation Policies	12
	Ratio of CEO Compensation to Workforce Compensation	39
QUALITY OF INVESTOR COMMUNICATIONS	Management Credibility	2
	Accessibility of Management	26
	Quality of Guidance	29
	Knowledge and Experience of Investor Relations Contact	31
	Quality of Published Materials	34
QUALITY OF PRODUCTS AND SERVICES	Quality of Major Business Processes	10
	Customer Perceived Quality	15
	Product Defect Rates/Service Failure Rates	25
	Product Durability	27
	Product Quality Awards	35
	Process Quality Awards	36
LEVEL OF CUSTOMER SATISFACTION	Customer Satisfaction Level	11
	Repeat Sales Level	19
	Number of Customer Complaints	32
	Quality of Customer Service Department	33

Source : Ernst & Young LLP.[44]

According to the portfolio managers that were questioned for this study, non-financial information are important indicators, allowing them to evaluate the intern workings of an company, as well as its application of the strategy. When asked how important these factors were in their decision-making, for 25% of them, non-financial information influenced more than 50% of the decision; for 60% of them, it influenced between 20 and 50% of it. In average, 35% of the investment decision is determined by non-financial decisions. The figure goes up to 67% if including the company's image in the non-financial data.[45]

This data is largely confirmed by Andrieu and Frottiée[46] in their study of the quantification of non-concrete elements in companies' valuation:

Figure 2.2: The stated usefulness of non-financial data

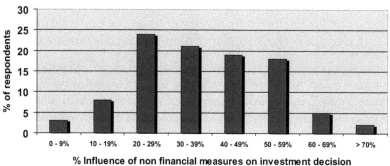

The same study shows that some non-financial information is particularly important for investors. Three out of five indicators considered important by more than 90% of investors are financial, while five out of ten indicators important for more than 80% of investors are non-financial.

Table 2.3: Significance of indicators

Indicator Financial (F) vs. Non Financial (NF)	Significance
Market growth (NF)	92%
Profit (F)	92%
Investment (F)	90%
New products (NF)	90%
Cash flow (F)	90%
Strategy (NF)	86%
Products quality (NF)	84%
Investment (R&D) (F)	84%
Production cost (F)	84%
Market share (NF)	82%
Division results (F)	77%
Work productivity (NF)	73%
Customer loyalty (NF)	64%
Return on investment (R&D) (NF)	61%
Intellectual property (NF)	59%
Customer satisfaction (NF)	57%
Industrial process quality (NF)	55%

The diversity of factors considered important in the analysis of a company's economical situation shows that investors take into account a large number of indicators in making asset management decisions. Non-financial information allow the investors to go beyond a superficial analysis (limited by the filter of accounting, even expert and technically sophisticated), by integrating strategic and organizational elements and immaterial assets. The focalization of fund managers on short-term rentability is more social representation than fact; the investor's expectations cannot be summed up at a better return on investment than average. The weight and diversity of big institutional investors would not easily allow them too out-perform the market.

Conclusion: the Necessity of Non-Financial Information

The pressure put on firms by investors through road shows and investigations indicates a search for information allowing them to control companies. This pressure results from a growth of Corporate Governance demands, which leads to a more important role of the information intended for the investors, notably through accounting and audits. It is expressed by the investor's will to evaluate not only the financial value of the company through accounting, leading to the evolution of accounting standards through the IFRS, but also by the demand of additional information able to go beyond the limits of purely financial information.

Indeed, an analysis' performance depends not only on the quality of the provided financial information, but also on non-financial knowledge. It has been shown that an analysis's precision, all things being equal, increases with the analyst's experience with the studied society, and decreases, all things being equal, with the geographical and industrial diversity of the studied society. (Mangot, 2005). The experience with the studied society results from a non-financial knowledge of the company's inner workings, through its previous decisions and reactions. Likewise, information on the local or sector-based particularities (which is also non-financial) make a difference in an analyst's performance. If non-financial analysis appears like a way to better an analyst's precision, it can also be the best means of prediction ; in the case of quick-growing firms (recently created or not), financial indicators are insufficient to build an viable analysis. In that case, non-financial indicators will better allow the analyst to give an opinion about the company's potentialities and inform investment decisions.

The IASB consultation concerning 'management commentaries' in October 2005 ended in January 2007 and led IASB to launch a new step of its rule-elaboration process. Despite a certain reluctance from the auditing and accounting professionals (61% of them are against those 'management commentaries' being added to the financial report, particularly because of the risks of this document's certification, even if the German example shows that it is possible). IASB is conscient of the importance of building a report's framework to obtain more precise financial information. Thus, quite paradoxically, the tendency towards financialization of the economical information that seemed to begin with the adoption of the IFRS leads, because it aims to better the financial market's efficiency, to increase the value of non-financial information, and consequently to increase the value of strategical elements that do not directly impact the short-term return on investment of the title. (Boyer[47] shows the negative impact of redundancies on stock-market and economical performances). Numerous studies show that the coherence between financial and non-financial information obtained from specific reports filed in financial reports is the more useful for investors in making good decisions in their middle- and long-term portfolio management.[48]

3 THE LESSONS OF LUXEMBOURG'S FINANCIAL CENTRE: TOWARDS A CERTIFICATION OF ETHICS FOR FINANCIAL CENTRES TO REPLACE CURRENT ASSESSMENTS

Jérôme Turquey

Luxembourg, under the spotlight over its banking secrecy, is defending its 'philosophical' choice, denying it is a 'tax haven' in a time of global financial instability when tax havens are in question. 'To equate banking secrecy with a tax haven does not make sense', Luxembourg Prime Minister Jean-Claude Juncker said on French television on 21 October 2008 after a critical report on his jurisdiction by the channel.

Prime Minister Jean-Claude Juncker stated an opinion that is shared by every professional and politician in Luxembourg. In answer to a question from the Member of Parliament Lucien Thiel, who is the former chairman of the ABBL (the Luxembourg Bankers' Association) and advisor to its board of directors,[1] Luc Frieden, who is Minister of Justice and Minister for the Treasury and Budget, specified that he wanted to make known the reality of the Luxembourg financial centre.[2] The same Luc Frieden had affirmed before the IMF in 2002: 'Personally, I have no doubt that my country can lead by example in promoting good governance, in fighting against the financing of terrorism and against money laundering, and in actively promoting development policies'.[3]

It is true that the IMF issued a good report[4] on the normative framework of the financial centre that would take into account the FATF recommendations, on which the financial sector and the political authorities communicate[5] to repudiate critics on the functioning of the jurisdiction.

However, the normative framework and the declarations are not enough to assess the actual ethical values of a financial centre: it is necessary to observe on the one hand the functioning of its institutions and on the other facts of business life. This is not exactly what the international assessors do; they are like Catherine II visiting the Potemkine villages while sticking with the apparent legal and regulatory framework or soothing declarations from officials, which, unfortunately, very often constitute a frontage.

As Christian Maréchal said, 'Behind the frontage of Professional standing, if there is another world, it is difficult to maintain the coexistence of both worlds durably. At one time, an error takes place, something is no longer compatible'.[6]

It is time to analyse official and public national and international sources to appreciate the ethics of the Luxembourg's financial centre beyond the split with on the one hand its exponents who deny dysfunctions and formulate the charge of gossip and polemic every time these dysfunctions are underlined, and on the other hand its detractors, that deny the positive and demonize finance and business in general: *In medio stat virtus.*[7]

After pointing out the social and political framework in Luxembourg (I), we will show that Luxembourg, by the functioning of its 'system' is a 'laboratory' of carelessness, bad practices of management and governance, which demonstrates a perfectible business ethics (II).

1. The Social and Political Framework in Luxembourg

1.1. Institutions

Official institutions[8]

The Grand Duchy of Luxembourg has been an independent sovereign state since the Treaty of London was signed on 19 April 1839. The country is a parliamentary democracy in the form of a constitutional monarchy.

Legislative power resides in the joint action of Parliament (Chambre des députés), Government and Council of State. Each entity serves a wholly separate function. Parliament is made up of sixty Members of Parliament (MPs) elected for a five-year term. The Government has a right of initiative in legislative matters known as 'governmental initiative', which allows it to table draft bills. After being examined by the Council of State, draft bills are put to the vote before Parliament. The Council of State is composed of twenty-one councillors. State Councillors are formally appointed and dismissed by the Grand Duke. In Luxembourg's unicameral system, the Council of State acts as a second legislative assembly. It is required to voice its opinion on all items of legislation, namely on all draft and private bills tabled before the Chamber prior to voting by the Members of Parliament.

Executive power is under the constitution of 1868, as amended by the Grand Duke and the Council of Government (cabinet), which consists of a prime minister and several other ministers. The Grand Duke is head of state.

As far as the judicial power is concerned, there are two branches of jurisdiction in Luxembourg: the judicial order and the administrative order. The Constitutional Court ranks on top of the judicial hierarchy. The three Magistrates' Courts are the first rank of the judicial hierarchy. The country is divided into the two judicial districts of Luxembourg and Diekirch, each of which has a district court. These courts hear and determine civil, commercial and criminal cases in the criminal or correctional division. The Supreme Court of Justice includes a Court of Appeals, divided into chambers where some thirty appeal-court judges sit and a Court of Cassation, consisting of a chamber in which five judges sit. The administrative courts are assigned by the Constitution to deal with administrative and fiscal cases. The Administrative Tribunal hears and determines in the first instance appeals against any administrative decisions. The Administrative Court is an appeal body.

The Constitutional Court is composed of nine members and sits in Luxembourg. As its name suggests, it rules on the conformity of laws with the Constitution, apart from those laws approving treaties

Official publications are released in the Memorial: Memorial A for the legal and regulatory texts, Memorial B for the administrative texts and Memorial C for the publications relating to the companies.

Financial Institutions: 'Fourth Power' in Luxembourg? Their Weight in the International Financial System

In any democracy, the fourth estate is normally exerted by the press. The GRECO noted its weakness in Luxembourg in 2001[9]. It is necessary, however, to underline recent positive evolutions with the Law of 8 June 2004 on the freedom of expression in the media, and several articles published in particular in *Agefi Luxembourg*, *Lëtzebuerger Land* and *Paperjam*. But we are far from an actual fourth estate as the press is not independent enough because it requires public financing to ensure a plurality of newspapers.

The function of the fourth estate in Luxembourg is exerted in practice by the financial institutions because of their weight in the economy allowing them a strong lobbying.

The Luxembourg financial centre holds 16% of the total offshore assets.[10] The STATEC (central Service of the statistics and the economic surveys in Luxembourg) underlined the importance of the sector for the growth of the country.[11]

The main associations of the financial sector are for bankers are the ABBL (Association Banques & Banquiers Luxembourg), for UCITS the ALFI (Association Luxembourgeoise des Fonds d'Investissement). Their members do not limit themselves to the financial companies because these associations also gather law firms, Big Four firms...[12]

Associations representative of professionals in charge of business ethics are, for internal auditors, the IIA Luxembourg (Institute of Internal Auditors Luxembourg), for compliance officers the ALCO (Association Luxembourgeoise des Compliance Officers) and for risk managers PRIM (Professionals of Risk

Management). The IRE (Institut des Réviseurs d'Entreprises) is responsible for the supervision of external registered auditors.

The professionals of finance are supervised, as regards AML-CFT, by two institutions: on the one hand the CSSF (Commission de Surveillance du Secteur Financier), which is in charge of the prudential monitoring and on the other hand, the CRF (Cellule de Renseignements Financiers): the CRF is the Luxembourg FIU (Financial Intelligence Unit), whose characteristic is to be the prosecuting authorities and not an administrative body, which is definitely an element of effectiveness in its duty.

The financial centre is growing and some actors see the financial crisis and the fight against tax havens (Luxembourg not being one of them in their opinion) as an opportunity to grow more. This is for example what Didier Mouget, who is PwC Luxembourg Territory Senior Partner thought.[13]

Several sectors depend on the financial sector: external auditors, cabinets of recruitment and IT service providers. The result is a pressure on public policies.

1.2. The System of Governance

The system of governance in place has two major characteristics: conservatism and on the dangerous influence of the financial sector on the State.

The Dangerous Influence of the Financial Sector on Public Policies

As Anouk Dumont explains,[14] banking secrecy in Luxembourg stems from the influence of the bankers on the legislator: Since 1956, the ABBL postulated the thesis of the existence of banking secrecy. This opinion was supported by the doctrine and has not been contested since then.

The law of 5 April 1993, relating to the financial sector, confirms and reinforces the principle of banking secrecy by stating in its article 41 that it is applicable to all the professionals of the financial sector. Exceptions to this requirement can only occur the law.[15] So according to some, banking secrecy is seen as linked to public order.[16]

At the time of the elections of 2004 the inappropriate footbridges between politics and financial sector were clear with, in particular, the election of the chairman of the ABBL, Lucien Thiel, at the Chamber of Deputies under the banner of the Prime Minister's party, while preserving a role of advisor at the ABBL. Beside him, Kik Schneider, Director at Fortis,[17] is a member of the executive committee of the DP (Demokratesch Partei) being its national treasurer.[18]

Conservatism

A characteristic of Luxembourg is the culture of dialogue and negotiation. In a general way any project of reform gives place to debate. It remains that there is a cultural difficulty to be called into question, which stems from the motto *Mir wëlle bleiwe wat mir sin* (We want to remain what we are).

The speech of defence of Luxembourg's financial centre against the charges and/or the requirements of the other countries must be analysed in this context.

1.3. The Defence of the Whole of the 'System' Against the Charges and Requirements of Other Countries

Marco Zwick made an objective presentation of the legal framework to the beginning of the twenty-first century. He pointed out strengths but also weaknesses and threats, among which was a trend to act on national views.[19]

There are incontestably positive elements that demonstrate a will to fight against criminality. for example, the Jurado affair – arrested, judged, condemned, imprisoned then extradited to the USA at the beginning of the 1990s for money laundering – was internationally acclaimed.[20] Jurado is mentioned twice in the Montebourg-Peillon[21] report without giving credit to Luxembourg. The affair, which was processed in an exemplary way in Luxembourg, is not promoted by the professionals of the financial sector who could have proven the partiality of the Montebourg-Peillon report when it was issued.

The Luxembourg Fonds de Lutte contre le Trafic des Stupéfiants (Fund for the Fight against Drug Trafficking)[22] was founded on 29 January 1993. The existence of this fund and the actual commitment of the country in the international fight against drug, greeted by the executive director of the United Nations International Drug Control Programme (UNDCP),[23] is not taken into consideration by the Montebourg-Peillon report. The 2005 report of the fund presented on 6 October 2006 at the Council of Government, but the professionals of the sector do not communicate on the exemplary work that is done.

The law of 5 April 1993, on the financial sector specifies provisions relating to business standing and experience (Article 7 for banks or credit institutions established under Luxembourg law and Article 19 for other professionals). In both articles it is stated that 'business standing shall be assessed on the basis of police records and of any evidence tending to show that the persons concerned are of good repute and offering every guarantee of irreproachable conduct on the part of those persons'. One can formulate three observations on this requirement of 'every guarantee of irreproachable conduct': first of all, the 'and' is cumulative; then the wording goes much further in that the applicable requirement for an audit, less constraining, which would simply specify 'the reasonable insurance' of an irreproachable conduct and not 'every guarantee'; finally, the word 'irreproachable' has a meaning more extensive than the words 'licit' or 'irreprehensible' and mechanically sanctions any behaviour of bad management and/or bad governance.

In 2002, Luxembourg was at the heart of an affair involving the Swiss ambassador Peter Friederich, who was tried in Switzerland. The Swiss penal Supreme

Court noted in particular that the first judge, examining the Luxembourg law, concluded that this one knew a broader notion of forgery than the Swiss law and than the sanctions envisaged were more serious'.[24]

In December 2006, new recommendations relating to AML-CFT were published, resulting from a pilot scheme by Marco Zwick for the industry of investment funds in Luxembourg.[25]

There are indisputable elements of business ethics in Luxembourg. However, many scandals occur periodically in Luxembourg. For example, Luxembourg is regularly involved in tax and money laundering cases: for example, an investigation was opened in late 2003 concerning all Luxembourg companies in which the Parmalat Company had a direct or indirect link. The investigation put forward the question of the large facility to create a business in Luxembourg in Luxembourg, of the screen companies and of the laxity of banks.[26] Another example, on 6 March 2006 the French police force found in Paris a fraud based on a fictitious company located in Luxembourg.[27] In another instance, the Spanish Guardia Civil and the national office of investigation of frauds (ONIF) blocked bank accounts for an amount higher than €1.8 billion after having detected a tax evasion which could affect many accounts. Later, according to the Guardia Civil 'the money was undoubtedly sent on other accounts abroad for finally reconsidering accounts to Spain, via Luxembourg'.[28] More scandal occurred when the air company Sabena was suspected of tax evasion: it tried to use a black case to pay its executives, via a subsidiary company in Bermuda and a bank account in Luxembourg. In an interview in January 2007, Pierre Godfroid, who was the head of Sabena between 1991 and 1996, admitted the Luxembourg window, which he learned of in 1995 and explained he thought that the bonuses were paid directly via the company in Bermuda, without passing through Luxembourg.[29] In late February 2007 AOL was fined in France by the fiscal administration[30] for its hub in Luxembourg allowing the invoicing of French clients with a VAT of only 15% instead of 19.6%. The tax department in France estimated that the French clients must be subjected to French, not Luxembourgian, VAT.

More recently, in September 2008, the media reported[31] that a Luxembourg-based company would have been used to bypass the OECD Anti-Bribery Convention. The Luxembourg-based company was used as the starting hub; then the money went to Ireland, then the Isle of Man, then the Bahamas, then the Caiman Islands and finally the BVI. These examples are not exhaustive.

However, in spite of frequent affairs with a root in Luxembourg, the country seems to refuse to officially recognize dysfunctions and the perfectibility of its legal and regulatory framework. There is no questioning; on the contrary, dysfunctions are denied as nobody is actually willing to tighten up the ship.

2. Business in Practice in Official and Public Sources

The denial of issues and the belief in self-regulation in a small place where everybody knows everyone and are informed of what others are doing, as expressed with the GRECO or OECD[32] leads both to self-satisfaction and inaction vis-à-vis to official facts of negligence, bad management and bad governance that demonstrate a perfectible business ethics.

2.1. Pressure / Motivation to Commit Fraud is Verified on the Field

In an exceptional way, with the observation of the functioning of the business in the country, it appears that the three components of the 'fraud' (pressure/motivation, opportunity and rationalization) 'stream on the surface', which is all the less acceptable given that the financial centre is small (approximately 2,500 km²) and could actually monitor what is going on, which is not possible because of the importance of relationships and networks of decision-makers.

The criterion of the pressure/motivation to commit fraud appears on the field with the reading of what the ABBL/Chamber of Commerce[33] said about the draft law relating to the transposition of the second directive.[34] Bankers wrote that the noble goals of the fight money laundering and the financing of terrorism, supporting a serene image of the financial centre must be combined with the economic interests of the country and the commercial objectives of the professionals.

One will note reserved and distant semantics ('noble goals') in opposition to semantics like 'the pressing need', which would represent a true adhesion with the fight against money laundering and the financing of terrorism.

The pressure/motivation appears especially with the primacy given to the economic interests of the country and the commercial objectives of the professionals concerned. In their opinion, the prosecuting authorities[35] observed that 'in a context of increasing penalization, it is not tolerable that professionals being in the presence of an infringement close the eyes and continue to seek what they qualify their 'commercial objectives''.

2.2. Opportunity to Commit Fraud is Verified on the Field

As Noël Pons wrote, 'It is the feeling of impunity which causes the fraud'.[36] The criterion of opportunity to commit fraud is verified on the field by a lax and permissive environment favourable to fraud which is found in the standards as in businesses.

Standards

The Ten Principles of Corporate Governance of the Luxembourg Stock Exchange were issued in April 2006.[37] They are the deliverable of the 'Corporate Governance' working group, which was set up to draft the general principles of best practice in corporate governance for all Luxembourg companies listed on the Stock Exchange. The reliability and integrity of the financial information provided by the company is only the ninth recommendation under the ninth principle, which states that 'The board will establish strict rules, designed to protect the company's interests, in the areas of financial reporting, internal control and risk management': 'strict rules' does not mean integrity and only principles are mandatory (comply).[38]

The law of 10 August 1915 relating to commercial companies requires neither the independence nor the qualification of the person that audit the accounts.[39] Additionally the Mémorial C shows many statutory auditors that are located in exotic jurisdictions, which means that nobody controls them.

The introduction of the penal responsibility for legal persons results from international commitments of Luxembourg, but there are resistances in the name of the reputation of financial centre.[40] The Council of State confirmed 'the absence, in Luxembourg positive criminal law, of a penal responsibility for legal persons'.[41] Early in 2008, the OECD Working Group on Bribery urged Luxembourg to introduce liability of legal persons: the press release dated 3 March 2008 states that Luxembourg urgently needs to establish liability against legal persons for foreign bribery and put in place sanctions that are effective, proportionate and dissuasive. The bill currently before Parliament, designed to introduce this responsibility in Luxembourg law, should be amended to ensure that it meets the requirements of the OECD Anti-bribery Convention. The main recommendations of the Working Group are that Luxembourg should:

- introduce promptly liability of legal persons for foreign bribery. Currently, prosecution and thus conviction of companies that engage in bribery remains impossible because legal persons cannot be held liable for criminal offences,
- reinforce its mechanisms for combatting bribery by making it easier for its judicial authorities to obtain information held by banking institutions in the Grand Duchy.
- introduce effective, dissuasive and proportionate sanctions for companies and guarantee the jurisdiction of the Luxembourg courts over acts of bribery committed abroad by Luxembourg companies,
- step up its efforts to make SMEs aware of the crime of bribing foreign public officials, and introduce a whistleblower protection system.

The first project of quality control for registered auditors that was circulated in October 2006 contained in its drafting the elements of its inefficiency by allowing in particular the auditor controlled by a fellow-member to be opposed to the examination of files 'being regarded as dispute'. Such wording can only lead in practice to drifts to draw aside the files that are not correct on the pretext they are 'being regarded as dispute'.

Business Life and Behaviours

On 17 January 2002, Jos Nickts, a Union chairman, was placed in preventive detention on suspicion of defrauding the 560 union members of about €5 million, although not all the mechanisms employed in this alleged embezzlement have yet been discovered. Mr Nickts has been charged with forgery, the use of forgeries, false entry, breach of trust, confidence trickery and common theft. He was also accused of carrying out rash transactions, particularly in Switzerland, and of financial speculation and personal enrichment, exemplified by the alleged purchase of an estate and a yacht in Palma de Mallorca. At the time of the trial, his collaborators said he was 'a chairman praising his relationships with the politico-financial world'[42]: this sentence underlines the major risk of Luxembourg: wide and varied speculation in a small place where everyone knows everyone, makes regulation difficult as there are too many conflicts of interest.

The knowing hiring of dishonest employees is standardized in a way by the semantics used by the regulator, which is disturbing:

> in too many cases, the persons responsible for reprehensible acts do not suffer the consequences with regard to the continuation of their occupation. The person responsible for such an act is often simply removed from management while being granted compensations, which largely exceed normal expectations. Sometimes, the impression could arise that crime pays, which soils the reputation of a financial centre. Moreover, it can be observed on too many occasions that when such professionals seek new employment, the new employers tend to somewhat close their eyes to the problem, while knowingly taking the risk that the persons concerned could again perform reprehensible acts[43]

The words 'too many', indicate an excess semantically contrary to an alternative formulation like 'many', 'a lot of', 'some'..., seems to say that the writer accepts the principle of such collaborators while deploring the excess of cases.

Denials that the country is a banking, tax or legal haven is contradicted by the dubious communication on the field by some professionals, which can only attract fraudsters:

SOPARFI states that

> Despite moderate taxes rates Luxembourg is not a tax haven. There are taxes for individuals and companies. More than a tax haven, Luxembourg gathers the advantages of an on shore jurisdiction because it is in Europe and the advantages of off shore states taxes of which are similar to a tax haven for Holding 1929 companies, Holding companies

in other words being a member of the European Union is a blanket allowing activities of tax haven;

Let's see what was said by another professional on the advantages of the centre:

> Banking secrecy is integral part of the Luxembourg legislative system. ... The abuse of social goods and tax evasion are non-existent in the Luxembourg law ... Trust is a notion that does not exist in the French legislation ... The application of trust makes it possible to manage business while preserving anonymity. ... Thanks to X and its partners Attorney and Lawyers, you can within the framework of an economic beneficiary, own and manage your business without appearing officially. That can be useful for the detention of goods and real estate or for the continuation of an activity.[44]

On the legal page, the fiduciary explained that it does not support fraud, and it is not responsible for verifying the compliance with laws and regulation, which is up to the client. This company does not exist anymore but there are many businesses that go on selling publicly the same services that definitely attract fraudsters.

The hub that was created by AOL to reduce VAT despite an incompatibility with the tax doctrine in France was even promoted by bankers[45] and the main big four in Luxembourg[46] to incite other companies to create the same kind of hub.

This situation of recurring implications of Luxembourg and lax environment was regularly deplored by the tax administration AED (Administration de l'Enregistrement et des Domaines),[47] which observed in the 2007 report that for the first time since many years, the stress was laid straightforwardly on the more systematic research of the national fraud.

2.3. Rationalization to Commit Fraud is Verified on the Field

The criterion of rationalization to commit fraud was verified on the field at the time of the debate relating to the transposition of the second European directive.[48]

The ABBL and the Chamber of Commerce wrote that in their opinion 'offences such as forgery, use of forgery, false balance sheets, use of false balance sheets or unauthorized use of corporate property should not be included. These are offences with financial connotations which are confused with laundering for the sole purpose of applying exceptional powers to these vague offences' and 'The legal initiatives of our neighbours have a clear tendency to concentrate on the laundering of this kind of ambiguous offences. But it is not a reason to imitate them in this way which caused troubles in the financial centre in various cases'.

Such an official opinion involves the entire Luxembourg financial sector including Big Four firms as members of the ABBL: in other words, accounting offences that were the charges in cases like Enron, Parmalat and other scandals of the early 2000s are vague and ambiguous for professionals in Luxembourg that never repudiated official opinion, including that of audit firms responsible for certifying the account and providing stakeholders with confidence.

The opinion of the Council of State showed how much it is under the influence of politicians and professionals: from its composition leading to the conflict of interest, it is not able to take a truly neutral position. One can be bank manager, treasurer of a political party and member of the Council of State.[49] On the contrary, the opinion of the prosecuting authorities in this debate demonstrated their rigour and their undeniable will to abide by international commitments.

But under pressure from the professionals and the Council of State, sensitive provisions were removed, which resulted in a late final text envisaging fines with weak financial stake and removing negligence from penal responsibility,[50] to bring closer a reality described by the UN in 1999 that

> Many lawyers, accountants and bankers are (often unselfconsciously) adept at not asking questions that would require them to refuse business or even to report their clients or potential clients to the authorities. But a major component of the motivation for crime is also the expected probability and scale of reward, while the reverse is the expectation (if contemplated) of prevention and/or salient punishment. Any form of crime for economic gain can have its relative attractiveness rating altered significantly by changes in detection and sanction levels both for it and for other crimes such as narcotics sales.[51]

The official state of mind of management in a business world sullied by the scandals (Enron, Parmalat, Worldcom etc.) and the current financial crisis is a major problem for external auditors who have a commercial contract with important financial stakes, and for internal auditors or compliance officers who have a link of subordination. The mechanisms of control of companies in the country do not present all the guarantees of effectiveness.

The state of mind of Luxembourg in its approach to money laundering traditionally consisted in *'leaving to the economic actors enough breath and spaces of freedom to open out their activities'* as the Council of State wrote at the time of the debate, was sanctioned by Luxembourg justice on 12 October 2006 because it appeared that attempting to launder money is not punishable in Luxembourg. This judgement put forward a gigantic bug in the national repressive legal and regulatory framework: the offence must be 'consumed' for the tribunal sanction the launderers. Even though the Court of Appeal created jurisprudence on 4 July 2007 to rectify the situation, the strict wording of the penal law complies neither with the FATF requirements, nor the European requirements.

The Importance of Relationships and Networks of Decision-Makers

In this small country where everyone knows everyone and where there supposedly 'self regulation', the study, exclusively based on sources that are public and/or official, of the business life around a financial director[52] allows a diagnosis on Luxembourg, where the law applicable to the financial sector requires both business standing and experience (article 7 for banks or credit institutions established under Luxembourg law and article 19 for other professionals)

A judgement of the Court of Appeal dated 12 October 2006 between a company and its former financial director, who it had fired in 2003, shows that the established irregularities committed by the person in charge of the department responsible for managing finances of the employer are likely to have definitively broken the essential relations of confidence between the employer and an employee responsible for managing finances of a company, position with high responsibility.[53]

The financial director had won the litigation at the previous stage,[54] possibly because the Company had made inaccurate statements at the time of the first audience in 2004 about its shareholder, a thing that would have been easy to check and which weakened its credibility before the tribunal,[55] at the Court of Appeal, however, the financial director lost his credibility by making contradictory statements.[56]

If a lack of competence were not proved by the Company before the Court of Appeal,[57] it appears that the financial director had made an abusive use of the protected title of Chartered Accountant,[58] in 2002, in the Corporate Registration, but was not dismissed despite this indication of poor qualification[59] for a professional of an accounting and finance function:[60] the fact was neither raised at the tribunal nor at the court by the employer.

This error is all the more unacceptable than other texts of Memorial C when we learn that it had been from 1999[61] to late 2001[62] financial director of the Big Four in Luxembourg, where the chairman of the registered external auditors in Luxembourg comes from.[63] This Big Four stated early 2002 that 'firms like ours are a fish-tank of experienced staff'.[64]

If self-regulation worked, the Big Four, which is member of the ALFI and the ABBL, and whose direction in function at the time of the financial director[65] said at the beginning of 2002 that 'it is the role of each one – leader banks, service provider, supervision authority – to play their part of guard of the temple of the respectability of the centre. We must be very vigilant on the respect of the rules and our responsibilities'[66] would undoubtedly not have kept the financial director for a two-year period, and its direction would certainly not have kept relationships with management of a company[67] who made visible on the public place the behaviour of the financial director that is neither compatible with the ethics of the Big Four nor the ethics of the financial centre. Especially the big four would not have been involved with the company in the creation of an association dedicated to Corporate Social Responsibility[68] and the former Territory Senior Partner of the big four, who left the audit firm early 2007, would not have joined the board of the Company early 2008[69] especially at the highest level of chairperson[70] all the more than there is a visible turnover of financial directors and above all of commercial directors, which is a red flag for any serious audit professional as it corroborates an aggressive will to grow with relating risks[71].

If self-regulation worked, the minister responsible for the supervision of the financial sector would probably not have written in a publication issued by the Company in 2003[72] that he was pleased with *'clear and pragmatic legal rules'*[73] in Luxembourg, wording rephrased by management of the company[74], and would not have recognized as Professional of the Financial Sector (PSF) the Company because of the accumulation of negligence and public and official facts of bad management and bad governance that do not comply with the strict requirement of *'every guarantee of irreproachable conduct'* and with the ethical communication of the Company itself on trust and integrity values.

If self-regulation worked, the financial director, who found a position in the Luxembourg financial sector shortly after his dismissal, would not, at the end of 2006, shortly after the judgement of appeal, have been responsible for the recruitment of lawyers for a large law firm located in Luxembourg[75] that belongs to the same professional circles as his successive employers and specifying the ethics of his collaborators. He would not have been appointed early 2008 as managing director responsible for finance and management of a real estate company located in Luxembourg, the statutory auditor of which is not registered in Luxembourg but is located in the British Virgin Islands,[76] meaning that this auditor is controlled neither by Luxembourg-registered auditors nor Luxembourg chartered accountants.

The above facts, that involve some of Luxembourg leading people, actually demonstrate the importance of networks and relationships in the Luxembourg society. This was admitted for the first time in the last GRECO report about Luxembourg[77] to explain why the number of cases coming before the courts appeared very small (the same goes for the small number of declarations of suspicion and the 'scarce number of financial crime cases' as the US Department of State wrote).[78] Neither the GRECO nor the OECD had pointed out before in their respective previous reports this huge problem of networks and relationships that explains the reason why Luxembourg is so interesting a jurisdiction, because the negative effects of conflicts of interest are visible.

Conclusion: What Lessons to Draw from the Luxembourg Laboratory?

Decision-makers, usually either professionals or politicians, in Luxembourg are not reliable because public and official negligence and poor governance are supported and even considered as indicators of success:[79] business stakes and promiscuity in the networks prevent criticism even when official and public facts are compatible neither with the ethical communication nor the requirement of professional standing and experience. Everybody meets everyone and no one is willing to take the risk of being excluded (either for jobs or business contracts) by deploring dysfunctions, even though these exist in official and public sources. Furthermore, as the GRECO had stated in 2004

> The often cited small size of the country, the fact that everyone knows everyone else (thus encouraging self-regulation) and the high level of incomes cannot therefore be taken to be a sufficient safeguard and could even have the opposite effect, with everyone sheltering behind a complicit silence rather than running the risk of being considered indelicate.[80]

Beyond law, training and international controls that are definitely a front, it is the deep culture of politicians and professionals that is relevant to assess the ethics of a financial centre, and inertia in Luxembourg is particularly important to allow an aggiornamento because business progresses anyway, even when there is no sanction.

This is the reason why some leaders in Luxembourg go on promoting fraud: in the context of the massive tax evasion through Liechtenstein that emerged early 2008, Lucien Thiel, who is the former chairman of the Luxembourg Bankers' Association (ABBL) and current Member of Parliament in the same party as the Prime Minister, stated in an interview[81] that 'It is not our duty to control if the tax payer was honest' and 'Banking secrecy remains: Luxembourg is not compelled to communicate its clients' data'. In a couple of sentences Lucien Thiel publicly admits that Luxembourg actually does not care about the fight against fraud or international cooperation. What counts is making money and growing financially. Money over ethics is unfortunately Luxembourg's business doctrine.

This is the reason why the FATF made a mistake that weakens the credibility of its assignment: it is said in the FATF Annual Report 2006–7 states that

> Thanks to a generous grant from Luxembourg, the FATF has been working to improve its information technology systems, with a view to providing FATF delegations with better access to confidential documents. This system will be strengthened over the coming year and the FATF will then be in a position to enhance its public website.[82]

The FATF should definitely not accept a grant from any country,[83] especially not Luxembourg, all the more because there are many warning signs in this small jurisdiction that does not implement the GRECO or OECD Recs, and because institutions that are critical to the fight against fraud and money laundering (such as police, justice and tax administration) lack means. One may find it strange that a small jurisdiction that finds the money for its promotion, with for example LuxembourgForFinance,[84] should be unable to invest in the means required to correct its dysfunctions. It is their choice of business over ethics.

Time is up for head offices, and bank head offices or audit firms head offices must realize the risks for their brand in a centre where both politicians and professionals definitelyfail in their duty: there should be no tolerance for professionals who have replaced actual pragmatism with that which is supported by negligence and who deny dysfunctions, which standardize bad management and bad governance with all potential risks. By excluding those who do not condone public or official issues, professionals demonstrate that their ethical and compliance frameworks turn out to be a charade, which weakens the credibility of financial centres and financial institutions worldwide.

The lack of responsibility of many decision-makers allows identifying ethical weaknesses, and realizing the limits of current international assessments in business ethics: assessments do not comply with reality as many financial centres still do not respect international recommendations, in the name of 'pragmatism', the magic word that weakens the enforcement of ethical laws and regulations.

In the context of the financial crisis, a certification to ethics for financial centre should be implemented. Such certification could be based on six criteria:

1. Credibility of statements

A financial centre cannot be ethical when official statements do not comply with reality. In such cases, the centre cannot be trusted. This area is probably more sensitive for small centres where dysfunctions are much more visible than in a larger centre.

2. Means for detection

A financial centre cannot be ethical if organizations that are responsible for detection and sanctions, either administrative (regulatory body) or judiciary (FIU), do not have the relevant means.

3. Credibility of sanctions

A financial centre cannot be ethical if sanctions for professionals who do not have a proper business conduct are not dissuasive enough. If the sanctions are ridiculous compared to the amounts of money laundering or frauds, there is no dissuasion.

4. Transparency

A financial centre cannot be ethical if issues are hidden or denied to show a clean Potemkine village. Two sub-areas should be especially taken into account:
– On the one hand, the behaviour of the media: do they play their role of watchdog or not?
– On the other hand, the transparency of justice: are cases easily available or not?

5. Independence of auditors

A financial centre cannot be ethical if auditors are close to auditees and could be influenced by them. This area is probably more significant for small centres where dysfunctions are more visible than in a larger centre.

6. Protection of the client

A financial centre cannot be ethical if the client is not protected.

4 IS ECONOMIC EFFICIENCY A MEANINGFUL DEVICE WITH WHICH TO ASSESS INSOLVENCY LAWS?

Nadine Levratto

The recent financial and economic crisis reminds us, if still necessary, that company default is an inseparable component of any market economy. In such a system, the survival of producers is conditioned in the short term by liquidity and in the long term by solvency. Failure to comply with the latter condition, defined in accounting terms as insufficient available assets to meet current liabilities, endangers the company and may be grounds for proceedings that could lead to ending the business. These financial considerations suggest a clear-cut separation between healthy and failing companies, either based on accounts or almost naturally. The origins of bankruptcy law show that this is not the case and while the nature of the default is obviously economic, it is also, and to the same extent, legal. The source of this twofold connection lies in the definition of bankruptcy, which means a trader is unable to honour his payments. As Pierre-Claude Bravard-Veyrières[1] emphasized, this definition presupposes that two conditions are met, for 'to be in default, it is necessary to have stopped his payments and to have stopped them as a trader'.[2] Thus, this twofold condition will underlie our discussion of the evolution of the law and litigation practices pertaining to bankruptcy, which today is largely dominated by viewing the law in terms of economic efficiency.

The idea that the law evolves with a view to attaining a greater degree of efficiency is directly inherited from work by scholars focusing on the economic efficiency of law and economics and the comparative analysis of legal systems, led by the emblematic figures of La Porta, Lopez de Silanes, Shleifer and Vishny,[3] abbreviated below as LLSV, who have produced numerous disciples in the field of business financing[4] and bankruptcy.[5] In general, these works help to show the superiority of bankruptcy law based on the common law tradition over the legal system of cessation of payment developed in countries with a civil or Roman legal code. The final proof of good performance in bankruptcy treatment by common law is presented under the heading 'Closing a business' in the annual World Bank survey on 'Doing business'. Referring to the English law on bankruptcies in 1732 as the source of modern bankruptcy law, the authors of the reports view the greater experience authorized by this seniority as the cause of the efficiency of the legal systems that flow from it. Indeed, they have come further on the path towards efficiency and, for that reason, among others, are said to come closer than the other legal systems to achieving the three 'universal goals of bankruptcy'.[6] Maximizing the value of liquidated assets through swift winding up, rescuing viable businesses and complying with the rank of creditors. The annual ranking, an extract of which is shown below (Table 4.1), drawn up on the basis of three indicators of legal efficiency – the duration of liquidation proceedings, the cost of bankruptcy as a percentage of assets and the rate of recovery – shows excellent performance in Canada, the Scandinavian countries, Japan and, to a lesser extent, the United Kingdom, considered as common law countries as far as insolvency is concerned, compared with the very mediocre position of France, an archetype of the civil legal system.

Here we find the clearest manifestation of the economic view of bankruptcy law designed as an instrument to achieve the best possible result.[7]

Table 4.1: Extract of the ranking of insolvency proceeding efficiency

	Length of proceedings (in years)	Cost (% of assets)	Recovery rate (in %)
Australia	1.0	8.0	78.8
Canada	0.8	4.0	88.7
Denmark	3.0	4.0	86.5
Finland	0.9	4.0	87.3
France	1.9	9.0	44.7
Japan	0.6	4.0	92.5
Norway	0.9	1.0	89.0
Sweden	2.0	9.0	75.1
United Kingdom	1.0	6.0	84.2
United States	1.5	7.0	76.0

(Source: 'Closing a business', Doing Business, www.doingbusiness.org)

Instead of this normative view of the law, and in keeping with the distinction made by Kirat,[8] we will substitute a view of the movement of law within a dynamic historical framework combining autonomy and heteronomy that underlies the pragmatist analysis of law in action. In so doing, we move away from the linear schema according to which the emergence of new institutions results from tendencies outside the individuals that take part in this construction and adopt instead the institutionalist viewpoint, notably due to Commons, for whom the enforcement of a rule, like its construction, contributes to producing the law. The legal proceedings determined by the strategies of the economic actors that initiate them thus contribute in fact to achieving an effect that complies with the one expected by lawmakers.[9]

Two elements will guide us in developing this point of view: firstly, how the judge qualifies the state of bankruptcy and secondly, the determination, by law, of trader status. Together, these two pillars delimit the scope of application of the rules governing bankruptcy and thereby influence the quantitative size of the legal proceedings initiated by the report of cessation of payments. This initial relationship between the scope of application of the law and the activity of the courts will constitute the first point in support of our analysis. It will be supplemented by questioning the meaning of the relationship as a dynamic factor in the law, which constitutes the second focal point of our work. These two foundations have been presented in earlier work.[10] This twofold framework leads us to a critique of the opposition between pro-debtor and pro-creditor bankruptcy law as a guide to assessing efficiency in this area, which the *Law and Economics* approach has adopted based on the analytic grid it has developed and the assessment method it uses. Then we will propose a new reading of the evolution of bankruptcy law as a capitalist institution, which will give us a grid for a new interpretation of the evolution of the law and practices relating to cessation of payments. We will rely on two phenomena for this purpose: the extension of the scope of application, on the one hand, and the opposition between bankruptcy law that organizes an optimum mode of sharing company assets and the law governing companies in financial distress aimed at correcting earlier market mistakes such as granting excessive loans, on the other.

1. Spatial and Historical Breaks: Questionable Keys for an Institutional Interpretation

The renown of the economic approach to law maintained by LLSV rests on an analysis of the evolution of the law and rules governing bankruptcy that relies on a methodology characterized by considerable recourse to econometrics. It helps to substantiate the framework for interpretation constructed by the authors linked to a purely economic interpretation of insolvency laws. This framework is rooted in a preconception that can be assimilated to a Coasean bargaining situation.[11] Situations are compared to a sort of ideal benchmark that defines a normative standard, prompting Djankov et al. to say that 'in a theoretical model of an ideal court, a conflict between two neighbours can be settled equitably by a third party, with a little bit of knowledge and limited use of the law, without lawyers or written proceedings, without procedural constraints regarding the manner of investigation, testimony, the way of presenting arguments, and without appeals'.[12] When a 'good' law is defined as one that does not exist, a series of often quantitative arguments will be mobilized to demonstrate the superiority of interpersonal relationships over legal proceedings and of common law over civil law. By focusing our approach on the treatment of companies in financial distress, we are seeking here to deconstruct the method and its presuppositions (Section 1.1) before giving an account of the fragility of the identified divisions (Section 1.2).

1.1. Theoretical and Methodological Issues

When applied to bankruptcy, the approach adopted in *Law and Economics,* which is essentially positive, presupposes that reforms of the legal system are necessary because the procedures in force are not efficient in most countries. This results in limited use of the rules in place for fear of seeing either the asset value diminish to such an extent that the creditors will only recover a small part of their due, or an exclusion from business life that prompts the entrepreneur to dissimulate his problems. On the contrary, when bankruptcy law is 'good', companies in financial distress and their suppliers do not hesitate to have recourse to proceedings from which they expect quick and efficient results. In addition to these direct advantages, the business climate is said to improve as a result of tidying up bankruptcy law. Two dimensions of the application of the LLSV approach are examined in depth here: the systematic and exclusive minimization of transaction costs (see 1.1.1.), and the methodology underlying the construction of performance indicators (see 1.1.2.)

1.1.1. A Quest for the Grail: the Minimization of Transaction Costs

The inclusion of bankruptcy law in an economic perspective centred on the distribution of assets is characteristic of the penetration of the law by the economic policy objectives characteristic of the recent period. By including procedures relating to cessation of payments in the policy agenda to stimulate a sort of growth based on the production of wealth by companies, legislators in most OECD countries gave up a moral and social vision of bankruptcy law. In so doing, they embed it in a private framework guaranteeing company prosperity or turnaround, or in a worst-case scenario, a quick liquidation of the business in such a way as to favour the reuse of production machinery in another framework. The utilitarian approach that prevails here is especially obvious in 'Doing Business' which argues in favour of a 'modernization of the law' based exclusively on practical considerations. Thus one of the two French partners in the survey maintains that the law must be tidied up due to the globalization of trade, that 'the relative efficiency of the law is obviously a factor in economic productivity and [that] in this area, France must do better by pragmatically agreeing to seek greater efficiency...'[13]

Two questions flow from the positive view of bankruptcy law. Both of them are related to the efficiency of the procedures within the scope of a market economy which orients the content of the research carried out. An initial level of analysis asks what means are available in collective proceedings to distribute the risks among all the actors in a market economy in a predictable, fair and transparent way. In addition to this question, the work seeks to identify what incentive mechanisms collective proceedings have acquired to encourage market economy actors to make sound decisions. Helping to resolve these questions will guarantee the introduction of efficient law, i.e. bankruptcy law in which the proceedings fulfil a twofold function:

- they give rise to good incentives for debtors and creditors in such a way as to encourage entrepreneurship,
- they ensure a good selection of companies by eliminating from the market those that are performing poorly and rescuing the others.

Seen in this light, bankruptcy law is essentially designed to keep businesses going and protect the value of the company in the interest of all the stakeholders. To achieve this objective, collective proceedings must avoid dangerous competition among creditors and enable viable businesses with temporary problems to be filtered out from those with a structurally-compromised future. According to LLSV, this aim would be achieved through English common law, which favours private arrangements among debtors and creditors. French law, on the other hand, is held to be inefficient because it is too costly, with low recovery rates of the amounts due to creditors and too favourable to the debtor.[14] The changes to be made in procedures for handling cessations of payment thus depend on the level of the country's score and rank in the World Bank classification. In general, they must help improve the level of at least one of the criteria presented above (the length of time required to process a bankruptcy case, the cost of the bankruptcy itself and the rate of claim recovery). Two types of efficiency will then be attained:

- *ex ante* efficiency consisting in encouraging the actors in a market economy (mainly company directors and shareholders, as well as banks in their decision to grant credit) to make the right decisions in order to avoid situations resulting in shortfalls of short-term liquidity and medium- or long-term insolvency. Here again the means available to collective proceedings must be balanced so as not to appear too disadvantageous and discourage the risk-taking inherent in entrepreneurship and the smooth workings of the market economy.
- *ex post* efficiency consists in liquidating only non-viable companies and maximizing, or at least protecting, the value of the company in the interest of all the stakeholders and the economy in general. This first principle explains the intrinsically collective nature of this type of procedure: individual proceedings by creditors to recover their claims would result in

piecemeal sale of the company that would prevent it from obtaining the best price for the disposal of its assets. The number of stakeholders (creditors with absolute priority, secured or unsecured creditors, shareholders, government administrations and social organizations, potential buyers, society, etc.) generates a variety of often conflicting interests.

Underlying these two types of efficiency, we find the utilitarian conception of bankruptcy law as the guarantor of the smooth operation of the economy in so far as it prevents creditors holding securities from collectively initiating a downward spiral of foreclosures and bank defaults that could cause a worldwide crisis like the one in 1933.[15] The positive view of law adopted here is also the source of the univocal association of procedural complexity with legal complexity, captured by the indicator that measures the time required to apply the measures provided for first in the commercial code and secondly in company bankruptcy law. As a result, the analysis leaves aside the social norms and extralegal factors that should be taken into account in any analysis of comparative law,[16] especially as 'a specific function may be assumed by a legal rule in one country and by an extralegal phenomenon in another country'.[17] The question that arises is thus the method to adopt and the sources to use in order to take into account the interdependence of institutions or laws, i.e. to carry out an endogenous assessment of national systems of economic rules and regulations. How can we get beyond a self-centred analysis of bankruptcy law and establish links between company law, credit law and insolvency law to escape the univocal positivism characteristic of *Law and Economics* and enrich it with a more diverse view of capitalism?

1.1.2. An Essentially Textual Knowledge at the Origin of Performance

This reading of bankruptcy law in terms of efficiency relies on a certain reading of the individual laws comprising it The paradigm established around LLSV gives rise to a sort of paradox because, on the one hand, they are writing under the influence of the works of North who insists on the role of institutions as a basis of property and the rights associated with contracts,[18] and on the other hand, they produce a totally a-historical analysis of the interaction between institutions and economic development. The result of this ambiguity lies in producing performance measurement indicators by processing questionnaires based on content derived directly from the 'law in the books'. By adopting this approach, LLSV are reviving a sort of legal formalism criticized by many authors in France, such as Raymond Saleilles[19] and François Gény, and by the Realists in the United States. According to Saleilles, this traditional method of interpreting the law 'consists in taking a code as a self-sufficient whole, which, without living an organized life (in fact, far from it), is content to draw the logical consequences of its own underpinnings, so as to present, through a process of narrow deductions, a series of abstract constructs that come only from itself and include nothing from outside'.[20] Although these reservations are well known, they have not kept the supporters of the positivist conception of law from using that method.

This first methodological bias is patently obvious in the item 'Closing a business' in the 'Doing Business' survey. This heading is built entirely on the assumption that 'reformed bankruptcy rules allow viable businesses to get through liquidity crises and quickly eliminate insolvent companies'.[21] Economic analysis is then used to argue in favour of this idea, without discussing it, whereas bankruptcy law also contains a significant moral aspect and has oscillated, since the beginning, between a will to exclude and a need for rehabilitation.[22] Like the laws governing property rights to which it is closely related, bankruptcy law and its need to evolve into a system that enhances company business rests on a form of fictional economy[23] in which growth is the consequence of flexible laws. The means used to foster dynamic entrepreneurship and encourage direct arrangements between debtors and creditors and thereby keep businesses in operation – because the value of a concern is higher when it is operating[24] – are defined with a high degree of precision, without any analysis or prior verification of alternative possibilities. It is as if the constructed indicators had to reinforce the conclusion reached from the outset, which consists in saying that preference should be given to out-of-court bankruptcy procedures. This is explicitly indicated by the preparatory work for the French insolvency laws in 1984 and 2005, which specifies that 'one of the causes of the failure of current procedures is their complexity' and consequently, 'it is advisable to simplify them by encouraging negotiation rather than court intervention' as quoted in the report of the National Assembly in, 2005, which nevertheless resulted in a conciliation procedure with approval by the commercial court.[25]

In answer to these remarks, which emphasize the deficiencies in an approach exclusively centred on formal law, one could retort that the questionnaires sent to bankruptcy practitioners originally came from databases created to measure the efficiency of the law. Hence, they are intended to evaluate practices and not written rules. This counterargument does not hold, however, because LLSV are not irreproachable even as regards the database content.

The nature of the collected information is thus the source of the second identified bias. It must be examined to show the limits of the World Bank indicators established through questionnaires filled out by national expert-practitioners (usually legal firms, including an American one operating in Paris), again for the 'Closing a business' section. The data, gathered by consulting correspondents, does not aim to be exhaustive or even representative; at best, it conveys the feelings or impressions of professionals in the field – whose scope of action is never specified – in their particular area of work. Their perceptions are interesting in that they reflect the current climate and, in this respect, are justified by specialists such as Kaufman et al. who stress that 'the subjective perceptions of governance are often as important as the legal reality'.[26] This is especially the case with regard to the actual length of the proceedings, the estimate of which can only be made by a practitioner, based on local experience, which gives no assurance of representing the overall situation. This method nevertheless reveals a significant amount of observational bias, a drawback that the survey attempts to avoid by discussing de facto situations that enable an assessment of 'law in action' independently of the opinions of certain experts regarding the way the laws function. Recourse to experts in a survey on objective legal data, which at best provides descriptions of positive law in force, nevertheless does not prevent the use of databases developed with econometric tools from which the international rankings of bankruptcy law efficiency are drawn.[27]

Thirdly, the World Bank method is, to a certain extent, unsatisfactory because the selected indicators measure the procedural rules in force and not how they are actually used in situations when companies find themselves in financial distress. For example, the duration of proceedings varies considerably depending on the type of commencement of insolvency and the procedures adopted (see Table 4.2 below). Immediate liquidations take place within a period of 1.7 months after the case is brought to court, with half the immediate liquidations ordered in less than two weeks. Liquidations following an observation period are ordered on average within 6.4 months, and half of these procedures last less than five months. Reorganization plans take much longer to decide. In 2005, the average time between bringing the case before the court and the adoption of a plan was 8 months when it led to winding up the company and 12.4 months when it resulted in continuing operations. Nevertheless, many recovery packages require far more time: 10% of continuation plans took more than 19 months to complete and 10% of sale plans necessitated more than 15 months. Whenever liquidation is ordered (immediately or after an observation period), the final closure decision takes place on average after three or four years. These time periods, which may be much longer, allow the liquidator to exercise the rights and actions relative to the debtor's estate, to divide up the proceeds of sales among the creditors, and update the accounts.[28] None of the variations in relation to a standard time for processing cases (as fictional as it is reductive) is mentioned in the work of the World Bank.

Table 4.2: Decisions of commercial courts regarding companies in financial distress

	2001	2002	2003	2004	2005	Evolution 2005/2004 (in %)
Liquidation proceedings	38,062	39,389	40,380	42,792	45146	+5.5
Type of liquidation						
Immediate liquidation	28,204	29,441	30,355	32,192	33,971	+5.5
Average time (in months)	2.0	2.0	1.7	1.6	1.7	

	2001	2002	2003	2004	2005	Evolution 2005/2004 (in %)
Liquidation after an observation period	9,858	9,948	10,025	10,600	11,175	+5.4
Average time (in months)	6.9	6.9	6.6	6.4	6.4	
Reorganization plans	4,458	4,390	4,699	4,960	5,290	+6.7
Type of reorganization plan						
Continuation plan	3,573	3,424	3,676	4,024	4,448	+10.5
Average time (in months)	13.3	12.8	12.4	12.1	12.4	
Sale plan	885	966	1 023	936	842	−10.0
Average time (in months)	7.9	7.6	8.0	8.0	8.0	
Decisions to close liquidation proceedings	42,742	40,360	39,842	44,059	41,710	−5.3
Reason for closure						
Insufficient assets	41,979	39,614	39,047	43,096	40,511	−6.0
Average time (in months)	42.8	43.0	45.0	44.8	45.1	
Termination of liabilities	783	746	795	963	1,051	+9.1
Average time (in months)	52.1	57.6	59.4	60.3	61.3	

Source: SD SED – general civil repertory[88]

Between the abrupt use of a single yardstick, i.e. the length of insolvency proceedings proposed by 'Doing business' and the nuances contributed by the statistical data of the Ministry of Justice, it should once again be emphasized that the first approach does not shed light on the actual workings of justice. On the contrary, this requires an examination of bankruptcy files and practices in addition to the legal framework.[29] We can therefore reproach these indicators, constructed on the basis of a standard reference, for providing a literal reading of the rules and playing an active role in forming the types of legal systems that will result from their use.

One may wonder, then, to what extent the three biases we have noted influence the assessment of bankruptcy laws and the recommendations regarding their evolution. Is there not a danger of skewering the results?

1.2. A Look at the Categories

The information collected and processed by the World Bank, together with the macroeconomic databases and datasheets specific to bankruptcies, allow the upholders of *Law and Economics* to propose a twofold division in the modes of handling the legal proceedings resulting from cessation of payments. The first is part of a comparative perspective and applies at a given moment in time; it differentiates rules first of all according to the interests they protect and ends by identifying pro-creditor and pro-trade creditor rules (Section 1.2.1). The second division intersects with the previous one; temporal and historical in nature, it finds the cause of the differences in the degree of bankruptcy legislation efficiency in the opposition between civil law and common law treatment (Section

1.2.2). We are seeking to show here in what way these divisions are sensitive to the selected method and the analytic framework.

1.2.1. A Clear-Cut Pro-Debtor vs Pro-Creditor Division to be Demonstrated.

In the literature devoted to demonstrating the optimum form for handling cessation of payments, two main issues are debated: first, the aspect of the balance sheet (assets or liabilities) which have to be restructured and second, the consequences of a breach of financial contract by the company's managing director.

- Restructuring the debt or the assets of a company in financial distress: In a context in which the stakeholders' support for a company project, whether sound or not, is presented as a key factor in success, the main arguments in favour of renegotiating debts concern the need to associate all the creditors in the decision-making process.[30] This same argument prevailed in the reform of the law on insolvent companies as demonstrated by the presence of an amicable settlement procedure, introduced for bankruptcies in 1985, known as the Badinter Act,[31] which was confirmed by the law of 10 June 1994[32] and reformed by the company protection law which came into force on 1 January 2006,[33] this called for the intervention of a judge to keep certain creditors from early renegotiation of the debt to dispense themselves from taking part in a collective renegotiation. This solution is widely preferred to the piecemeal disposal of assets, which is reputed to be favourable to creditors because the costs of liquidation are taken out of the revenue.[34] Yet, while the choice between these two avenues depends on the characteristics of the company and the investment decisions of its management,[35] it is also influenced by the legal context, the second point debated by the authors.
- The type of legal framework to adopt according to its repercussions on the various actors involved in the crisis (debtors, employee claimants, etc.): Taking into consideration the effects of the law on the behaviour of debtors and creditors leads to the question of which type of rules will best ensure debt-restructuring for economically viable companies with temporary financial problems on the one hand and the liquidation of inefficient companies on the other.[36] With a view to determining the characteristics of a law that would limit behavioural deviation on the part of company management and court errors, Aghion, Hart and Moore[37] began to wonder about the beneficial effects of strict laws against managing directors who display imprudence or whose management is marked by incompetence. Their model reveals the disciplinary effect of systems in which company insolvency ends either in eviction of the company management or liquidation of the business, with the entire procedure under

the supervision of a judge. In addition to its *ex ante* effect of encouraging caution, this so-called pro-creditor rule (in the sense that it attributes to creditors rights over the management and capital of the company)[38] should make it possible to avoid inefficient restructurings. The British system is traditionally held to be in keeping with this logic insofar as the administrative receivership procedure initiated by a creditor holding a floating charge[39] then takes place under the supervision of a professional appointed by the initiator of the procedure with a view to being paid off.[40] The introduction of reforms in 1986, which was supposed to turn company rescue into 'a genuine institution'[41] did not alter the desire for vengeance and exclusion that characterizes the Insolvency Act of 1986.[42] The same holds for the Canadian law governing companies in financial distress.

These pro-creditor systems are not exempt, however, from harmful effects, ranging from premature liquidation to liquidation of efficient companies, in cases grouped together by White[43] under the name Type II error.[44] Several works show that they could be avoided by introducing a greater degree of clemency into the formal proceedings to encourage managing directors to behave in such a way as to optimize their investment plans and financing structures. This is the case of the Berkovitch, Israel and Zender model,[45] which shows that as the human capital accumulated by the managing director which is specific to the business determines the value of the company, it may be untimely and costly to replace the existing team if the poor results obtained are caused by the current economic situation. Similarly, the sanctions associated with a bankruptcy caused by what could be interpreted as excess investment might lead to excessive caution on the part of the managing director, under-investment harmful to company performance, and consequently to an increased risk of bankruptcy. Most of the authors[46] consider that American law, marked by the determination to preserve the company, the most visible manifestation of which is the famous Chapter 11,[47] is typical of a pro-debtor system. In France, the company rescue law adopted on 26 July 2005[48] also seeks to protect the business, and through it, the debtor. The negative effects of these rules have often been underscored in the case of the United States, where air-freight, energy and automotive industry companies in particular are put under the protection offered by Chapter 11 and thus escape from many creditors, including the bodies that dispense employee social protection and old-age pensions.

Several works attempt to bring out the superiority of one model over the other without succeeding in establishing a stable hierarchy between the various systems of *prise en charge* by the law of cessation of payment. The theoretical models[49] seek to identify the prerequisites for avoiding the occurrence of strategy failures on the part of company managers or of Type I and II errors. With a scope often reduced by the restrictive assumptions on which they are based and by the problems they encounter in trying to grasp the strategies of the various categories of actors involved, these models result at best in a typology of bankruptcy systems.[50] The empirical research seeking to pinpoint the most efficient bankruptcy system has also been impeded by heavy reliance on assumptions, the sensitivity of the results to the selected criteria and the fragility of the established hierarchies.[51] These studies mainly reveal the generally poor performance of the various types of laws governing companies in financial distress. But this overall conclusion is nuanced by taking into consideration the type of country in which the rules are applied: 'In the richest countries, the most efficient procedure is reorganization. In the lower middle income countries, attempts to rehabilitate the firm almost always fail, so the best procedure is foreclosure.'[52] It is also tempered by the study of the rights acquired by creditors.[53] In the end, the quoted authors unanimously acknowledge that the threat of eviction looming over management is far from the sole factor explaining efficient bankruptcy law; other factors also play an important role, such as how the business is authorized to continue, and even more, the attraction exerted by the commencement of legal proceedings from the viewpoint of direct out-of-court renegotiation, and, another essential characteristic point of *Law and Economics*, the legal origin of the rules.

1.2.2. What About the Convergence and Mixing of Legal Systems?

In the area of bankruptcy, the opposition between the flexibility of common law and the formalism of civil law leads to the conclusion that the former is more efficient than the latter. The international comparisons carried out insist on the inefficiency of the French system, which limits the rights of creditors and dilutes the value of collateral, including the sizeable personal collateral required by banks, without resulting in a satisfactory rate of recovery. The German and English legal systems, which give greater control and decision-making power to creditors while limiting formalism, guarantee higher recovery rates. However, these three countries demonstrate perceptibly equivalent performance when one observes private, out-of-court renegotiation procedures between debtors and creditors.[54] The factors that explain these variations usually concern the legal origin of the rules, which would explain the shareholder structure of the companies, the efficiency of the financial markets, the financial fragility of the systems, macroeconomic growth and the cost-effectiveness of company liquidations.[55]

 We will limit ourselves here to recalling the main characteristics attributed to the two types of system. Civil law designates the set of fundamental rules of private law – the general principles of law, the rules concerning the status of persons and of the family, the system of property and the theory of obligations – that make up the general law. It is often defined as a law originating in Roman law, but this definition reveals only part of its essence, for although most civil law countries include rules that can be traced back to Roman law, they usually also have rules that come from canon or customary law. Common law is more recent; it was gradually developed by the royal courts that sought to create a uniform law in opposition to local customs, based on a general – and fictional – custom applicable throughout the kingdom. As a work of judges, it is therefore a law that finds its source in court activity,[56] a characteristic that often leads to assimilating it with unwritten law, based on case law, as opposed to rules flowing from legislative sources. Nevertheless, this method and inductive reasoning which consists in generalizing from precedents by observing the analogies between them, are above all what distinguish common law from civil law. The latter is presented as more rational; it is characterized by its deductive method and its will to generalize.

Denounced in its principle, the opposition between bankruptcy law that is rigid because it comes from civil law and an adaptable law arising from its customary nature is not relevant to making international comparisons in the area of debt renegotiation and company liquidation. The most relevant criticisms are expressed by Siems[57] and Lele and Siems[58] who deconstruct the groupings created by supporters of the *Law and Finance* approach and conclude that the character of the legal subsets they constitute is totally artificial. Firstly, because only temporal arguments are used to justify considering two countries as coming under the same legal tradition (e.g. Austria and Switzerland are viewed together because their civil codes were constructed simultaneously). Secondly, because the identified legal families[59] are based on a priori ideas and incomplete cultural constructs since they eliminate, among other things, any reference to an Islamic legal tradition. This decentring of the perspective leads to aggregating the countries of Eastern Europe, Asia and Africa, strongly marked by arbitrariness.[60] The failure to take equally important factors into consideration regarding legal origins also weakens the typology and conclusions of LLSV. Among these criteria, we find the forms of colonization and their impact on the laws in force in the colonies, the language in which the laws are written and the degree of independence of the magistrates which, when taken into account, results in forming other subsets accompanied by statistical tests that are as significant as those exhibited by LLSV.[61]

The introduction of the historical dynamic undertaken by these authors opens the way to recognizing the process of convergence of national legal systems, which, although strengthened by the development of international trade in the contemporary period, dates back to the eighteenth century. But it was in the nineteenth century that the greatest awareness of the need for harmonization of commercial law in general and bankruptcy law in particular developed. Locré (1827–32) was especially clear on the subject during the debates on Book III of the French Commercial Code[62] and the will to harmonize it with other European legal systems, notably English law, among the legal experts who drafted it. Even if significant differences remain[63] and the will to harmonize did not always result in a process of effective convergence, one will note with Sgard[64] that, in some respects, it is impossible to differentiate the various national laws. This legal mixing has taken different forms depending on the country and ranges from a fully bi-legal system as is the case of Canadian law on bankruptcy and insolvency[65] to borrowing rules such as the introduction of a form of amicable agreement inspired by the American Chapter 11 in the French reform of collective proceedings. This concern about harmonization is especially strong at the European level where, despite the uncertainties generated by the recent bankruptcy proceedings regulation of 20 May 2000 which came into force on 31 May 2002, one must acknowledge that the effort conveyed by this law to bring concepts and procedures closer together has already produced tangible effects.[66]

All in all, whether the resulting mix stems from political will, the action of history or commercial necessity, the various national bankruptcy laws present significant similarities and, for that reason, cannot be classified solely on the basis of their origin. This weakens the typology and hierarchy established by LLSV. What can be substituted for this positive approach to law?

2. Bankruptcy Law, a Capitalist Institution: a Reinterpretation of Reforms of the Law Governing Companies in Financial Distress

A distinction is generally made between the handling of cessation of payments proposed by civil law inherited from the strict Commercial Code which seeks to exclude debtors from economic, political and even social life by keeping them in disgrace and the process authorized by customary law which is flexible and therefore favourable to an entrepreneurial spirit. In place of this distinction, we propose a division based on the nature of the assets at stake in the contract between debtors and creditors and the underlying vision of the firm. This change of viewpoint is legitimated by the transition that took place in the second half of the nineteenth century between a moral, individual and social conception and a commercial, capitalist vision of bankruptcy. The optimum sharing of the debtor company's assets and the inquisitorial procedure used to carry out this total dismemberment was substituted by a search for means to reinsert bankrupt company owners and the assets they managed into the life of the economy. These measures were first found in the practice of law, and were later given renewed codification. This is the case with the law governing bankruptcy of 23 May 1838 aimed at encouraging the survival of efficient businesses, particularly through the introduction of a court-approved arrangement with creditors. It is also true for the law of 4 March 1889 which instituted liquidation. Instead of a punitive law resulting in dismembering the failing company's assets, a moral and economic sanction was introduced, on which the smooth running of society as a whole depended, through successive reforms designed to substitute laws more favourable to the continuation of company activity. This appears quite early in the decisions of the commercial courts, notably that of the Seine department, which frequently ruled in favour of excusing the bankrupt trader and keeping him at the head of the company, starting in the 1840s. These decisions reflected a desire to keep the company in the market rather than exclude it. Indeed, they can be interpreted as a mean to correct earlier market failures such as granting excessive or untimely loans, and planning mistakes arising from poor information or outside shock effects causing the insufficient liquidity or even insolvency of some companies.

Two sets of elements that come under the scope of the law governing companies in financial distress and the change of status of the parties support the thesis of a bankruptcy law more concerned with the recovery of entrepreneurs than their exclusion from business life. The first is the establishment of a line of demarcation between situations of insufficient liquidity and those of insolvency (Section 2.1); the second is the arbitration between the respective rights and interests of the creditors and the debtors (Section 2.2).

2.1. A Law for Traders Applied by Traders

Systematically decried by legal experts, debtors, bankers and chambers of commerce, as attested by the criticisms levelled against Book III of the French Commercial Code upon its promulgation, bankruptcy law, originally reserved for traders, nevertheless exercised such a strong attraction for other categories of the population that its scope was widened to include individuals. Beginning in the nineteenth century, commercial law manuals insisted on specifying the definition and identification of the rights and duties with which 'those who exercise commercial acts and make them their usual profession' had to comply (Commercial Code, Book I; Title 1). Among them, we are particularly interested in the determination of who would benefit from trader status, and hence from bankruptcy law and the operation of the commercial courts where disputes between debtors and creditors were settled.

2.1.1. Who is a Trader?

The term 'trader' was introduced by the commercial code of 1807. Formerly, one spoke of merchants, wholesalers, bankers and artisans. At the end of the Ancien Régime, commercial courts had jurisdiction *ratione personae* to handle disputes between traders, but the law did not define this term and mere membership in a guild was not considered proof of status. The nobles, who were prohibited from engaging in commerce on pain of exclusion, skirted this rule by becoming sleeping partners, and some of them thus interfered in company management without trader status.[67] With the introduction of the Civil Code, the scope of trader status constantly expanded, conveying the will of participants in the business world to benefit from the treatment provided for by the Commercial Code, particularly as regards bankruptcy. The widening scope of the law led some authors (Marco in 1992 and Di Martino in 2005),[68] to see this as the explanation for the steady rise in the number of bankruptcies during the nineteenth century.

The question that arises is what led debtors to prefer the application of bankruptcy laws to bankruptcy as an offence (*banqueroute*)? Was it due to a greater ability to begin new trading activity authorized by the former, which, ever since the 'decodification' of 1838, showed itself increasingly favourable to the survival of companies and maintaining entrepreneurs in the economic world? This interpretation is supported by the introduction of the composition by relinquishment of assets introduced by the law of 17 July 1856, which released the bankrupt owner from administration of his estate, allowed him to return to commercial life after an arrangement with his creditors and halted his exposure to legal action by creditors. In contrast, the system of bankruptcy offence still favourable to traders would gradually become obsolete. Indeed, negligent bankruptcies could no longer benefit from liquidation and fraudulent bankruptcies could no longer hope for an arrangement with creditors, or to be excused or rehabilitated.[69] With regard to non-trading cessations of payments, failure in no way protected the business: collective procedure was not applied, especially as no organized party requested it whereas it would have been highly advantageous, and the fear of expropriating peasants led to removing them permanently from the scope of bankruptcy law. In the face of these disadvantages, a few courts sought to avoid them by creating the name of 'civil receivership' for procedures that resembled bankruptcies.[70]

The advantages that traders obtained from a law made for them and applied by them explain in large part the abundance of case law relative to Section 1 of Article 437 devoted to the definition of trader status at the beginning of Book III 'bankruptcies and bankruptcy offences'. Some 101 commentaries were noted by Dalloz and Vergé;[71] the same task of listing examples of the doctrine in this area was carried out by Tripier,[72] thus demonstrating the intensity of the debates over the interpretation of trader status and the possibility of acquiring it. The evolution of bankruptcy law observed in France testifies to the unification of commercial and civil law which admitted bankruptcy of corporations under non-trading private law (non-commercial partnerships, associations, trade unions, cooperatives), authorised receivership for artisans in 1985 and for farmers in 1988 and allowed the liquidation of companies to be extended to their managing directors who still did not have legal trader status. The same phenomenon of unification occurred in other countries in Europe, albeit at very different periods: in England, the Insolvency Act (1986) applied to all debtors, in Germany, the procedure ensuring equal rights to payment upon enforcement to unsecured creditors (1877) was also applied to all insolvent debtors (which explains why this particular system was maintained in the three recovered departments of Alsace-Lorraine), as well as in the Netherlands.[73]

The bankruptcy system and the protection it offers were therefore valued by debtors who, owing to the compulsory 'class', did not run the risk of finding themselves confronted by isolated creditors seeking to commence proceedings first, for fear of being overtaken by the others.

2.1.2. Commercial Judges with Essential Attributions

Commercial courts, which are special courts within the judiciary system, are systematically criticized for their mode of operation. Since they were first instituted, their prerogatives in bankruptcy proceedings have nevertheless been confirmed. As the arbiters who determine the moment when a firm leaves the world of the commercial economy dominated by contracts and private property to enter that of litigation which organises the legal expropriation of the owners, judges appear to be key components of bankruptcy as a capitalist institution.

As bankruptcy is in no way a natural state, the question of defining the date on which the cessation of payments occurred arose very early for the courts and the authors of manuals and user guides for practitioners. In volume 1 of the '*Dictionnaire des faillites*', Mascret listed the various conceptions of the state of cessation of payment and recalled the point of view of P.-S. Boulier Paty expressed in the book '*Des faillites et banqueroutes*', in which he maintained 'it is less a question ... of the trader being solvent or insolvent, than of knowing if, in fact, he pays or does not pay: whatever his assets, even if they are superior to his liabilities, if he stops paying, he is in a state of bankruptcy. On the contrary, if, through sustained credit, he constantly honours his commitments, even if he owes more than he possesses, he is not bankrupt'.[74] The analytical commentary on the law of 8 June 1838 written by F. Lainné in 1839 seems to have dissociated the accounting situation of the business from bankruptcy, as the author considered that '...it is up to the judges to decide, in view of the circumstances, if the suspension of payments is equivalent to a real cessation ...'[75]

Beyond the control they exercise over the methods of applying the law, commercial judges possess above all the power to discriminate between a temporary situation of insufficient liquidity and a situation of insolvency, the latter being a necessary but not sufficient preliminary condition for bankruptcy. This provision appeared early on, for while the outdated legislation provided within a civil framework mainly for enforcement procedures that could vary according to local suzerainties, Title IX of the commercial order of 1673 stipulated that 'Bankruptcy or bankruptcy offences will be considered to commence on the date that the debtor withdraws or an official seal is placed on his property'.[76] This '...will of the royal legislator to bring legal clarity to the commencement of the proceedings'[77] enshrined the absence of any absolute criterion used to define bankruptcy and, consequently, the importance of the judgement exercised by the courts. Commercial law manuals are clear on this point: the mission of the courts is to declare cessation of payments; they are also sovereign in their assessment of the circumstances and the facts related to cessation of payments, which leads them in particular to fix the date of cessation of payments.[78] This provision is essential, for the date of commencement of bankruptcy makes it possible to fix the observation period, i.e. the period preceding bankruptcy commencement during which the debtor may have executed more or less fraudulent legal instruments, for which the creditors may request termination.

The key role played by the judges in the bankruptcy decision definitively distances this procedure from the image of a struggle of the weak (the debtors) against the strong (the creditors) with which the law of the market is often associated. Nevertheless, a breach of contract by the entrepreneur does not put him out of action. On the contrary, he leaves one instituted system – the monetized market, regulated by the discipline of contracts and property rights – to enter into a judicial mechanism of governance and distribution of income. Like any transitional phase, this passage carries with it certain risks and the actors should be protected from them. Filing for bankruptcy, which the entrepreneur is asked to do to signify his honesty and spirit of cooperation[79] to his creditors, flows from the same logic. This also applies to the creditors who, from the start of the proceedings, are prohibited from access to individual instruments for protecting their contractual rights which were available to them when the company was still in the market: seizure of assets, complaints to the prosecuting authority, etc.[80] The acknowledgement of the failure of business owners and the organization of the sharing of assets under the control of the courts removes the multiple contractual ties binding the firm to the commercial framework and places it in the world of sharing debts among the various creditors, asset takeover by investors and a fresh start which, at the outcome of a procedure completely foreign to an individualist, contractual logic, authorizes its return to the market.[81]

2.2. From Protection of the Rights of Creditors to That of the Business: a Capitalist Evolution

Historically, the repayment of debt was considered as a moral act and the inability to comply with this rule implied prohibition from any contractual activity as well as the suspension of all civic rights. By excluding bankrupt owners simultaneously from the market and civil society, the first bankruptcy procedures merged the civic and economic dimensions of society. While the use of the rules in the nineteenth century conveyed a concern for reinsertion manifested by the trader-judges, the crises of the twentieth century were to make the rehabilitation of the bankrupt trader and the protection of the business more systematic. We are going to look at this dimension through two elements: first, the establishment of a hierarchy among creditors so as to eliminate the race to the courts (2.2.1) and secondly, the replacement of exclusion by protection (2.2.2).

2.2.1. *The Redistribution of Assets: Between Hierarchy and Collective Proceedings*

Splitting assets among creditors is the core redistributive challenge of bankruptcy. With the passage of time, successive reforms have constantly sought to attenuate the risk of a race to the courts fostered by the principle of 'first come, first served', in force for a long time, for example in German law. Whereas the judge takes official note of the failure of the business, the owner-entrepreneur or the shareholders are formally and legally expropriated. This removal is required in liquidation and the accompanying disposal of assets. This is the stage in the procedure when conflicts emerge among the various categories of stakeholders, which have been given considerable attention in the literature on bankruptcy. Overall, the law provides that the payment of creditors shall be based on the price of the sale or the proceeds from the liquidation, with the income serving to repay creditors. Here a new level of bankruptcy organization appears with a view to ordering the actual losses which until then were potential and now become real, and as a result, charged to the balance sheets of the various partners. The amount depends on the rank of the creditor's claim in the order of repayment: legally or conventionally secured creditors (the State, employees, secured suppliers) are repaid in order of priority according to the rank and extent of their privilege from the proceeds of the sale of the pledged property. In every case, their repayment takes place before that of creditors who relied on the debtor's ability to pay (unsecured creditors), who are then paid in proportion to the amount of their verified, accepted claims out of the amount remaining after payment of the privileged creditors. These dividends are often low and in many cases unsecured creditors receive nothing.

These differences of status and the resulting variations in payment explain why unsecured creditors, especially banks in the recent period, continually denounce the unfair treatment reserved for them. Hence, it seems timely to study the internal conflicts within the class of creditors to understand the observable differences in the order of priority and the numerous reorganizations they have brought about since the procedure took on a collective character.[82] By emphasizing the existing tensions between the personal interests of the creditors and those of the mass to which they nevertheless belong, we can shed new light on the conflict between the need for swift liquidation of a business in cessation of payments and the attempts to protect the company and maintain its business which benefit not only ordinary creditors but also third parties either directly (employees, for example) or indirectly (local authorities, etc.).

The recent modifications introduced in French law reveal the will of creditors to be given a priority rank that will allow them to anticipate a higher payout than that granted to ordinary unsecured creditors. The order of payment instituted by article L.622–17–II of the Commercial Code establishes the following ranking among earlier and later claims:

1. the highest privilege of employees,
2. the privilege of court fees prior to the decision to commence collective proceedings,
3. the privilege of conciliation (see Article L.611-11 of the Commercial Code),
4. later claims eligible for preferential treatment,
5. in the event of the sale of property subject to a special actual pledge (special privilege, pledge, mortgage) during the observation period or during the execution of a protection or rehabilitation plan, the holders of special pledges will be paid:
   – before later creditors not entitled to preferential treatment and earlier creditors,
   – but after later creditors entitled to preferential treatment.
6. later claims not entitled to preferential treatment and later claims.

The law of 26 July 2005 introduced a distinction among the later claims[83] and provides that only those creditors whose claims are 'useful' to collective proceedings shall benefit from favourable treatment. This modification corresponds to a new privilege in favour of later creditors, consisting of payment priority for later claims defined in articles L.622-17-I and L.641-13-I, in the event of failure to pay these claims by the debtor. This is a privilege in so far as the benefit of payment priority is maintained, even if further collective proceedings are subsequently initiated, regardless of whether they involve receivership or liquidation. This means that the 'useful' later claims of the first proceedings will retain their payment priority over the earlier claims of the second. They will, however, be ranked after the new 'useful' later claims of the second collective proceedings.

This provision, which improved the rank of bank claims, was introduced to give creditors an incentive to take part in company receivership. Does this mean that, even if the outcome of the proceedings is market-oriented, a dividing line can be traced between the liquidated assets that will be put back into the market by the buyers who will attempt to enhance the value of the machines and technologies included in those assets, on the one hand, and the rescue of viable companies that will be able to face the commercial world after restructuring their assets and liabilities, on the other?

2.2.2. Company Protection or Liquidation of Assets?

The fate of the company is one of the major concerns of the various actors involved in the bankruptcy process. The future of the firm's productive assets – both tangible and increasingly intangible – is indeed important not only to the owner but also to commercial judge, the court-appointed administrator and the creditors who, from the nineteenth century onwards, have worried about the loss entailed by the cessation of business. Early on, reports by court-appointed administrators and the minutes of general assemblies of creditors expressed this fear linked to the loss of what would later be called 'goodwill', by pointing out the damaging effects of interrupting business on the amount of payout? to creditors. The latter, grouped together and assumed to play a key role in settling the bankruptcy through general assemblies, soon realised the antagonism that existed between their interests and those of the court-appointed administrator:

- the creditors, like the entrepreneur to a certain extent, see their interests preserved by continuing the business which enables receipts to come in instead of having only disbursements to record,
- the court-appointed administrator often finds it advantageous to keep the proceedings going, for his remuneration depends on the number of steps carried out and because he may have connections with other entrepreneurs with an interest in taking part in the dismemberment of other companies to boost the growth of their own businesses.

Here again, in the face of deviations from the doctrine revealed by an interpretive reading, we observe that very early on the commercial courts demonstrated imagination in getting beyond the lack of definitions of the basic concepts of bankruptcy to assess as best they could the complex situations experienced by bankrupt companies.[84] Often deviating from the legislation condemning most bankrupt owners, the victims of events beyond their control, the actors in the proceedings (magistrates, agents, court-appointed administrators, and creditors) seem to be largely free from the weight and rigidity of an essentially repressive procedure to adopt an economic attitude towards failing companies authorized by their experience and familiarity with the local business network. While this practice would initially result in protection of creditors whose interests were affected by the complexity and length of the proceedings as well as the loss of assets following the shutdown of business operations, it would also be concerned with the interests of the debtor. In this respect, although attenuated by the law of 28 May 1838, the extremely strict provisions introduced by legislators in 1807 were soon be skirted by the judges who often favoured continuing business activity. During the nineteenth century, the latter would also mean almost systematically recognizing the excusable character of the bankruptcy and a tendency to easily obtain the rehabilitation of the bankrupt owner, allowing the latter to begin commercial activity anew.

The will of French legislators to promote the survival of companies in financial distress is visible above all in legislation in 1955, 1967, 1985, 1994 and 2005.[85] It also distinguished itself by granting essential authority to the courts and by the prevalence of the rights of debtors over those of creditors. The concern for continuing the business usually means deciding on a receivership procedure, which attributes to the judge the power to set, only in the cases where receivership is not manifestly impossible, an observation period which may last from six to twenty months, during which the management of the company is placed under direct or indirect court control. At the end of the observation period, the court may decide to liquidate the company or impose a receivership plan on the debtor and all the creditors. As the procedure almost always results in liquidation of the firm, the law of 2005 sought to strengthen the means implemented in favour of protection and to do whatever was necessary to give the prevention of company failure precedence over receivership.

Here again, we see that the various legal systems for handling bankruptcy have resulted in a sort of convergence tending to favour keeping companies alive, as the value of a 'going concern' is systematically assumed to be superior to the value of dismembered assets. In this case, it should be recognized that French bankruptcy law, represented today by the company protection law, authorized very early on an explicit distinction between the prevention of problems and their treatment.[86] The priority given to the survival of the business is therefore presented as a supplementary objective to the minimization of transaction costs which consequently cannot constitute the sole criterion for assessing the efficiency of the law governing the end of operations. In any case, the legislators and court actors raised the question at an early date concerning returning the unused assets of companies involved in litigation to the market. Thus, they met capitalism's need for self-regulation, which, more than the simultaneous exclusion from the market and civil society in force in outdated law, requires setting up a system that authorizes the cancellation of debts after liquidation of assets and decriminalization. This dissociation of the economic order from that of civil society makes it possible to close the economic cycle by charging losses to balance sheets, returning part of creditors' capital so they can reinvest it and giving the debtor a chance to engage in business once again.

Conclusion

As a symptomatic treatment of market failure, bankruptcy law is still subject to criticism, despite an increasingly pronounced will to protect businesses in every country, in the name of economic imperatives and efficiency. Ignoring the fact that 'beyond its economic objective, aside from the repayment of creditors, the essential function of a law on collective proceedings is to soothe minds and channel individualism,'[87] supporters of an approach gauged in terms of efficiency recommend introducing a system of managing bankruptcy solely for economic purposes. Conceived as an extension of company law and a necessary counterpart to contract law, LLSV maintains that the function of bankruptcy law should be reduced to setting up efficient means to ensure the redistribution of assets from an estate perspective. In the French case, this form of pragmatism appears untenable at two levels:

- First, at the empirical level, which refers to our deconstruction of the indicators used in 'Doing business' and of the categories on which they are based. The distributive imperative that underlies them and the minimization of the time spent outside the market – a situation considered abnormal and useless by LLSV – can be explained by assimilating the company exclusively to an economic entity that should be sent back into the market if it is viable or eliminated as soon as possible if it is not. In both cases, a profitable allocation of productive financial resources must result. This conception of protection in the name of particular economic interests has the defect of ignoring social issues and the conception of an enterprise as a mode of organization bringing several groups of actors into play. It also leaves aside the debates raised by the question of the status and role of bankruptcy law in history and the status of a public concern which bankruptcy has acquired over time.

- Next, at the theoretical level, since we have replaced the search for the economic efficiency of bankruptcy law by a conception of bankruptcy as a capitalist institution. Within the scope of this work, we have been able to show that bankruptcy does not correspond to any 'natural' situation but rather that its occurrence depends merely on the existence of the laws that define and treat it. We have suggested here that there cannot be bankruptcy if there is no legal system to qualify a situation of insolvency as bankruptcy. This conception has allowed us to develop the thesis of a bankruptcy law that would have neither a vocation to make society more ethical nor an exclusive mission to allocate assets efficiently. Beyond these two objectives, bankruptcy law would determine who makes up a company, the performance criteria to attain and consequently, the mode of governance of firms. In this regard, the question of the rights of stakeholders other than the creditors and the managers/owners, especially the employees, in the course of the proceedings deserves to be explicitly raised, in addition to their right to be paid the wages they are due.

Our main theoretical claim here is that bankruptcy is not a clear-cut common-knowledge fact, a situation in which a firm is and one that the court can recognize and settle. To enter a bankruptcy procedure is a choice which depends partly from the situation of the firm as known by the actor making the choice, partly from what he expects from the decision to enter the procedure, which depends on bankruptcy law and the behaviours of all other actors concerned. This 'realist' epistemological choice leads to emphasize the strategic and the information dimensions in the bankruptcy process, as well as the characteristics of the legal system and the economic environment.

In the end, the laws governing companies in financial distress must respond to more than the opposing interests of categories that are held to play essential roles because they make resources available (creditors) or enhance their value (debtors) or to an exclusively economic logic. It must respond to the question of how this legal institution can solve failures in the market. In our view, that is the meaning of the successive phases of the proceedings: i) the insolvent trader is prohibited from exercising or placed under the control of a court-appointed administrator, ii) the creditors are brought together in a 'compulsory class' in such a way as to give a collective character to cessation of payments and replace individual arbitrations by a collective mode of resolution of the problem and iii) the owners and creditors are released from their previous commitments, which allows them to engage once again in a new activity. This three-stage sequencing enables continuity between cessation of payments and the disengagement of the parties involved. Thus, far from being solely a selection method that purges the market of its failing agents, bankruptcy law opens up a space for resolving market failures in a non-commercial way, which authorises the actors to return to the world of business by freeing them from their previous constraints.

Acknowledgement

This work is greatly indebted to the research on the evolution of law and litigation practices pertaining to bankruptcy before World War II that I am currently conducting with Pierre-Cyrille Hautcoeur (Ecole des Hautes Etudes en Sciences Sociales et Paris-Jourdan Sciences Economiques, UMR CNRS-EHESS-ENPC-ENS) and to various discussions with the members of the ACI 'Histoire du contentieux' directed by Alessandro Stanziani (IDHE, ENS Cachan, CNRS). I also wish to thank Evelyne Serverin (IRERP, Université de Paris 10 Nanterre, CNRS) and Thierry Kirat (IRISES, Université Paris Dauphine, CNRS) for the time they devoted to me and their generous advice and suggestions. In keeping with custom, none of them are responsible for any errors or omission in this text.

5 FINANCIALIZATION OF EUROPEAN ECONOMIES

Miia Parnaudeau

The credit market[1] plays an essential role in financing European companies. In 2004, stock market capitalization accounted for 53% of Euro zone GNP. The size of the banking sector and the depth of the intermediation process are also considerable: bank assets compared with GNP reached almost 281%. Domestic credit to the private sector (compared with GNP) represents 114%. This strong shift towards financialization today comes hand in hand with enhanced variability of inflation. We can, however, ask ourselves if inflation is still the only factor to provide a relevant indicator of economic fluctuations' overheating: what about financial assets' influence?

The current context of financial instability affecting economic agents requires that we again question the types of expectations they are making. In the systemic analysis of H. P. Minsky,[2] the free play of individual behaviour and the competitive environment lead agents to create their own instability. But it is also because banks are capable of financing themselves that a true imbalance can occur. This second financing mode, which interacts with bank credit, has consequences on the nature of agents' expectations. If the Central Bank continues today to limit the credit supply of commercial banks, the fact that the latter are increasingly turning to the markets to finance themselves creates further uncertainty. The ignorance facing economic agents drives them to develop herding behaviour (Section 1).

We aim to verify that this behaviour results above all in self-fulfilling expectations of the real price of assets. Based on a database supplied by the Bank for International Settlements (elaborated by S. V. Arthur, C. Borio and P. Lowe) we introduce the evolution of the real price of assets in Wicksellian rate differentials aimed at recounting the direction taken by the business cycles of four European countries (Germany, Spain, France and Italy). Our results tend to show that a reduction of the monetary interest rate is a warning signal for long-term growth cycles. The latter, are then clearly illustrated by the agents' expectations of the evolution of the real price of assets (Section 2).

1. Financial Instability and Speculative Investment Decision: the Contribution of the Austrian Tradition

The Austrian business cycle theory provides a connection between productive structures and agents' multiple investment decisions, in the context of decentralized economies, with intensive use of capital. When a more accommodating monetary policy encourages commercial banks to reduce their interest rates, entrepreneurs have easier access to credit to develop their projects. However, the expansion in which the economy enters is not sustainable insofar as it is not financed by real saving. Entrepreneurs are mistaken in imagining that the increased supply of bank credit is related to a voluntary postponement of household consumption.

As they are launched, investment projects become increasingly risky. Increased risk and inflationary pressures, approximating full employment, drive banks to raise their interest rates, plunging the economy into crisis. Business cycles are the result of banks' decisions: their lending activity creates instability. In his analysis, K. Wicksell seeks to explain the direction that business cycles take when a reduction of the monetary interest rate disrupts the investment decisions of economic agents. These investment decisions are motivated by the gaps established, in their respective business sectors, between the real interest rate and its natural level.

Based on the works of K. Wicksell, we extend the analysis to the market of real and financial assets. The study therefore relates to a monetary economy, where the creation of money is the result of debt from resorting to credit. A distinction should be made between this framework and an economy of financial markets, where the creation of money results from the transformation of previously accumulated saving resources.[3]

1.1. The Market of Real and Financial Assets: Self-Fulfilment of Expectations

The inclusion of real and financial assets markets increases the potential instability of the traditional Austrian model in which credit (already responsible for a cumulative imbalance) was indirectly supervised by the Central Bank (by means of the nominal interest rate and the level of reserves).

While the Central Bank continues to limit the credit supply of commercial banks, the fact that banks are increasingly turning to the markets to finance themselves creates further uncertainty for economic agents.

Indeed, in a world of partial ignorance where expectations on the price of assets do not have any real anchor, the economy constructs in itself a potential for instability with increasingly blurred limits, which results in a self-fulfilment of the agents' expectations. The diagram (Figure 5.1) proposed by C. Aubin, J.P. Berdot and J. Leonard specify the conditions for this process.

Figure 5.1: A debt economy

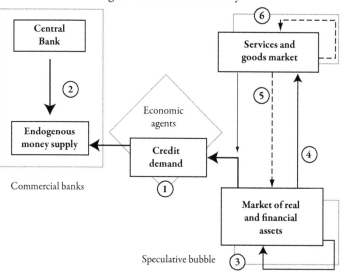

In this representation, credit demand is associated with economic agents' two distinct financing needs (**1**). The first relates to their activities in the goods and services market, and the second to their desire to accumulate a certain number of real and financial assets.

This demand for credit should elicit a response from the commercial banks, only if the Central Bank allows it (**2**). The credit distribution thus authorized confirms the agents' bullish expectations on the price of assets: they are self-fulfilling. Rising asset prices improve agents' balance sheets, further increasing their capacity to borrow. Increased use of credit frees up expenditure on the goods and services market but also on the real and financial asset market. This results in the formation of a speculative bubble (**3**), due to rising appreciation of real and financial assets, and to beneficial effects (growth, employment, etc.) on the goods and services market (**4** and **6**). The draught effect thus generated in this market further encourages speculation (**5**).

Economic agents make rational expectations limited by the partial ignorance (the absence of real anchors, whether for the supply of money or the price of assets) with which they compose. They are not irrational or blind.[4] Economic agents use debt as a competitive instrument, creating cumulative financial instability in the economy. The money supply becomes endogenous, and expectations are self-fulfilling. As long as the Central Bank retains an accommodating position, authorizing the distribution of credit, agents will remain confident and the bubble will grow. Increased debt and asset appreciation create a self-maintaining effect of (artificial) wealth, showing favourable economic signals, particularly in terms of employment and growth. In economies with moderate inflation variability, it then can be a while before overheating is checked by rising nominal interest rates.

In the Austrian business cycle analysis,[5] two factors can cause a reversal (nominal interest rate increase): drying up of loanable funds and the desire of the Central Bank to fight inflationary pressures. Today, the growing use of market financing allows commercial banks to continue finding the funds that they need to supply the demand for credit.

Due to its low variability, inflation no longer provides the same overheating indicator highlighted by K. Wicksell in an aggregated plan or by F. A. Von Hayek in a sectoral plan. An increase of the nominal interest rate is still the starting point for the reversal, and the financial crisis is inevitable given the artificial nature of the boom. However, the reversal seems to be more closely associated with a change of direction in the expectations of economic agents. Rising asset prices and associated risks cannot continue indefinitely.

When the latter lead to a gradual disappearance of capital gains,[6] agents will reconsider their enthusiasm and banks will very rapidly increase their nominal interest rates. Agents' expectations are always made with partial ignorance of future events; they are rational in the sense put forward by L. Von Mises,[7] but due to the endemic nature of debt, they are above all self-fulfilling. In such a context, two new business 'overheating' variables must be considered: the real price of assets and economic agents' debt.

1.2. Integration of the Price of Assets and Debt in a Wicksellian Rate Differential

Our initial aim is to take into account the wealth effect (associated with appreciation of the value of assets), but also the rising debts (the importance of which was mentioned when defining agents' expectations, as well as in the cumulative imbalance affecting the economy).

Then we aim to verify the capacity of inflation to provide a relevant 'overheating indicator' despite its persistent nature.[8] P. Artus[9] suggested a framework specifying the conditions for transmitting a bearish shock of the nominal interest rate (see Figure 5.2). The author uses a dynamic model to determine production, inflation and rate of interest. To this he adds a determination (and an effect) of the value of assets and debt among economic agents. Production is a (negative) function of the nominal interest rate, (positive) of inflation, (positive) of the value of real assets, (negative) of real debt and (positive) of demand (assumed to be exogenous).

Figure 5.2: Theoretical model of a debt economy – P. Artus

The monetary economy of production is characterized by the following relations:

(1) $y = -\alpha(i - \pi) + \beta a - \gamma c + \bar{y}$ (1) **Production** of the economy

(2) $\pi = \vartheta(y - z)$ (2) **Inflation**

(3) $\dot{a} = \rho a + (i - \pi) - \sigma y$ (3) **Growth rate of real assets**

(4) $\dot{c} = \varphi(a - \lambda(i - \pi) + \bar{c} - c)$ (4) **Real debt rate of the agents**

(5) $i = \bar{i} + A\pi + Ba + Dc$ (5) **Central Bank's Interest rate rule**

Where

y is the log of *the production* of the ecomony and $\bar{y}$ is the log of the exogenous component of the demand;

$(i - \pi)$ is the *real interest rate*, where i is the nominal interest rate and π is inflation;

a is the log of the *real value* (deflated by the price of goods) of *assets*;

c is the log of the *real value of debt*, $\bar{c}$ being that of its reference value;

and $a - \lambda(i - \pi) + \bar{c}$ is the *optimum debt of the agents*;

$\alpha, \beta, \gamma, \vartheta, \rho, \varphi$ are constants;

z is the log of the exogenous supply of goods and services;

σy is the log of the *profit from production*;

$\bar{i}$ is the 'reference' interest rate or the *equilibrium interest rate*;

With $A > 1, B > 0, D > 0$.

The difference between supply (assumed to be exogenous) and demand for goods and services determines the level of inflation. The growth rate of the real value of assets depends on their actual return, the real interest rate,[10] and (negatively) on the profit made[11] by entrepreneurs.

The real rate of debt among agents depends on the difference between debt and its reference level (the level that is acceptable for the agents) as well as on the value of real assets and the real interest rate.

This real debt rate is assumed to adjust itself to an optimal level, characterized by the real value of the assets, the real interest rate and the level of debt desired by the agents. Finally, the author provides the Central Bank interest rate rule in which he introduces, in addition to the equilibrium interest rate, the value of real assets, as well as the value of actual debt among agents. In this model, a bearish shock of the interest rate causes a long-term increase of debt and the value of assets,[12] but the impact on production remains ambiguous.[13]

We suggest using the interest rate rule created by the author (expression 5, Figure 5.2), to 'increase' the Wicksellian rate differential with the price of assets and agents' debts. The initial situation of the economy is full-employment equilibrium, where the following relations hold true:

$$i_t - \pi_t = r_t = t_n^*, \text{ with } \pi_t = 0, i_t = r_t = t_n^* \ (1)$$

Where i_t is the nominal interest rate, π_t the inflation, r_t the real rate, and t_n^* the natural interest rate according to K. Wicksell.

According to P. Artus, the nominal interest rate depends on its reference value ($\bar{\imath}$), inflation (π), the price of assets (a) and agent debt (c):

$$i = \bar{\imath} + A\pi + Ba + Dc, \text{ which can be rewritten}^{14} \text{ as } (i_t - \pi_t) = r_t + a_t + c_t \ (2)$$

Where $r = \bar{\imath}$ is the real interest rate, a the log of the real value of assets, and c the log of the real value of agent debt.

According to this approach, a reduction of the nominal interest rate drives the real rate under its equilibrium level, which generates inflationary pressures, increasing debt and rising value of real assets. This pressure plunges the economy into a cumulative instability characterized by self-fulfilment of agents' expectations ($\pi_{at} = \pi_t, a_{at} = a_t$). This instability will be followed sooner or later by raising the nominal interest rate.

According to M. Aglietta,[15] 'credit variation in the private sector is closely associated with asset price variations, but does not influence the GDP deflator'. In his Wicksellian monetary model, the demand for credit depends on the difference between the return expected from newly created capital and the cost of capital. K. Wicksell's natural interest rate is the expected rate of return from the capital, adjusted for the risk incurred[16].

This rate is linked, in accordance with Wicksell's hypotheses, to macroeconomic equilibrium. In this model, the natural rate t_n is the rate at which the expected return on the capital r^a (corrected for the risks incurred) is equal to the real interest rate (nominal interest rate i corrected for agents' inflation expectations). The dynamic equation of the natural interest rate (expressed as units of work) therefore provides the balanced inflation value for the economy. Inflation is an increasing function of the difference between the entrepreneurs' decisions ('animal spirits') to invest and households' decisions to save.

In this context, the dynamic equilibrium is compatible with all types of inflation. Price stability means that $r^a = i$, but such an adjustment is impossible in reality. No market mechanisms exist that can adjust inflation and the nominal interest rate to their natural levels.

Demand conditions depend on production conditions. They change when an additional supply of money is offered to the economic agents. It is no longer possible therefore to depend on 'exogenous' anchors (of the natural rate) to determine the optimum (equilibrium) level of inflation in the economy.

Since financial deregulation has essentially rendered money supply endogenous, the reference values of the economy change regularly.[17] Inflation of the general price level plays a completely secondary role in the analysis of cumulative processes. The approach proposed by M. Aglietta does not agree, furthermore, with Lachmann's vision of the Austrian tradition, in which disequilibrium is the norm. On the contrary, inflation remains a target variable in so far as, due to the fluctuations that affect the economy, it is more likely to be in disequilibrium than in equilibrium.

This equilibrium, however fragile, is still possible: equilibrium is 'dynamic', 'on a razor-edge'. The henceforth volatile nature of the natural interest rate invalidates any approach based on the establishment of reference values.

And, in so far as a nominal interest rate lower than its natural level automatically leads to a distortion of real asset prices, inflation can still be an eventuality to be observed. The analysis must therefore be approached differently and take into consideration the variability of the price of assets.

2. Economic Financialization: an Indicator

The conditions for transmission within the economy of a bearish shock of the monetary interest rate are complicated in their explicit consideration of the price of assets. Their integration in the analysis of long-term European cycles allows us however, to highlight an important phenomenon.

This phenomenon is the potential for economic instability. In such a context, expectations no longer have any lasting basis in reality, and herding behaviour seems to offer the only solution for economic actors. The hypothesis according to which they mainly make self-fulfilling expectations on the real price of assets therefore seems to be the most plausible. In order to verify it, we have studied the causality of impulses including two types of expectation on the evolution of the real price of assets. The estimation of various indicators for long-term European growth cycles is then proposed.

2.1. Causality Tests

Based on the interest rate rule put forward by Artus,[18] we suggest taking into consideration, in a Wicksellian impulse (defined by a divergence between the monetary interest rate and the real interest rate), the evolution of the real price of assets.

The Wicksellian impulse$(i_t - r_t)$, assumed to illustrate the direction taken by the long-term growth cycle in Europe, is therefore increased by the evolution of the real price of assets (a):[19]

$$IW_t = (i_t - r_t) + a_t \quad (3)$$

Where i_t is the monetary interest rate, r_t the real interest rate and a_t the evolution of the price of real assets (price of assets deflated by current inflation).

When a falling monetary interest rate forces the real interest rate under its equilibrium level, the economy is characterized by inflationary pressures and an increase in the value of real assets. The resulting cumulative instability is assumed to result in self-fulfilment of economic agents' expectations.

2.1.1 Naïve Expectations

The eventuality according to which economic agents produce naïve expectations (on the evolution of the real price of assets and on the price of services and goods) can be verified using the following Wicksellian impulse:

$$IW_t^1 = (i_t - r_{at}) + a_{at} \quad (4)$$

$$\text{With } \pi_{at} = \pi_{t-1}; a_{at} = a_{t-1}$$

This Wicksellian impulse in fact has a solid, unidirectional causal link to the long-term growth cycle[20] in the four European countries studied. The most solid link is found in the French case; the weakest in Germany (Table 5.1).

Table 5.1: Causality of an impulse on the long-term European cycle

1 lag (1991–2004)	Granger causality of the Wicksellian impulse (IW_t^1) on the long-term cycle:	
Naïve expectations	The gap does not cause the cycle	The cycle does not cause the gap
Germany	3.46 (0.06)	0.74 (0.39)
France	**15.36 (0.00)**	**0.007 (0.93)**
Spain	4.18 (0.04)	0.07 (0.79)
Italy	6.60 (0.01)	0.09 (0.75)

2.1.2. Self-Fulfilling Expectations

When the expectations of economic agents are assumed to be self-fulfilling, the Wicksellian impulse is as follows:

$$IW_t^2 = (i_t - r_{at}) + a_{at} \quad (5)$$

$$\text{With } \pi_{at} = \pi_t \text{ and } a_{at} = a_t$$

The results improve in the case of self-fulfilling expectations. Causalities are increased, in fact, most considerably in the French case. Germany is the country with the weakest causal link.

Table 5.2: Causality of an impulse on the long-term European cycle

1 lag (1991–2004)	**Granger causality of the Wicksellian impulse (IW_t^2) on the long-term cycle:**	
Self-fulfilling expectations	The cycle does not cause the gap	The gap does not cause the cycle
Germany	*6.67 (0.01)*	*1.00 (0.32)*
France	**31.28 (1.0^E–06)**	**0.03 (0.85)**
Spain	7.24 (0.00)	0.13 (0.71)
Italy	11.31 (0.00)	0.00 (0.81)

2.2. Indicators for European Growth Cycles

Different indicators for the long-term cycles result from these two hypotheses. In its general form, the indicator is as follows:

$$J_t = fJ_{t-1} + g(i_r - r_t) + ha_t + k \tag{6}$$

Where J_t is the long-term growth cycle,[21] $(i_r - r_t)$ is the gap between the monetary interest rate and the real interest rate, a_t the rate of growth of the real price of assets and k is a constant.

In this expression, the long-term cycle depends on its value in the preceding period, on a 'classic' Wicksellian rate differential, on the evolution of the real price of assets and on a constant. Two types of expectations are tested: naïve and self-fulfilling.

2.2.1. Naïve Expectations

When agent expectations are assumed to be naïve, the indicator provided for the long-term cycle in the four European countries, is defined as follows:

$$J_t = fJ_{t-1} + g(i_r - r_{at}) + ha_{at} + k \tag{6–a}$$

$$\pi_{at} = \pi_{t-1} \text{ and } a_{at} = a_{t-1}$$

The agents' expectations of inflation are naïve, since the inflation used to calculate the expected real interest rate (r_{at}) is the inflation for the preceding period (π_{t-1}). In the same manner, it is assumed that the agents' expectations on the future evolution of the real price of assets (a_{at}) are naïve, as they are equal to their past value.

Financial Markets and the Banking Sector

Table 5.3: Indicators including the price of assets – naïve expectations

$$\pi_{at} = \pi_{t-1}$$
$$J_t = fJ_{t-1} + g(i_r - r_{at}) + ha_{at} + k \text{ (6-a)}$$
$$a_{at} = a_{t-1}$$
(1991–2004)
$$J_t = fJ_{t-1} + ha_{at} + k \text{ (6-b)}$$

MMG[22]	f	g	h	k	R^2	DW	I
Germany	108.30	-0.93	*0.52*	4.48	0.9913	2.01	10
	(0.00)	(0.35)	*(0.60)*	(0.00)			
	82.51		3.67	0.90	0.9910	1.99	6
	(0.00)		(0.00)	(0.36)			
France	250.18	-1.16	5.47	1.66	0.9984	2.13	10
	(0.00)	(0.24)	(0.00)	(0.10)			
	177.49		5.57	0.71	0.9983	1.90	6
	(0.00)		(0.00)	(0.48)			
Spain	–	–	–	–	–	–	–
	281.66		2.06	1.15	0.9980	1.97	6
	(0.00)		(0.04)	(0.25)			
Italy	112.69	0.14	3.97	4.13	0.9932	1.06	10
	(0.00)	(0.88)	(0.00)	(0.00)			
	86.40		3.34	3.66	0.9933	0.98	6
	(0.00)		(0.00)	(0.00)			

The first important result emerging from GMM estimates of the expression (6–a) in all the European countries (Table 5.3) is the lack of a significant Wicksellian rate differential. The inflationary pressures resulting from the gap between monetary interest rate and real interest rate do not provide a variable that can explain the long-term cycles, regardless of the country selected for analysis. The introduction of an additional explanatory variable therefore casts doubt on the capacity of inflation (in the case of naïve expectations) to provide a relevant indication of overheating.

Removing the Wicksellian rate differential from the regressions does not at all modify the explanatory power exerted by the evolution of the real price of assets (6–b), except in the case of Germany, for which it was not significant in the first estimation (6–a).

When the agents' expectations are assumed to be self-fulfilling, the indicator used in the four European countries is as follows:

$$J_t = fJ_{t-1} + g(i_r - r_{at}) + ha_{at} + k \text{ (6-c)}$$
$$\text{With } \pi_{at} = \pi_t \text{ and } a_{at} = a_t$$

In this expression, the agents' expectations of inflation are self-fulfilling, since the inflation used to calculate the expected real interest rate (r_{at}) is the inflation for the current period (π_t). In the same manner, the agents' expectations on the future evolution of the real price of assets (a_{at}) are self-fulfilling, as they are equal to their present value.

In expression (6–c) the interest rate differentials are not significant, except in the case of Spain. In the other European countries, the interest rate differential constructed on the hypothesis of self-fulfilling expectations of inflation is not noticeably different to zero (and for only 10% in Germany). The evolution of the real price of assets constitutes, on the other hand, a relevant explanatory variable of the direction taken by the long-term cycles in the four European countries tested.

However, it is difficult to decide between the regressions (6–a and b, Table 5.3) and (6–c and d, Table 5.4). In fact, they are relatively similar to one another.

As the unidirectional causalities (in the sense put forward by Granger) obtained in the preceding section were slightly improved under the hypothesis of self-fulfilling expectations, we have tended to prefer the associated regressions (6–c and d) as indicators for the long-term cycles.

Table 5.4: Indicators including the price of assets – self-fulfilling expectations

$$\pi_{at} = \pi_t \qquad J_t = fJ_{t-1} + g(i_r - r_{at}) + ha_{at} + k \ (6\text{–c})$$
$$a_{at} = a_t$$
$$(1991\text{–}2004) \qquad J_t = fJ_{t-1} + ha_{at} + k \ (6\text{–d})$$

MMG	f	g	h	k	R^2	DW	I
Germany	85.83	-1.66	0.29	4.09	0.9902	1.68	10
	(0.00)	(0.10)	(0.76)	(0.00)			
	87.55		4.11	0.67	0.9916	2.09	6
	(0.00)		(0.00)	(0.50)			
France	231.86	-0.71	7.36	0.48	0.9984	2.03	10
	(0.00)	(0.47)	(0.00)	(0.62)			
	184.39		8.63	0.10	0.9985	1.97	6
	(0.00)		(0.00)	(0.91)			
Spain	305.96	-2.59	1.50	1.58	0.9980	2.07	10
	(0.00)	(0.01)	(0.14)	(0.12)			
	359.30		3.53	0.63	0.9981	2.01	6
	(0.00)		(0.00)	(0.52)			
Italy	99.21	-0.13	2.65	3.59	0.9934	1.12	10
	(0.00)	(0.89)	(0.01)	(0.00)			
	87.59		3.00	3.10	0.9937	1.18	6
	(0.00)		(0.00)	(0.00)			

Although the classic Wicksellian impulse, increased by the evolution of the real price of assets has a solid unidirectional causal link with the long-term cycle in all the European countries, it no longer constitutes a relevant indicator for this cycle when an explicit consideration of the real price of assets is added to the GMM regressions.

In other words, the monetary interest rate still provides a warning signal for the cumulative process. However, the long-term cycles then appear to be better illustrated by the evolution of the real price of assets, due to the weak variability of the inflation of the price of goods and services throughout the entire study period. Overall (summary of results, Table 5.5), the best indicators for the long-term European cycles are those based on the evolution of the real price of assets (6–d).

Table 5.5: Summary of results – Indicators selected for long-term cycles

	Indicators for long-term growth cycles based on:					
	A Wicksellian impulse increased by the evolution of the real price of assets:				**An impulse based only on the evolution of the real price of assets:**	
	In the case of naïve expectations (6–a)		In the case of self-fulfilling expectations (6–c)		In the case of naïve expectations (6–b)	**In the case of self-fulfilling expectations (6–d)**
	$(i_t - r_{at})$	a_{at}	$(i_t - r_{at})$	a_{at}		
Germany			$s^{[23]}$		s	s
France		s		s	s	s
Spain			s	s	s	s
Italy		s		s	s	s

Conclusion

The various indicators proposed for the long-term European growth cycles (Germany, Spain, France, Italy) are based on investment decisions made by economic agents. However, the idea that the latter produce self-fulfilling expectations of inflation only provides a partial illustration of the interactions that take place between economic agents. The analysis has therefore been extended by taking into consideration the financial market. In fact, in the self-maintained cumulative framework that now characterize contemporary debt economies, investment decisions also affect the price of financial assets.

With the hypothesis that economic agents are only concerned with future price evolutions, we have sought to separate indicators based on expectations of inflation from indicators based on expectations of the evolution of the real price of assets. The indicators that only use expectations on the evolution of the real price of assets have proven to be more efficient. The starting point for the loops of activity is still provided by a reduction of the monetary interest rate, but the long-term cycles are then proven to be better illustrated by the evolution of the real price of assets than by inflation of the price of goods and services.

This result leads us to discuss the targeting of asset prices by the Central Bank. If it included targeting the price of assets under an interest rate rule, the monetary policy would gain the means for preventing and fighting against the financial imbalance that currently guides the long-term condition of the economy. The question regarding the conditions for intervention, *ex post* or *ex ante*, by the monetary policy on the price of assets remains open. And yet the results obtained in this paper suggest that, in addition to the Central Bank's credibility for optimising this type of targeting, it is necessary to compare the effectiveness of a monetary policy with an enhanced and clear prudential policy.

Acknowledgement

I would like to thank Stephan Arthur for providing the AAPI data used in this text. I also wish to thank Jacques Leonard (CRIEF, University of Poitiers, EIA CNRS) for his comments. Any errors or omissions remain my own responsibility.

PART 2: GLOBALIZATION AND BANKING INSTITUTIONS: EVOLUTION OF THEIR ROLE AND INSTITUTIONAL ASPECTS

In the actual global context, banks have seen their contribution to investment change according to the place accorded to financial markets. Their structure, mainly universal has enabled bankers to undertake many types of activity. This trend has induced an increasing profitability for most institutions, in particular the biggest ones.

From the 1980s to the beginning of our century, financial places have played an important role in the financing of enterprise projects. This is largely due to the favourable economic context and administrative facilities given to newly-created firms to have access to liquidity for productive investments. The recent volatility of markets has reversed the trend in favour of banks. Several speculative bubbles have occurred since the last thirty years:

- Financial Krach financier 1987
- Patrimonial depreciation in Japan in 1990–1 (the financial and property sector were concerned)
- General property and banking crisis at the beginning of the 90s (in the United States with the Savings and Loans, United Kingdom, the Scandinavian countries, the Credit Lyonnais)
- The Mexican crisis 1994–5
- The Asian crisis 1997–8
- The Russian crisis
- The NTC crisis from 2000 to 2003
- The Argentina crisis 2001
- The credit and information crisis (for example Enron) from 2002
- The subprime crisis from 2007 onwards

During these events, banking institutions have sacrificed their primary function, which is to grant credit and assume risk, to concentrate their main activities to maximize their profit. The subprime crisis illustrates this point; the core lesson issued from this last situation is then twofold:

- first, banks have created an amount of money superior to the liquidity really needed by the global system,
- second, they have transferred risks to private agents, risks that should be normally supported by the banking institutions.

The evolution of banking structures since the 80s towards universalism, general mergers and acquisitions process show the strengths and weaknesses of our global world. If universal banks seem to be more capable of resisting to actual financial disorders, all institutions should seriously reconsider to focus on their core activity: retail banking. To attract new clients, they have to be consistent with societal pressures and propose more financial products, whose main objective is to realize safe investment on a long term basis. This new orientation, if valuable, is not so easy to undertake. Banks run their activities in a very competitive environment, which sometimes oblige them to have risky attitudes. The entire goal for the next decades will then be to prove that profitability and ethical factors in financial questions are not antonymic. Their concomitance could lead to a new form of profit both for the banks and the economic system as a whole. This second part intends to gradually lead to a new concept of banking activity by including economic performance and social values.

6 EUROPEAN BANKING: A REVIEW OF TRENDS AND POLICIES FOR REASSESSMENT OF BANK REFORM AND DEVELOPMENT IN BRAZIL AND LATIN AMERICA

Kurt Mettenheim

Continental European banking and finance provide important references for Latin America. This chapter focuses on relations between banking and political development in the traditional sense of democratization; the inclusion of social classes in political institutions. Unfortunately, there are few precedents for this type of analysis. Since US Treasury Secretary Douglas's testimony to Congress in 1941,[1] or Gabriel Ardant's overview of finance in Western European states published in 1975,[2] we were unable to find a compelling discussion of finance, banking and *political* development. Moreover, Ardant's synthesis of theory and European history concludes by warning scholars and policymakers in developing countries that experiences from Europe do not apply because 'numerous bottlenecks intervene between demand and any response of agriculture or industry' and, therefore, 'solutions must be sought in different forms'.[3] This chapter begs to differ, somewhat, by reviewing several 'different forms' for reassessment of policies in Brazil and Latin America, specifically, development banks, savings banks and policies from coordinated market economies.

This effort is part of a broader re-evaluation of market-centred paradigms in developing countries. Long before the current financial crisis, Pinheiro argued that crises in emerging markets encouraged economists and policymakers to search for alternative 'post-liberal' policies.[4] Bresser-Pereira argues for a new developmentalism to replace policies of privatization and liberalization in Brazil that have slowed growth.[5] Cornia and contributors argue that financial liberalization tends to worsen domestic income distribution in developing and emerging economies.[6] Amsden broadens debates by arguing that classic themes about production and government policies in late development remain timely.[7] Evans and Chang remind us that most states embed and underpin economic policies and development, and that the market-centrism of recent social science lost this fundamental insight.[8] Finally, Stallings & Studart bring our object of inquiry into focus by reviewing finance policies for sustainable development in Latin America and other developing regions.[9] This chapter briefly examines banking and finance policies in Europe in an effort to identify institutions and policies able to deepen credit and finance, accelerate economic growth, improve income distribution and promote social inclusion and citizenship in Brazil and Latin America.

1. Development Banking

Although absent in liberal market economies, development banking was essential for industrialization during late development across Continental Europe, Asia and Latin America.[10] These public institutions were created to provide finance and credit on terms beyond those which private banks or capital markets were willing to provide. The reality that private banks were unable to measure or cover long-term risks associated with infrastructure investments led Continental European governments to found industrial development banks in the early nineteenth century.[11] By financing railroads and industry in France, the Credit Mobilier became a model abroad and shareholder in other European development banks.[12] It also became a model for banks in Asia, such as the Industrial Bank of Japan and India.[13] Development banks were also founded after World War I by European governments to infuse cash, subsidize loans and guarantee bank bonds to capitalize reconstruction.[14] The Kreditanstalt fur Weideraufbau (KfW: Reconstruction Credit Agency) and the Development Bank of Japan were created after World War II to channel foreign funds for reconstruction. However, these institutions have continued to evolve since, adopting new policies and strategies for domestic and foreign development.[15] Many developing countries also created development banks after World War II to channel World Bank loans, foreign aid and domestic savings. Gerschenkron, Myrdhal, Lewis and other economists argued that banking and government intervention were essential to accelerate industrialization in late development. Johnson's study of the Japanese Ministry of Technology and Industry (MITI) remains a classic account of finance, late development and government intervention.[16] Hirschman also argued that inducement mechanisms and policy coordination were needed to manage foreign assistance and public and private investments in Latin America. Government development banks and agencies are also cited as critical agents for accelerated growth across developing countries of Asia.[17]

Nonetheless, the modernization of manufacturing, information technology, financial markets, and banking in the twenty-first century suggest that more complex tradeoffs between free markets and development banks have arisen. Critics such as Woo-Cummings emphasize three problems with development banks.[18] First, because development banks tend to deeply leverage large industrial groups with bank credit, firms tend to avoid going public through the issue of equities. Second, given the scale and scope of political and economic interests involved, development banks often increase moral hazard and require costly bailouts. Third, development banks tend to impede economic innovation, slow adjustment, escape accountability, and reproduce bad equilibrium through inflationary finance or infusions of equity that transfer losses to government accounts. The Asian financial crisis of 1997–8 reinforced the view, among critics, that development banking tends to distort domestic economies and increase risk.[19] Development banks also invest in large projects often notorious for their negative impact on the environment.

Studies of the Brazilian development bank (Banco Nacional de Desenvolvimento Econômico e Social, BNDES) also suggest mismanagement under military rule and during the political vacuum of prolonged transition to civilian rule. Nonetheless, reforms since democratization amidst repeated financial crises in emerging markets from 1994–2003 placed this bank, once again, at the center of policy prerogatives and state capacities. Indeed, since its creation in 1952 as part of US–Brazil bilateral commission recommendations, the BNDE(S) repeatedly recast policies in response to changing circumstances. The BNDE first underwrote infrastructure investments from 1952 until the breakdown of democracy in 1964. Under military government, the BNDE channelled vast funds from world liquidity and forced domestic savings programs from 1964–82 through financial markets to private and state owned enterprises. As foreign debt and fiscal crisis deepened during the 1980s, the BNDES (S, for 'Social', was added in 1982) shifted to market-centred policies and explored privatizations. After 1990, the BNDES became primary agent for privatization of state-owned enterprises, the globalization of large Brazilian firms and new policies designed to maximize the gains of liberalization and market forces. Charges of inside information and phone tapping among BNDES officials during privatizations shook the bank and the Cardoso government in the late 1990s. However, the BNDES has since provided critical counter-cyclical credits and finance to Brazilian firms to counter capital outflows from 2001–3, helped underwrite the booming stock market and increased growth from 2004–8, and once again has appeared as critical source for counter-cyclical credit as the international financial crisis hit the Brazilian economy during 2008.

The combination of financial repression *and* political repression under military rule in Brazil suggests that democratization may improve the corporate governance and accountability of development banks. Critics of these institutions underestimate the importance of transparency, accountability, legislative oversight and judicial review for averting mismanagement. Since return to civilian rule in 1985, the BNDES became primary agent of privatizations and critical policy tool for financial, fiscal, and administrative reforms during two terms under President Cardoso (1995–2002). This endowed President Lula's PT coalition government (2003 onward) with a very large development bank able to pursue policies despite capital flight, perceptions of political risk among foreign investors, and lack of confidence in private finance and banking early in his presidential term. In this respect, the BNDES has returned to its origins as an institution designed to encourage collaboration between the public and private sectors, and domestic and foreign capital, to overcome infrastructure bottlenecks and the aversion of private investors to underwrite long-term projects. Since 1952, the BNDE(S) has maintained credit and finance flows when markets collapse, capital flees and private banks refuse to lend. Indeed, throughout Latin America, development banks (often renamed development agencies) have once again increased their role in domestic finance, especially during downturns and financial crises.[20] The history and rich current variety of policies of Continental European development banks thus provide important models for alternative development strategies in Latin America. Development banks in Europe and Asia have been leading agents for new market-centred policies designed to increase sustainable development and social investments. Given the maturity of capital markets in Brazil and other countries in Latin America, policies of development banks in advanced economies provide new opportunities for long-term strategies designed to sustain social inclusion, environmentally sound initiatives and productive processes while maintaining transparent financial reporting and accounting standards.

2. Savings Banks

The original intent of savings banks was to teach popular classes the habit of saving, increase the liquidity of capital, and spur economic growth. Government savings banks were founded across Continental Europe in the early nineteenth century, while government guarantees provided incentives for a variety of private, community, cooperative and mutual savings banks in the Netherlands, England, Italy and the United States. In 1906, almost a century after the *Caisse d'Epargne* was founded in France, Charles Gide argued that savings banks should serve a limited role, comparable to piggy banks in terms of collecting small amounts of capital and savings. This now appears overoptimistic. The first Brazilian government savings bank, Caixa Econômica e Monte de Socorro was founded in 1860. If savings banks are temporary and limited in character, why were an estimated 80% of Brazilians still *sem conta* (bankless), that is to say without checking accounts, savings deposits or bank cards in 2000? If other banks and credit institutions are more efficient, why do government savings banks still provide roughly 20% of credit in Brazil and retain over 20% of savings deposits?

And why, after two decades of a Washington Consensus about the need to privatize state firms and liberalize (especially banking and finance) industries, did the Caixa remain the third largest bank in Brazil (depending on measure)? In June 2004, the Caixa maintained 60,402 employees, 2013 branches, more than R$82 billion in deposits, and over R$166 billion in assets.[21]

Our answer is twofold. First, savings banks retain significant institutional foundations for competitive advantages as banks such as greater client and public confidence and longstanding, highly valued, brand names. Second, savings banks remain institutions necessary to counter the imperfections of markets and private banks, imperfections that the pressures of globalization and liberalization tend to exacerbate. In this respect, the refinancing (2001) and strategic reorientation (2002 onward) of the Brazilian Caixa provide an important case study for the ability of public savings banks to encourage popular savings without crowding out market forces or succumbing to the politicization of credit and/or outright fraud associated with government banking in the past.

Before turning to recent developments, it should be noted that government savings banks have a long history at the centre of Brazilian political economy. Although sparse, the evidence suggests that government savings banks expanded under Empire from 1860 to 1889 but declined during the economic liberalism of the Old Republic (1889–1930). After the 1930 revolution, savings banks became central to national populist strategies of capital mobilization and import substitution industrialization. Balance sheet problems during the late 1950s appear to be due primarily to rising inflation (that led clients to withdraw funds from savings accounts earning fixed 6% annual returns), while rising administrative costs also appear to indicate lax management and politicization. After the breakdown of democracy, the indexation of savings in 1965 led to a recovery of deposits at government savings banks while reforms in 1970 centralized control over the preceding federalist structure. During the 1980s, high, 'inertial' inflation and monetary chaos left the bank as one of the few major lenders; providing up to 50% of domestic lending during periods of instability. During and after price stability (1994 onward), the Caixa was used to cushion the cost of adjustment through purchase of bad credits at private and public banks before their resale or privatization. The Caixa also became a 'domestic IMF', providing conditional loans to state and municipal governments that required payroll reductions, reforms and privatizations to adjust accounts to price stability.

Since capitalization of the bank in 2001, the Caixa has led in core business areas of housing, urban development and sanitation while remaining the central agent for government social policies. A sanitized portfolio combining high interest bearing government paper and low interest savings deposits helped produce strong profits, permitting the bank to pursue a dual strategy of expanding both upmarket investment bank operations and new downmarket popular credit and savings programmes. The Caixa has reported strong profits each quarter since capitalization in 2001. Furthermore, as agent of federal government social programs, the Caixa distributed citizenship cards (Caixa ATM cards) and family grants that have contributed to significant improvement of those worst off in Brazil. Neri suggests that correspondent banking and family grants distributed through Caixa ATM cards have contributed to placing Brazil well ahead of millennium goals to reduce extreme poverty.[22]

This social role of the Brazilian Caixa is not an exception. Savings banks have proved critical agents for social inclusion and sustainable development throughout Latin America. Mena and Errázuriz´s review of savings banks in Chile over 150 years concludes that these institutions are still necessary to promote financial inclusion, banking competition, and the mobilization of household savings.[23] The BancoEstado also retains a mandate to promote entrepreneurship, invest in human capital and culture, lead infrastructure investment, finance social policies and contribute to financial stability and public confidence in the banking system. With over $20.5 billion in assets, the largest network of bank branches and ATM machines in Chile, holder of half of savings accounts and two-thirds of mortgages in Chile, processor of 60% of domestic payments, a 45% market share of small enterprise banking and 80% of public sector bank services and loans, the BancoEstado remains a critical institution for Chilean development. Recent modernization of information technology, administrative reforms and new micro-credit policies suggest that the bank is at the centre of efforts by President Bachelet to reverse the substantial increase of inequality experienced by Chileans during the last decades.

The European Savings Bank Group and World Savings Bank Institute have been particularly active in promoting savings bank and postal bank modernization in advanced, developing and transition countries. However, like development banks, savings banks have critics. The proposed privatization of the Japanese Postal Bank system (and Development Bank of Japan) provides important examples of how political coalitions attempt to use financial liberalization and privatizations against entrenched interests.[24]

In sum, this brief review of development banks and savings banks suggests the value of looking at Continental European experiences for alternative policies for banking in Latin America. These financial institutions are at the heart of policy coordination and imply a very different variety of financial capitalism than the highly leveraged financial markets and private banking that tend to predominate in liberal market economies.

3. Varieties of *Financial* Capitalism: Banks and Coordinated Market Economies

Core differences between coordinated and liberal market economies have to do with development banks and public savings banks. Comparison of banks and financial markets can thus reveal much about how different varieties of capitalism work. Since publication of Hall and Soskice's *Varieties of Capitalism* in 2001,[25] scholars have focused on matters of classification,[26] corporate governance,[27] policy complementarity,[28] regulatory convergence[29] and the applicability of concepts to Latin America.[30] Although debates continue, one conclusion is clear: Theories and policies from market-centred financial systems and liberal-market economies such as the US and UK are often amiss or out of place in Latin America and Brazil. Instead, bank-centred financial systems and government banks have several advantages that are especially relevant to the Latin American context of late development, shallow markets, dismal income distribution, volatile business cycles, and dramatic periods of capital flight and financial crisis. Banks provide more patient capital than equity markets to help firms through adjustment during the larger economic shocks experienced in Latin America. Banks can monitor firms and the economy better where shallow markets lack information and efficient pricing. And government banks still provide longer time-horizons for infrastructure and social investments in which private agents remain unwilling to put money. Development banks and savings banks thus provide both institutional foundations of competitive advantage for firms and comparative advantages of policy coordination for national governments.

Hall and Soskice briefly note that the varieties of capitalism approach may be applied to Latin America.[31] Nonetheless, they underestimate both stark differences between developing and advanced economies *and* fundamental tensions between markets and institutions. In Latin America, policymaking involves fundamentally different realities that reproduce underdevelopment, social exclusion and market volatility. And despite recent transitions to democracy, Latin American economies remain far less settled and far less coordinated than Continental European ones, especially in the case of large amorphous federal polities such as Brazil. Latin America also pales in terms of political development. A standard distinction in political analysis turns on whether social classes have been included in political institutions. By the mid-twentieth century, this was largely the case in Europe, whether through democracy or dictatorship. Scholars of advanced capitalism therefore assume many parameters such as price stability, comparatively equitable levels of income distribution, widespread rule of law, significant government capacity and institutions for exercise of political accountability. In Latin America, policy disputes over credit and finance differ because the stakes are higher, the number of those excluded is greater and the parameters for policy constantly shift.

These differences are not simply of degree. Advanced economies have long-standing consolidated institutions and deeply embedded and stable markets. In Brazil and Latin America, firms, governments and citizens face volatile business cycles, shallow markets and political disjunctures. Conaghan & Malloy noted over a decade ago that transitions from authoritarianism in Latin America demonstrated remarkable political creativity.[32] However, another of their observations still rings true: Democracy in the region is neither based on underlying social pacts, nor on class compromises along the lines of European experiences with Keynesian policies and welfare states. Nor are the young and often embattled democracies in Latin America based on political regimes or policies of social inclusion comparable to past experiences in the region with national-populism and import substitution industrialization. Latin American politics therefore involves fundamental disagreements about markets, institutions, government, law and competing perceptions of social justice. In short, Latin American policymaking involves decisions during volatility, crisis and even catastrophe that sum to a different type of unsettling statecraft.[33] President Kirschner's nationalization of private pension funds during the financial crisis of 2008 suggests that politics continues to shape domestic financial systems along these lines.

These differences notwithstanding, a core distinction in financial economics (between bank-centred and market-centred financial systems)[34] fits closely with Hall and Soskice's two varieties of capitalism (coordinated and liberal market economies). This reinforces our argument that Continental European (and Asian) institutions and policies provide new perspectives on Latin American banking.[35] Liberal market-economies are driven by equity markets, thrive on public information and shun coordination. Coordinated market-economies are driven by bank credit, thrive on concealing (limited sharing) of firm strategy with financiers and shun markets for their excessive volatility. Different varieties of financial capitalism also tend to generate diametrically opposed policy recommendations. From a market-centred perspective, coordination and neo-institutionalism are nothing but neo-protectionism. From the perspective of coordinated capitalism, excessive financial liberalization and privatization of public banks would simply throw babies (institutions of social policy and domestic control) out with the bathwater.

Worse, these differences often tap fundamental differences across nations. Allen and Gale argue that markets, banks and corporate governance vary across the largest economies in ways consistent with the distinction between bank-centred and market-centred financial systems (and, we say, liberal *vs* coordinated market economies). On the left side of Figure 6.1 is the paradigmatic market-centred economy of the US that retains deeply leveraged liquid financial markets, a large number of banks that compete to provide financial services and credit, and where hostile takeovers and liquid equities reinforce financial markets and competition. On the right hand of Figure 6.1 is Germany, with comparatively small financial markets, the concentration of domestic banking in a few large institutions[36] and long-term relationships between banks and firms at the heart of political economy. Allen and Gale arrange the UK, Japan and France as intermediate financial systems along these three dimensions, suggesting that their financial markets, banks, and traditions of corporate governance tend to approximate the attributes more clearly embodied by the polar opposites of the US and Germany.

Figure 6.1: Banks in financial systems: comparative categories of Allen and Gale

	US	UK	Japan	France	Germany
Financial Markets	Hi	Hi	Moderate	Moderate	Low
Banks	Competition		↔		Concentration
Corporate Governance	Hostile takeover		Main bank		Hausbank

Source: F. Allen and D. Gale, *Comparing Financial Systems* (Cambridge, MA : MIT Press, 2000), p. 4.

Neat schemes fail to capture subtleties. However, these concepts and categories reinforce our core argument; that development banks and savings banks provide better models and comparisons for reassessing policies and banking in Brazil and Latin America. Allen and Gale present four further observations that also reinforce our claim about the misplaced character of policies from liberal market economies and market-centred financial systems in Brazil and South America:

1. In most countries, stock markets are unimportant.
2. Financial markets are primarily markets for government debt.
3. Firms obtain funds via capital markets or bank loans.
4. The ideal of frictionless markets is rarely achieved in practice.
   i. instead, 'intermediaries' are needed to overcome information barriers.
   ii. the traditional view of financial markets as ideal means of allocating resources is misplaced.[37]

Each of these observations raises complex matters beyond the scope of this chapter. However, they sum to suggest that Continental European banking and finance provide more adequate paradigms and policies in Latin America. A brief empirical comparison of domestic financial systems provides further evidence.

4. From Theory to Evidence: Observations on Financial Structure and Change

Figure 6.2 on the following page compares financial systems along two dimensions, the value of bank credit, and the value of capital in equities, as a percentage of GDP. Year-end average values of domestic bank credit and domestic equity market capitalization are drawn from the World Bank Financial Structure Data Base. The distribution of domestic banking and finance systems suggest the existence of *four* varieties of financial capitalism. The concepts of bank-centred and market-centred financial systems from comparative financial economics capture national experiences in the upper left and lower right cells of Figure 6.2. This suggests that the distinction between stock market centred economies and bank centered economies does indeed help explain differences across advanced political economies.

Again, these concepts from comparative financial economics fit closely with the core concepts used by Hall and Soskice to describe varieties of (advanced) capitalism. For Hall and Soskice, 'in liberal market economies, firms coordinate their activities via hierarchies and competitive market arrangements' while 'In coordinated market economies firms depend more heavily on non-market relationships to coordinate their endeavors with other actors and to construct core competencies'.[38] The first variety, liberal market economies, turn on traditional laws of free markets and forces of supply and demand. The second variety (coordinated market economies) turn on non-market relations, incomplete contracting, networks, inter-firm collaboration and other social and political factors that add up to a different type of market economy. Banks and financial markets are at the center of these differences across advanced economies.

However, most domestic financial systems are distributed across two further cells. We label these cells 'world finance centers' and 'underdeveloped financial systems'. For the purposes of comparison, world finance centers are defined as economies with capital in equity markets above 100% of GDP and bank credit above 75% of GDP. Finally, underdeveloped financial systems are defined as economies with bank credit below 75% of GDP and capital in equity markets below 100% of GDP. Although we do not mean to demarcate rigid types or categories, the data appears to support the following observations. First, regarding world finance centres, the data suggests that very few countries are able to position themselves at the center of global banking and international financial markets. As Smith and Walter note, policies in world finance centres seek to capture market share of international money and foreign currency exchange markets, primary and secondary debt and capital markets, international and offshore bank lending and other financial transactions.[39] Small island economies often specialize in this regard.[40] This suggests that, far from a widespread pattern of convergence across domestic financial systems toward private banking and financial markets, deeply leveraged financial systems arise instead from a particular, path dependent and exceptional character of select countries that serve as world finance centers. This implies that policies and political coalitions supporting financial liberalization and flexible accounting regulations are largely non-replicable.

Figure 6.2: Bank credit and equity market capitalization
(1995–2000 averages)

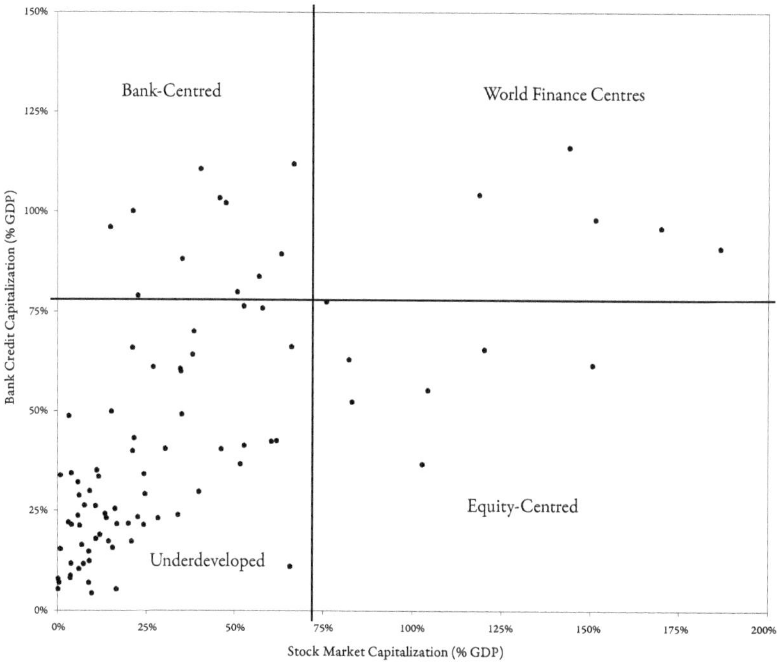

Source: World Bank Financial Structures Database
Note: Points = Mean of the year-end average values, 1995–2000

Finally, regarding the lower left cell of Figure 6.2, underdevelopment theory suggest that shallow finance and credit markets are caused and reproduced by vicious cycles and causal relations often shared by developing countries.[41] From this perspective, political economy and policymaking in developing countries involve fundamentally different realities of legal, institutional, and political underdevelopment amidst social exclusion and market volatility. Again, firms and governments in developing countries face more volatile business cycles and unstable markets that elevate risk perceptions and prices, drag economic growth and impede financial deepening.

Although descriptive, exploratory and limited in time span, the evidence suggests further implications that should be examined. First, if the data is accurate, financial development appears *not* to be an ordinal or linear process. The most leveraged domestic economies are not the most advanced economies but countries that occupy a particular place in the world economy as financial centres. The only countries in the World Bank Financial Structures data that reported capitalization of equity markets over 100% and domestic bank credit over 75% of GDP (1995–2000 averages) are the Netherlands, the UK, Singapore, Luxembourg, Hong Kong and Malaysia. This also implies that *particular configurations* exist for both comparative and competitive advantage in the international economy and the most appropriate set of banking and finance policies.

A second implication from this descriptive data is that equity-market-centred financial systems remain rare. Only the US, South Africa, Finland and Sweden report capitalization of equity markets above 100% of domestic GDP and bank credit at less than 75% of GDP. Contrary to the idea of convergence toward stock-market driven economies through privatizations and liberalization, this rough comparison suggests that these types of financial systems remain quite rare (note that data preceeds collapse of stock markets in 2007–8). Third, most advanced economies fall within the upper left-hand cell that we define as indicative of bank-centered financial systems. The countries that reported equity market capitalization less that 100% of GDP and domestic bank credit above 75% of GDP were Japan, Germany, Switzerland, Austria, France, Spain, Australia, New Zealand, Thailand, Belgium, Cyprus, China and Panama.

Finally, it bears repeating that most domestic financial systems report low values for *both* equity market capitalization and bank credit. Underdeveloped financial systems include, at the upper reaches of the cells in Figure 6.2, countries such as Chile, Canada, Israel and Korea, with substantial domestic financial markets and banking systems. However, the bulk of countries in this cell report capital in equity markets and bank credit at well below 50% of GDP. Although the causes and consequences of financial underdevelopment have been debated for decades, the data suggests that, in comparative perspective, most domestic financial systems remain substantially less leveraged than advanced economies (both bank and market centered) and a select number of world financial centres.

5. On the Financial Origins of Inequality

This section dares to paraphrase J. J. Rousseau to dramatize the lack of studies about the impact of domestic financial systems and policies on inequality. We briefly explore two questions. Are market-centred and bank-centred financial systems related to different levels of income distribution? Does financial liberalization increase inequality? Differences about the origins of inequality are also longstanding and contested. However, one shift in recent scholarship is marked. Past expectations that modernization would increase equality have been replaced by generalized concern that globalization may increase inequality. Indeed, since 2000, commissions have been created to investigate the causes and consequences of increasing inequality by the American Political Science Association, the United Nations and the World Bank, along with many other institutions and organizations.

We venture two claims. First, income distribution appears to differ across bank-centred and market-centred financial systems.[42] Further research is needed to understand causal mechanisms and control for other variables such as taxes and government transfers. However, a simple comparison of advanced economies during the 1980s and 90s suggests that bank-centred economies sustained significantly better distributions of income than market-centred political economies. These differences increase markedly during the recent decades of financial liberalization. First, Gini coefficients suggest substantially different distributions of income in countries with market-centered and bank-centred financial systems.[43] Based on data from the mid-1990s, the average Gini coefficient of countries with bank-centred financial systems is 0.248, while the average Gini coefficient of market-centred financial systems is over 0.336. Again, other factors (such as tax systems and social policies) must be considered. But this is a stark difference. Furthermore, these differences are consistent with both theories in financial economics about household savings patterns,[44] as well as empirical studies that emphasize the increasing upmarket strategies of private banking and free credit markets. Dymski argues that US banking has shifted away from the traditional 'one-bank-for-all' system at mid-twentieth century, largely because of upmarket strategies and predatory lending of lower-income clients.[45] Banking and finance thus appear to have contributed to the marked deterioration of income equality experienced by the US during the last decades.

Table 6.1: Income distribution in market-centred and bank-centred political economies

Market-Centred	Early 1970s	Early 1980s	Early 1990s	Late 1990s
United Kingdom	0.34	0.26	0.33	0.40
United States	0.34	0.36	0.39	0.37
Australia	0.32	0.40	0.41	0.41

New Zealand	0.30	0.34	0.40	0.37
Finland	0.31	0.31	0.25	0.28
Bank-Centred				
Canada	0.32	0.33	0.35	0.28
Denmark	0.22	0.21	0.39	0.36
France	0.44	0.35	0.46	0.29
Germany	0.39	0.31	0.26	0.32
Italy	0.38	0.33	0.28	0.36
Netherlands	0.34	0.33	0.30	0.32
Norway	0.30	0.27	0.32	0.32
Spain	0.37	0.34	0.33	0.25
Sweden	0.38	0.35	0.31	0.34

Source: Luxembourg Income Study. Available at www.lispect.org

Differences have increased over time. The US and UK, countries with paradigmatic market-centred financial systems, have experienced substantial deterioration in income equality since the mid-1970s. In comparison, Gini coefficients from Germany suggest that bank-centred financial systems contribute to maintaining more equitable societies.[46] The Gini coefficient for Germany remained stable at roughly 0.27 in the mid-1970s to 2000; compared to an increase in the US from 0.318 in the mid-1970s to an estimated 0.368 in 2000. Indeed, increasing inequality in the US has led political scientists to reassess traditional Tocquevillian views of a vibrant civil society and more equitable distribution of wealth in the US compared to Europe. The UK has also experienced a dramatic increase of inequality. Gini coefficients for the UK increased from 0.268 (mid-1970s) to an estimated 0.345 in 2000.

The characteristics of market-centred and bank-centred financial systems thus appear to be important determinants of inequality. Vitols and Dymski consider several causal mechanisms. Their claims mirror arguments about the allocation of savings and investments in the two varieties of capitalism defined by Hall and Soskice. For Vitols, wealthy individuals tend to prefer stocks and bonds, while middle-class savings tend to be kept as savings deposits in banks, while low income groups are able to save little, and keep whatever assets they accumulate as cash or liquid deposits in banks.[47] In sum, social classes save differently, and these differences reinforce the tendency for dynamic financial markets to coexist alongside worsening inequalities.

Vitols also emphasizes the importance of retirement savings programmes and pension funds. In market-centred financial systems, private pensions reinforce capital markets and the bifurcation of social classes. Indeed, Vitols notes that private pension funds are now among the largest holders of equities in market-centred systems such as the US and UK. By contrast, pensions and retirements in what Vitols described as 'solidaristic' systems provide income guarantees through families, firms or public social security systems, none of which involve assets in equity markets.[48] And while private pension funds drive equity markets in the US and UK, public pensions during the 1990s remained 68% of retirement income in Germany (compared to 33% in the US).[49]

Evidence from developing and emerging nations is also compelling. The evolution of Gini coefficients from the 1970s through the late 1990s confirms both substantial differences between market-centred and (public) bank-centred financial systems. Indeed, Brazil and Latin America stand out, in terms of higher levels of inequality, not only from advanced economies, but also most emerging economies, transition economies in Eastern Europe and the former Soviet Union, and Asia. In advanced economies, Gini coefficients largely vary between 0.2 and 0.4, while coefficients in developing nations often remain above 0.4. Gini coefficients for new republics of the former Soviet Union and satellite states suggest their more egalitarian point of departure for transitions from Stalinist rule and command economies. Gini coefficients from the mid-1970s under communist rule remained between 0.2 and 0.25. In comparison, most developing countries in Asia measure between 0.3 and 0.5, with examples of both improvement and deterioration. African countries consistently range much higher, reflecting stark inequalities. The evidence from Latin American countries suggests that the impact of financial liberalization has been significant. Brazil remains a notorious outlier in terms of income inequality. However, it is notable that both Mexico and Chile have experienced significant worsening of domestic income distributions, increasing from 0.46 and 0.45 in the mid 1970s to 0.56 and 0.52 respectively in the late 1990s.

In sum, descriptive comparisons suggest that bank-centred financial systems are related to more equitable distributions of income and that liberalization policies tend to increase inequality. Both findings reinforce our turn to Continental European institutions and policies for new ideas about development in Brazil and Latin America.

6. Brazilian Banking: A New Division of Financial Labour

The institutional foundations of competitive advantage of Brazilian federal government banks have produced an unexpected new division of financial labour involving private, government and foreign banks within a more transparent regulatory environment. Liberalization and privatizations reduced the role of state government banks and increased the importance of foreign banks.[50] In 1995, the Cardoso government ended protection of domestic finance set in the 1988 Constitution, permitted foreign participation in privatization auctions and provided new incentives for foreign investment in financial industries. From 1994 through 2002, foreign investment in the financial sector summed to US$19.8 billion or 15% of total direct foreign investment. However, instead of privatization, federal government banks were capitalized in 2001 to meet Basle II accord and tougher Central Bank of Brazil bank capital guidelines. From 2001–8, evidence suggests significant competitive advantages and fundamental roles for federal government banks. Brazil thus provides a critical case combining price stability, liberalization, reform and modernization of government banks amidst democratization after military rule.

But rather than a linear story of successes, advances tended to create new, often more serious, challenges. For example, price stability in 1994 required the creation of government programmes to save and sell failed private banks (PROER, 1995–7),[51] then to privatize indebted state government banks (PROES, 1997–9)[52] and, finally, to capitalize and reform federal government banks (PROEF, 1999–2001). Furthermore, after heterodox policies reduced inflation in 1994, a variety of new regulations, procedures and programmes were created at the Central Bank of Brazil to increase its capacity to supervise banks, regulate markets, and reduce risk.[53] Despite capital flight and opposition party programmes to reverse reforms, policies under the PT coalition government of President Lula (2003 onward) have maintained policies set in place during the 1990s.

Table 6.2: Bank assets in Brazil, 1996–2004

	1996	1997	1998	1999	2000	2001	2002	2003	2004
Other Gov't.	21.9	19.1	11.4	10.2	5.6	4.3	5.9	5.8	5.5
Banco do Brasil	12.5	14.4	17.4	15.8	15.6	16.8	17.1	18.4	17.4
Caixa	16.5	16.6	17.0	17.1	15.4	11.0	11.7	13.0	11.5
Private	38.3	36.8	35.3	33.1	35.2	37.2	36.9	40.8	41.7
Foreign	10.5	12.8	18.4	23.2	27.4	29.9	27.4	20.7	22.4
Credit Coops	0.3	0.4	0.5	0.7	0.8	0.9	1.0	1.3	1.4
Total	100	100	100	100	100	100	100	100	100
R$billion	487.0	682.4	673.4	717.8	823.8	938.1	1103.9	1184.0	1285.7

Source: Central Bank of Brazil, available at www.bcb.gov.br

This new division of financial labour in Brazil can first be seen in terms of bank assets. The declining share of government banks (other than the Banco do Brasil and Caixa Econômica) from 1996 through 2004 reflects the privatization of state government banks and the downsizing of federal government bank portfolios. Domestic private bank market share of bank assets increased slightly from 38.3% in 1996 to 41.7% of bank assets in 2004. Meanwhile, foreign banks increased their share of bank assets in Brazil from 10.5% in 1996 to 22.4% in 2004. In sum, financial liberalization led to the entry of new foreign banks into Brazil at greater levels than reported in European economies during monetary integration, most emerging economies in Asia and large emerging economies.

The increase of foreign bank branches (915 in 1995 to 3.799 in 2001) suggests the extent of liberalization and internationalization of banking in Brazil.

The reform of federal government banks during the 1990s can also be seen in the declining number of federal government bank branches from 7.232 to 5.611. The number of state government bank branches also declined sharply from 1.863 in 1995 to 1.084 in 2001 due to privatizations. However bank branches are not the most important story from Brazil.

New policies and strategies have reached clients and provided services through automated teller machines (ATMs) and bank outposts or correspondents (i.e. agreements with businesses or non-governmental organizations to provide banking services). These outlets have increased dramatically in Brazil since 1994. Furthermore, the predominance of domestic and government banks in this area has been marked. The number of bank branches in Brazil actually declined from 17.400 in 1994 to 17.049 in 2002 before expanding to 18.087 in 2006. The number of other points of service (mostly fully staffed mini-branches, *pontos de atendamento bancário,* PAB) also declined from 12.641 in 1994 to 2.274 by 2005. However, the number of alternative points that offer banking services increased dramatically. ATMs increased from 3.446 in 1994 to 31.279 in 2005. And while the number of 'bank outposts' declined from 2.506 in 1994 to 2.376 in 2002, new legislation defining 'bank correspondents' led to the establishment of 10.589 points of bank service in 2000, reaching 40.411 by 2005.

A World Bank survey of access to banking services in Brazil conducted during 2002 provides further evidence that government banks still maintain a critical role in the delivery of banking services, especially to underdeveloped regions.[54] The data is striking. A full 90% of survey respondents in the North region and 79% of respondents in the Northeast region reported having no bank deposits. In comparison, 66% of respondents in the Southeast region, 50% of respondents in the South, and 39% of respondents in the Centre-West reported having no bank deposits. The survey data casts further light on regional differences across Brazil: Of respondents reporting having deposits with financial institutions, public banks retained a larger market share than private banks in the South (33% *vs* 16%) and Northeast (10% *vs* 7%), while private banks retained larger shares in the North (6% *vs* 3%) Southeast (22% *vs* 11%) and Centre-West (30% *vs* 21%).

Market shares of payments and credits also suggest that government banks remain critical. With the exception of the sparsely settled Centre-West region, private banks retained half or less than half of credit and payment operations reported in the survey. In sum, the data counters expectations that policies of liberalization and privatization would free market forces to meet untapped demand for banking services in less developed areas. Instead, the evidence suggests a new division of financial labour between public and private banks, with the former assuming critical roles in terms of access to banking services.

Supply of credit also indicates a shift from government to private lenders, with the government bank share of total credit (other than the Banco do Brasil and Caixa Econômica) declining from 23.5% in 1996 to 4.4% by 2004. Meanwhile, private credit increased from 31.9% in 1996 to 41.3% in 2004, with foreign banks increasing their share from 5.2% in 1994 to 21.5% in 2004. This confirms the emphasis of Goldfajn et al about the liberalization of domestic Brazilian banking and comparative data on financial liberalization reported by Stallings and Studart.[55] However, the increase of Banco do Brasil market share of domestic credit from 10.6% in 1996 to 19.4% in 2004 and the decrease of Federal Government Savings Bank market share (dropping from 23.0% to 7.5% in 2004) suggest that policies and politics of these institutions remain central to adjustment, capitalization and domestic development.

Table 6.3: Credit, 1996–2004

	1996	1997	1998	1999	2000	2001	2002	2003	2004
Other Govt	23.5	10.3	8.9	8.1	5.1	3.1	4.8	4.5	4.4
Banco Brasil	10.6	11.0	12.1	10.6	11.0	14.5	16.2	20.4	19.4
Caixa	24.0	30.9	32.3	28.7	23.0	7.1	7.6	7.9	7.5
Private	31.9	35.4	31.0	31.7	34.5	42.1	39.7	41.3	41.3
Foreign	9.5	11.7	14.9	19.8	25.2	31.5	29.9	23.8	25.1
Credit Coops	0.5	0.7	0.9	1.1	1.2	1.6	1.8	2.1	2.3
Total	100	100	100	100	100	100	100	100	100
R$billion	192.1	184.7	186.6	193.7	228.3	233.2	259.2	284.6	342.0

Source: Central Bank of Brazil, available at www.bcb.gov.br

Comparison of the size of credits from government, domestic, foreign and non-bank loans helps further clarify the new division of financial labour in Brazil. Data from year-end 2002 reported by the Central Bank of Brazil suggests that government banks tend to concentrate in extending large and small loans, while domestic and foreign banks tend to specialize in the middle market, i.e. lending intermediate values of credits.[56] Although they remain a very small part of the domestic credit market, 'non-banks' such as cooperatives tend to concentrate on the concession of smaller loans. This suggests the specialization of domestic private, foreign and government banking institutions in different market segments. Credit cooperatives specialize downmarket, while government banks tend to either lend small amounts or very large amounts. In comparison, private and foreign banks lend more evenly spread across loans by value.

Credit leverage is another traditional indicator of bank behaviour. Credit leverage is simply the proportion of credit/assets. The difference between government, private and foreign banks suggests that these institutions have not converged toward similar practices and that different portfolio decisions and different business strategies persist.[57] The credit leverage of government banks declined from 10.32 in 1994 to 6.65 during 1999, but increased thereafter to

8.68 in 2000. In comparison, the credit leverage of foreign banks increased slightly from 2.33 to a peak of 3.11 in 1998, declined to 2.25 in 1999 and increased slightly to 2.47 in 2000. Meanwhile, the credit leverage of private domestic banks decreased from 8.98 in 1994 to 5.54 in 1999, increasing thereafter to 6.24 during 2000. In sum, government, private domestic and foreign banks appear to have significantly different strategies in the allocation of their portfolios. Foreign banks transform assets into credit at less than one-third of the levels reported by government banks, and less than half levels reported by domestic private banks. In this respect, international capital risk guidelines set by the BIS appear to reinforce a bias of foreign and private banks away from riskier credit allocation and towards holding government paper that is classified as zero (or low) risk. This suggests that government banks remain critical agents for provision of counter-cyclical credit during downturns in the Brazilian business cycle.

Perceptions of Brazilian political elites are consistent with this evidence about the roles of government banking. A survey of federal deputies conducted during 2002 found a tempered realism about the potential use of these institutions for electoral purposes but strong opposition to their privatization.[58] Of seventy-five federal deputies interviewed from a cross-sample of parties, regions and ideologies, 46.7% responded that they did not think federal banks will be used to influence elections, while 34.7% thought this use was possible and 16.0% likely. Politicians recognize the realities of electoral cycles and the risks of mismanagement. Nonetheless, privatization was opposed by an overwhelming majority of federal deputies. A full 89.3% opposed privatization of the Banco do Brasil or Caixa, while 90.7% opposed privatization of the BNDES.

In sum, bank change in Brazil suggests the cohabitation of private banks and equity markets alongside government development banks and savings banks. Instead of convergence toward private banking and a market-centred financial system through privatizations and liberalization, a new division of financial labour suggests the institutional foundations and competitive advantages of public banks. Federal government banks have modernized, reformed, and pursued new strategies, both up- and downmarket. Development banks and savings banks in coordinated market economies provide better references for understanding this new division of financial labour and new policies that may further promote social inclusion and sustainable development.

Conclusion

Brazilian federal government banks have adjusted to price stability (1994 onward), pursued new business strategies, and implemented new government policies in a context of greater transparency and accountability, tighter central bank supervision and democratization. From the perspective of politics and public policy, these institutions remain critical for social policy, popular credit and a variety of development roles. Brazilian federal government banks thus remain commanding heights. They are uniquely positioned to sustain growth, accelerate social inclusion and deepen citizenship. However, for these institutions to deepen domestic credit, finance, and democracy, they must also respect sound credit practices, prudent banking and economic constraints. Far from a Leninist conception that sees government banking as a means for capturing state and corporate power, our argument is 'Shonfieldian', a liberal-pluralist approach to statecrafting that emphasizes particular configurations and opportunities for building on existing institutions, especially during critical junctures. The coincidence between price stability and democratization in Brazil since 1994 provides such a critical juncture in terms of government policies that have sought to recast banking in a new direction.

The realities of banking and credit in Brazil are still sobering. Indeed, the financial crises faced by Brazil since 1994 (Mexico 1994–5, Asia 1997, Russia 1998, Brazil 1999, Argentina 2001, Brazil 2002–3, US 2008) have reinforced the aversion of Brazilians to credit and debt. For example, the FGV survey of CEOs and managers of Brazilian industrial firms suggested that investments would be made almost exclusively through cash during 2003.[59] Brazilian households have also long associated debt with a spiral that inexorably leads to bankruptcy and poverty. Far from irrational, this perception is based on the caution imposed by decades of economic instability where social mobility was measured more as the frightening likelihood of descent downward than entrepreneurial calculations of risk to improve social station. Perhaps this is the greatest, if still incremental, shift in Brazilian political economy. Popular credit in Brazil is not 'micro' in the sense of small volumes because of the still-terrible distribution of domestic income. The creation of over six million new accounts for bankless Brazilians at the Caixa since 2003 suggests that federal government banks provide large levers, not only for counter-cyclical policies, but also for policies of social inclusion and political socialization.

Since Zysman's work twenty-four years ago, scholars have clarified how bank-centred and market-centred financial systems work.[60] During the 1980s and 90s, specialists in financial markets expressed concern about the viability of traditional patterns of household savings and banking after financial liberalization due to increased competition. The evidence suggests the contrary. Most domestic banking systems appear to have retained and indeed reinforced traditional institutions, including non-profit and government-owned credit institutions such as cooperatives, mutual societies and savings banks. European experiences especially suggest the continued importance of differences rather than convergence toward private banking and market-centred financial systems.

Banks and markets thus appear to coexist after financial liberalization to a considerably greater degree than expected by theories of convergence. Domestic financial systems around the globe appear *not* to have converged toward equity markets and private banking along the lines of the US and UK.

These findings are controversial because scholars and policymakers retain core differences about government intervention, finance and credit in development and government ownership. Theories of financial repression see government presence in banking and credit as responsible for reproducing underdevelopment, and privatization and liberalization as necessary to free-market forces. Theories of comparative institutional advantage, relational banking and public and cooperative banking suggest that long-term relations between banks, local communities, political forces and firms are necessary to realize the gains of investments and social policies. That these relations be sheltered from short-term market forces is fundamentally at odds with core ideas about financial markets. Perhaps the central difference turns on liquidity. Advocates of markets suggest that liquidity, transparency, competition and market pricing produce higher levels of welfare. Advocates of bank-centred development and government value patient capital, networks, social policies, coordination and institutions that, in the long run, ensure higher rates of growth and welfare. The collapse of credit and capital markets during 2007–8 surely calls for more careful assessment of alternatives to market-based paradigms.

The evidence and debates explored herein provide new perspectives on politics and markets in a broader sense. Since the abandonment of the electoral road to socialism and the breakdown of democratic regimes in Latin America and other developing nations during the 1960s and 1970s, political and other social scientists have emphasized economic constraints on social policies, limits to popular inclusion and the perverse impact of politics on markets. The remarkable series of transitions from authoritarianism in several world regions that began in Southern Europe in the mid-1970s has done little to change the overwhelming sense that markets severely constrain governments and social policies. Meanwhile, in most advanced economies, neo-conservative politics and neo-liberal policies have dismantled welfare states and worsened inequalities. Given the unprecedented transparency and accountability provided by advances in banking and information technology, post-transition experiences of democratization in Brazil and Latin America provide an opportunity to reassess relations between politics, policies and social inclusion. Despite the recent onslaught of financial crisis, the achievements of financial integration and monetary policy in Europe also suggest that it is now possible to modernize public banks, tap the popular credit channel, retain social policies and pursue income policies without creating bad equilibrium or repressing free markets. New 'downmarket' policies of popular savings and credit have also brought large numbers of bankless Brazilians and Latin Americans into the formal economy and helped reverse forces of impoverishment and exclusion. Although a long sequence of financial crises wracked developing and emerging economies during the 1990s and early 2000s, their banking systems have emerged, phoenix-like, 'after the financial storms' to provide policy options, sustain better domestic income distribution and increase the pace of economic activity – despite the shocking news about financial crisis from advanced economies. The microeconomics of social inclusion have replaced the macroeconomics of populism.

7 MONETARY AND FISCAL POLICY CONFLICTS IN CENTRAL EUROPE: HOW CREDIBLY ARE MACRO POLICIES CHARACTERIZED IN THE PHASE OF PREPARATION FOR EMU?

Caroline Vincensini

This essay explores the challenges facing the policy mix in Central Europe (Hungary, Poland, Czech Republic) since 2000. At the turn of the century, their independent central banks implemented a monetary policy strategy of inflation targeting aiming for disinflation while the countries concomitantly started preparing their entry into the European Monetary Union (EMU), even before their accession to the EU in May 2004.[1] This period was characterized by several episodes of conflicts between the central banks' monetary policy and the governments' fiscal policies, which brings to mind the conflict that opposed the national governments and the European central bank (ECB) in the first years of EMU. This latter conflict has been interpreted in terms of the difficulty for the new ECB to establish its credibility, leading it to implement a perhaps excessively restrictive monetary policy.[2] Can the policy-mix conflicts in Central Europe in the 2000s be interpreted in the same framework? It seems that although the question of the central bank's credibility is relevant, the question of the government's fiscal policy credibility also arises, thus posing more generally the question of the credibility of macro-policies in the phase of preparation for EMU, in relation to their institutional framework.

We shall explore the credibility of monetary and fiscal policies in Central Europe, with a view to explaining the policy-mix conflicts observed and their resolution. The first two parts of the essay outline the institutional and economic framework of both macro policies. The third part exposes the conflicts observed. The fourth part explores whether they may be explained by a lack of central bank credibility and suggests that the problem also lies with fiscal policies. The fifth part argues that the conflicts may be interpreted in terms of imperfections of the institutional framework governing macro-policies and explains why the conflicts have been attenuated in recent years.

1. The Institutional and Economic Framework of Monetary Policy in Central Europe

The general framework of monetary policies includes the rules they are submitted to and their economic context.

1.1. Independence of Central Banks

In all three countries, central banks are highly independent, either since their creation, or since more recent legislation enacted just before the implementation of inflation targetting. Their independence concerns the use of monetary policy instruments as well as the definition of monetary policy objectives.

In Hungary, the two-tier banking system was reinstated on 1 January 1987, returning central bank status to the Magyar Nemzeti Bank (MNB). Its independence was guaranteed by the Act on the MNB in October 1991. In July 2001, a new Act on the MNB was voted to put its status in compliance with EU rules: it aligned the MNB's independence with EU regulations and made price stability its primary objective. This Act also defined the nomination rules of the members of the Monetary Council, the decision-making organ, who are appointed by the President of the Republic for a six-year term. The Governor of the MNB is also appointed by the President of the Republic for a six-year term, at the proposal of the Prime Minister (see www.mnb.hu). Contrarily to ECB practice, the MNB and the government jointly decide of inflation targets since 2001 (see p. 146, below).

In Poland, the Narodowy Bank Polski (NBP) was reinstated as a central bank in 1989 and was then entrusted with the value of the Polish currency. Its status was modified by the Constitution of 1997 and the Act on the NBP of 1997, which reinforced its independence and created the Monetary Policy Council (MPC). The MPC defines the objectives of monetary policy and the level of reference interest rates. It is chaired by the President of the NBP and its nine other members are appointed in equal numbers for a six-year term by the President of the Republic, the Sejm (the lower chamber of the Parliament) and the Senate. The President of the NBP is also appointed by the Sejm, for a six-year term, at the request of the President of the Republic (see www.nbp.pl).

In the Czech Republic, the central bank (Ceska Narodni Banka, CNB) was created on 1 January 1993, following partition with Slovakia. The Czech Constitution (1992) and the Act on the CNB of 1993 guarantee its independence. The seven members of the Bank Board, including the Governor, are appointed by the President of the Republic for a six-year term. The Bank Board, the decision-making organ, sets its inflation objectives and its monetary policy instruments (see www.cnb.cz).

In all three countries, the decision-making organ decides on the reference interest rates by a simple majority vote, the chairperson having the casting vote in case of a tie. Measures have also been taken in each country to improve transparency and accountability of central banks in the 2000s,[3] though there is still progress to be made.[4]

1.2. Monetary Policy Strategy, Objectives and Instruments

The primary objective of monetary policy defined by the three Acts on the central bank is price stability; without prejudice to this primary objective, the central banks support the general economic policies of their government.

Each central bank defines what it understands by price stability by setting an inflation target. The Czech Republic adopted inflation targeting in January 1998, Poland in January 1999 and Hungary in the summer 2001. They all chose a fast path to disinflation due to the objective of EMU accession in a near future. The chosen targets accompanied the disinflation process and have converged around 2.5%–3% (see Appendix 1). The common preferred monetary policy instrument is the two-week repo rate. The adoption of inflation targets as a nominal anchor follows (or shortly precedes) the abandon of fixed exchange rates, replaced by a managed float in the Czech Republic since 1997, a float in Poland since 2000 and an exchange-rate band of ±15% in Hungary between September 2001 and February 2008. Even if there was no full float in Hungary in this period, this greater exchange-rate flexibility allowed more autonomy for monetary policy to pursue disinflation, otherwise constrained by the fixed exchange rate (Mundell triangle). The fixed exchange-rate regime was abolished in February 2008 for the MNB to better achieve its inflation target.

Inflation targeting involves setting a publicly announced medium-term inflation objective and short-term yearly objectives. The central bank elaborates regular inflation forecasts, evaluates the risks of non-fulfilment of the target and decides whether to adjust its reference interest rate. In case of exceptional shocks on inflation steering it away from the target (e.g. major variations in oil or food prices, administrative changes in tax rules or in regulated prices), the central bank generally decides not to intervene. The Polish and Hungarian central banks will however act to prevent 'second round effects' on inflation (a build-up of inflationary expectations, a spill-over on wages...). The credibility of monetary policy hinges here on the central bank's capacity to justify its analysis of the shock and its policy decision.

1.3. Macroeconomic Context

In these countries, convergence of inflation to EMU levels is still hampered by the Balassa effect linked to catching-up and by the ongoing liberalization of administered prices, even though they are one-off. Therefore the inflation targets were initially set slightly above the ECB's objective of 2%. The three countries implemented the following monetary policies.

In Hungary, monetary policy has been rather tight since 2001, with interest rate cuts following declining inflation:[5] they fell from 11% in the summer of 2001 to 6.5% in January 2003. A strong tightening was necessary in 2003 following speculative attacks on the forint and rates had gone back up to 12.5% at the end of the year. Monetary policy has remained cautious since, with an easing in 2005 following disinflation (rates fell to 6% in September 2005) and a tightening in 2006 maintained up to November 2008. Rates thus inched up to 8.5% in May and then 11.5% in October 2008 (even if floating the forint in February 2008 and its subsequent appreciation had reduced the need for tightening), due to persistent inflationary pressures and, in the end, to the financial crisis accompanied by speculative attacks on the forint. Rates were then slightly reduced in November and December 2008 to 10% to support the liquidity of Hungarian financial markets.

In Poland, monetary policy is considered to have been rather excessively restrictive in 1999–2002.[6] During this time, reference interest rates, which were at 15.5% in January 1999, were brought to 19% in August 2000 and then declined but remained above 10% until January 2002 although disinflation had been important in 2000 and 2001. After a brief loosening in 2002, monetary policy was tight again in 2003–4: spectacular disinflation in 2003 was not offset by equivalent rate cuts as they remained around 5.5–6.6%. Monetary policy was more eased or at least neutral in 2005–6: further rate cuts mirrored continuing disinflation and rates reached their lowest level at 4% in March 2006. A small-scale tightening in 2007–8 due to renewed inflationary pressures brought rates back to 6% in June 2008. With the 2008 financial crisis, the stance was moved back to neutral in October 2008 and rates stood at 5% in December 2008.

In the Czech Republic, monetary policy has been restrictive in 1998–9 and 2003 and otherwise neutral or slightly expansive.[7] In January 1998, reference interest rates stood at 14.75% in the wake of the 1997 financial crisis which had forced the CNB to raise its rates to 39% in June and again to 18.5% in December. They were then, step by step, drastically reduced to 2% in August 2003, only barely following the fast pace of disinflation. Monetary policy has undergone cautious tightening since October 2005, rates being slowly increased to 3.75% in February 2008. This tightening was reversed in August 2008 due to the financial crisis and rates were brought down to 2.25% in December 2008, which is the lowest level in the EU27.

All three countries have achieved disinflation (Table 7.1). In Poland, the first stabilization of inflation expectations was recorded in 2000, then disinflation was observed as of 2001, with a high cost in terms of slowing growth. The NBP considers that the disinflationary process has been achieved in 2002.[8] Except for a rise to 3.5% in 2004 when it was fuelled by EU accession, inflation has since remained low due first to a restrictive monetary policy and then to the underestimation by the NBP of GDP growth and the overestimation of budget deficits and of rises of regulated prices.[9]

In the Czech Republic, disinflation was very swift in 1999, inflation flared up again in 2000–1 in a context of renewed growth, and disinflation seems durable since 2002, despite transitory increases in inflation expectations in 2003 due to a wavering credibility of the 2002 disinflation episode and despite growing uncertainties on public finances since 2000.

In Hungary, disinflation had been pursued since 1995 with the crawling-peg exchange rate regime, but had reached a limit in 1999–2000, inflation remaining around 10% with high inflation expectations.[10] With the inflation targeting strategy, disinflation resumed in 2002, was interrupted in 2004, proceeded further in 2005–6 upheld by low inflation expectations[11] and was once again halted in 2007. Disinflation is therefore not as definite in Hungary as in the other two countries as it is fuelled by the fiscal consolidation measures adopted in 2006 which have increased taxes and by increases in oil and food prices. Inflation expectations are not yet anchored at a low level.[12]

Table 7.1: Inflation (%)

	90	91	92	93	94	95	96	97	98	99	00	01	02	03	04	05	06	07
H	28.9	35.0	23.0	22.5	18.8	28.2	23.6	18.3	14.3	10.0	9.8	9.2	5.3	4.7	6.8	3.6	3.9	7.4
P	585.8	70.3	43.0	35.3	32.2	27.8	19.9	14.9	11.8	7.3	10.1	5.5	1.9	0.8	3.5	2.1	1.0	1.9
CR	9.7	52.0	11.1	20.8	9.9	9.6	8.9	8.4	10.6	2.1	4.0	4.7	1.8	0.2	2.8	1.8	2.5	2.8

Annual average increase in consumer prices. Source: EBRD 2007.

The institutional and macroeconomic framework in Central Europe thus seems to buttress the credibility of monetary policy: central banks are independent and pursue an objective of price stability through a strategy of direct inflation targeting which seems more transparent and more credible even than the double pillar strategy of the ECB.[13] Disinflation seems to have been achieved, at least for the moment.

2. The Institutional and Economic Framework of Fiscal Policy in Central Europe

2.1. New Member States and Maastricht Criteria

Governments of new members states (NMS) are submitted to EMU-related constraints on fiscal policy, in a specific manner: NMS participate in EMU as of their accession to the EU but with a derogation as they do not fulfil the Maastricht criteria. This implies first that they shall integrate EMU when they respect the Maastricht criteria and when they request it, but that they have no opting-out clause. Second, they must comply with general provisions of the EU Treaty on economic policy, including the avoidance of excessive deficits (public deficit below 3% of GDP and public debt below 60% of GDP). In case of an excessive deficit, NMS are exposed to recommendations from the European Council, but do not risk sanctions in case of non-compliance. At most, they risk suspension of all or part of Cohesion Fund assistance.[14] This is not anecdotal: in the very extreme case when all Cohesion Fund assistance were suspended, this would amount to three times the maximum fine of 0.5% GDP under the SGP sanctions (Appendix 2).

Finally, in addition to these constraints, Polish law includes further constraints on the public debt since November 1998. If the ratio of public debt to GDP: (i) is greater than 50% but not greater than 55% in year x, the draft budget for $x+2$ must stabilize the rate of increase of the debt; (ii) if it is between 55% and 60%, the draft budget for $x+2$ must reduce the ratio of public debt to GDP to a level lower than in year x; (iii) if it is equal or greater than 60%, the draft budget for $x+2$ must be balanced.

2.2. Fiscal Policy Objectives

Central European governments support the central bank's objective of price stability in the perspective of EMU accession, but they also pursue real objectives: they are much more sensitive to growth, development, employment and catching up with the EU average. This implies fiscal policies oriented towards structural reforms stimulating growth (e.g. infrastructure, education) and competitiveness, but also direct fiscal stimulation.

For example, the Hungarian government stated that it 'is committed to an economic policy which ... assures the restoration of the equilibrium and the stimulation of growth. Long-term objectives include the strengthening of social and economic cohesion, modernization and catching-up with Europe'.[15] The Polish government adopted the following strategic aims in October 2001: 'gradual return to the path of GDP growth, improvement in employability of the population and employment growth, effective absorption of European funds'.[16] The Czech government states that '[its] main economic objectives are to promote growth and employment by stimulating productivity and competitiveness and to get public finances under sustainable development. The aim is to accelerate the process of catching-up with the 'old' EU Member States, without neglecting environmental and social issues ... Fiscal policy must fulfil its macroeconomic stabilization function and be – at the same time – consistent with other structural policies promoting the competitiveness of the Czech economy on the single market'.[17] Due to these objectives and to historical specificities, Central European governments therefore still have reasons to engage in high public spending. Costly structural reforms are still needed to complete transition (pension reforms).

2.3. Macroeconomic Context

The growth path was contrasted in the three countries (Table 7.2). In Hungary, the disinflation process did not greatly hamper growth: it has remained above 4% since 1997, slowing only in 2007 to 1.3% for other reasons. In the Czech Republic, disinflation had a modest negative effect on growth: in 1999 it did not prevent economic recovery. The Czech growth rate was lower on average in 2000–04 than in the other two countries but for reasons relating more to structural problems than to disinflation. In Poland, disinflation in 2001 and 2002 was accompanied by a marked slowdown in growth from 4–5% in 1998–2000 to 1.2% in 2001 and 1.4% in 2002. Governments were therefore tempted, to varying extents in each country, to maintain high public spending in order to mitigate the real costs of disinflation. The following fiscal policies were implemented in the three countries.

Table 7.2: GDP growth and public finances

	Hungary			Poland			Czech Republic		
	Public deficit	Public debt	GDP growth	Public deficit	Public debt	GDP growth	Public deficit	Public debt	GDP growth
1996	–	71.7	1.3	−4.9	43.4	6.2	−3.3	12.5	4.0
1997	−5.8	62.3	4.6	−4.6	42.9	7.1	−3.8	13.1	−0.7
1998	−7.8	60.4	4.9	−4.3	38.9	5.0	−5.0	15.0	−0.8
1999	−5.3	59.5	4.2	−1.8	39.3	4.5	−3.7	16.4	1.3
2000	−2.9	54.2	5.2	−1.5	35.9	4.3	−3.7	18.5	3.6
2001	−4.1	52.1	4.1	−3.7	35.9	1.2	−5.7	25.1	2.5
2002	−9.0	55.6	4.4	−3.2	39.8	1.4	−6.8	28.5	1.9
2003	−7.2	58.0	4.2	−4.7	43.9	3.9	−12.6	30.1	3.6
2004	−6.5	59.4	4.8	−3.9	41.8	5.3	−2.9	30.7	4.5
2005	−7.8	61.7	4.1	−2.5	42.0	3.6	−3.6	30.4	6.4
2006	−9.2	65.6	3.9	−3.8	47.6	6.2	−2.7	29.4	6.4
2007	−5.5	66.0	1.3	−2.0	45.2	6.5	−1.6	28.7	6.6

Source: ECB *Convergence Report* 2004, 2006, 2008, ESCB and Commission data. Public deficit and public debt in % GDP, GDP growth in % change. Czech public deficit in 2003 is affected by the inclusion of state guarantees.

In Hungary, a right-wing government was in place from 1998 to 2002 and the socialists have been in power since 2002. After the difficulties related to the beginning of transition and following an austerity plan in 1995, public finances reached their least imbalanced situation since 1990 in 2000, with a deficit at 2.9% of GDP. This however was short-lived, as fiscal policy reverted to an expansionary stance and deficits have increased since: they have been above 3% of GDP since 2001 and above 6% from 2003 to 2006. In 2001 and 2002, fiscal policy was expansionary to counter deteriorating competitiveness and slower growth due, among other factors, to monetary policy. The Medgyessy government (summer 2002) further loosened fiscal policy and then again the Gyurcsany government (October 2004).

Although the Medgyessy government committed itself to fiscal restraint,[18] aiming to reduce the budget deficit to 3% in 2004, it appeared quickly that it would not succeed. In the same manner, the fiscal adjustment announced in the 2003 *Pre-Accession Programme* was not achieved because of expenditure slippage. The government's concern for growth and competitiveness slowed down fiscal adjustments, contrary to its commitments. Furthermore, it pursued in 2003 a policy in favour of competitiveness at odds with the MNB's policy, which it criticized for the excessive strengthening of the forint.[19] In order to attenuate this conflict (see below), the government agreed to tighten fiscal policy in 2003 to allow a relaxation of monetary policy, by aiming to restrict demand and reduce the deficit.[20] But *ex post*, this commitment did not prove credible. With a deficit at −7.2% of GDP in 2003, Hungary underwent an excessive deficit procedure as of May 2004, upon EU accession. The European Council recommended that the deficit should be brought below 3% by end 2008.

However, in October 2004, the Gyurcsany government introduced a further shift towards income redistribution and tax reductions without increasing fiscal revenues, implying further deficits. It considered that previous deficits were not the result of government decisions but of market processes (rising interest rates).[21] So fiscal policy still aimed to restrict demand to restore exports and a balanced growth, but at the same time structural reforms in the social and health systems and in education were launched, raising the target deficit. The reiterated commitment to control expenditures was still not credible. Therefore the European Council issued a second recommendation in March 2005 still requiring that the deficit be reduced to 3% of GDP by end 2008. But fiscal policy was further loosened in 2005 and the runup to the 2006 election as the government failed to take new measures to correct the deficit slippages and even implemented tax cuts as of 2006 which reduced revenues and abandoned the target deficit set in the updated Convergence Programme in December 2004. In November 2005, the European Commissioner for Monetary Affairs even threatened to suspend part of Hungary's structural funds.[22]

Finally, the re-elected Gyurcsany government (autumn 2006) seems credibly committed to turning around public finances. It states that 'the credibility of fiscal policy has been considerably undermined by the frequent modifications of the deficit targets and the failure to achieve the modified targets' and pursues the 'restoration of the credibility of fiscal policy'.[23] To this end, a fiscal austerity package was adopted in the summer of 2006, the New equilibrium programme, which reduced the growth rate to 1.3% in 2007 but also initiated a gradual deficit reduction from 9.2% in 2006 to 5.5% of GDP in 2007. Growth is expected to pick up in 2009.[24] Furthermore, the government has undertaken structural reforms of the public administration, of the health and education systems and of the rules of public spending, to reduce the share of non-productive expenses in public spending and to improve control of budgetary execution.[25] Although this fiscal consolidation seems credible, the government only aims to correct the excessive deficit by end 2009 instead of end 2008, so the Council issued a third recommendation in October 2006, pushing back the target date to end 2009. In June 2007, the Commission considered that Hungary had taken the necessary steps thanks to the implementation of the austerity package as of 2007, but it remains very watchful, assessing the sustainability of Hungarian public finances as highly risky.

In Poland, following a period of relative fiscal discipline (deficit of 1.5% of GDP in 2000), fiscal policy was rather lax under Miller's left-wing government (2001–5), in spite of the ambitious Hausner plan which was not entirely implemented. It remained lax in 2005–6 and the public deficit has exceeded 3% of GDP from 2001 to 2006 (except in 2005).

In 2001–3, fiscal policy was expansionary, essentially due to social spending, except in the first half of 2002 when Finance Minister Belka implemented an austerity programme. The latter was reversed in June 2002 by Finance Minister Kolodko, who nonetheless aimed to reduce the budget deficit, with little success. In January 2004, Finance Minister Hausner launched a *Programme for Rationalisation and Reduction of Public Expenditure* ('Hausner plan') to bring the public deficit under 3% of GDP by end 2007 by reducing social and administrative spending and increasing the efficiency of tax administration and increasing the tax base.[26] The government further intended to cap the level of the deficit at 30 billion zloty (this was applied for the first time in 2006 by the next government). But despite faster growth, none of the proposed measures were fully implemented and the deficit increased to –4.7% of GDP in 2003. In particular, growing political instability delayed the complete vote of the Hausner plan in Parliament. Its partial adoption explains, however, the reduction of the 2004 deficit to –3.9% of GDP. This being above the 3% threshold, Poland underwent an excessive deficit procedure as of May 2004, the European Council recommending that Poland should bring its deficit below 3% by 2007.

Fiscal policy was then relaxed in 2005 as the deficit target for 2007 was revised upwards, in spite of strong growth, due to the full inclusion of the costs of the 1999 pension reform in the public deficit in 2007, which increased the deficit by about 1.5 points. This implied that after an improvement in 2005 (–2.5% of GDP), the deficit deteriorated again in 2006 to 3.8% of GDP.

The new right-wing government (November 2005) announced it would seek to improve public finances through performance budgeting and the introduction of three-year budgeting for general government finance planning.[27] It further stated that its main objectives were improving the employment rate and living standards while respecting fiscal constraints but only in the long term: it aims to meet the reference value by end 2009 only and aims for close to equilibrium public finances in the sense of the SGP (–1% of GDP deficit) for end 2010 at the earliest.[28] However, this government continued to take many fiscal measures at odds with these objectives for populist reasons (income tax relief for families, reduction in social contributions...) and the deficit ran to –3.8% in 2006. The situation was not set to improve on the basis of the 2006 budget prepared by the right-wing government, so Poland incurred a second recommendation from the European Council in February 2007, which maintained the 2007 target date. But GDP growth was finally higher than expected, allowing lower than expected public expenditures (helped by the effects of some measures from the Hausner plan such as removal of indexation of pensions) and higher than expected revenues. Poland's public finances therefore dramatically improved in 2007 with a deficit at only 2% of GDP, the structural balance having improved by 1.5 points. The European Council therefore abrogated the excessive deficit procedure in June 2008.

The government elected in October 2007 headed by the liberals from PO (Civic Platform) then pledged to continue fiscal consolidation. The 2008 deficit is set to deteriorate because of measures adopted before the change of government, but the government presented an updated Convergence Programme in March 2008 that credibly aims for durable fiscal consolidation.

In the Czech Republic, after the right-wing government's conservative fiscal policy in 1993–8 aiming for a balanced budget, in 1998–2006 the successive left-wing governments have been more expansionary and the fiscal deficit has increased. It has exceeded the reference value from 1996 to 2005, with a worsening of the situation in 2002–3. Fiscal consolidation and favourable cyclical factors have allowed it to improve since 2005, despite a policy loosening in 2006.

The fiscal policy objective in 1998–2002 was to maintain balanced public finances, then the new Prime Minister Spidla, having campaigned in 2002 in favour of reinforcing the welfare state, switched to an explicit policy of fiscal deficits and created several off-budgetary institutions to carry out state interventions.[29] Therefore, he did not aim to reduce the fiscal deficit below 3% of GDP before 2010. In 2003, it reached 12.9% because of the one-off imputation of state guarantees representing 6–7% of GDP to government expenditure in line with ESA95 rules. Upon EU accession, the Czech Republic therefore underwent a procedure for excessive deficits and the European Council recommended it should bring its deficits below 3% by 2008.

Then the Spidla government, spurred by this procedure, decided to tackle the problem and designed in 2003 a consolidation plan for public finances which would bring the deficit under 3% in 2008 while avoiding a strong reduction in growth.[30] This would be achieved by a slightly restrictive fiscal policy and by structural changes in fiscal policy (first changing the structure of taxes and government expenditure and budgetary rules, then introducing tax incentives for growth while maintaining fiscal neutrality). So fiscal consolidation started in 2004 and was pursued by the Gross government (July 2004) with the introduction in September 2004 of fiscal targeting, which includes binding medium-term expenditure ceilings. A deep pension reform is also under discussion. At the end of 2004, the Commission concluded in that effective action had been taken and that no further steps were necessary. But it became apparent that these measures would not be sufficient as public expenditure reform was not pursued consistently, so the 2005 budget included further discretionary cuts.

Fiscal targets seem to have been met in 2004, 2005 and 2006, but in a larger part thanks to better than expected growth and revenues than to fiscal consolidation, which has wavered (e.g. the medium-term ceilings were exceeded several times in 2005–7). Furthermore, fiscal policy was once again loosened in 2006, an election year, and in 2007 the strong growth reduced the pressure on the government to improve public finances and the windfall revenues were used to increase expenditures instead of reducing the structural deficit. Thus the 2007 budget and March 2007 Convergence Programme do not respect former engagements on fiscal consolidation and the European Council issued a new recommendation in October 2007. But fiscal developments proved surprisingly favourable in 2007 due to unexpectedly high growth and revenues coupled with lower than expected expenditures (especially social expenditures and public sector salaries). The government has also increased taxes, allowing for a credible and sustainable improvement of public finances, so the Council abrogated the excessive deficit procedure against the Czech Republic in June 2008. Fiscal sustainability remains at risk, however, as deep structural fiscal reforms have still not been undertaken (especially of pensions and healthcare). This explains that further fiscal stabilization measures were taken in September 2008, transferring the tax burden from direct to indirect taxes and cutting social benefits, which resulted in a restrictive fiscal policy for 2008.

Fiscal policies in NMS are thus subject to precise rules, which have not proved very effective up to 2007 in curbing fiscal deficits due to their weak credibility (absence of sanctions) and to the real objectives of fiscal policies. An improvement in fiscal deficits has been observed since 2006–7 in Hungary and the Czech Republic and since 2007 in Poland, seemingly more because of unexpected growth than thanks to sound fiscal policies.

3. Conflicts Between Central Banks and Governments in Central Europe

Given this institutional set up and diverging objectives between central banks and governments, conflicts could be expected between monetary and fiscal policy and have been observed to varying degrees in the three countries since the beginning of the 2000s. They concern the macro-policy mix and the status of the central bank.

3.1. Conflicts in Hungary

A first conflict between monetary and fiscal polices appeared in 2001–2. While the central bank was implementing a disinflationary policy, the governments slowed down fiscal adjustments and sought interest rates and exchange rates reductions from the MNB. Far from complying, when it appeared that the deficit would actually amount to 9% in 2002 and that fiscal policy was not credible, the MNB tightened its monetary policy in May and July.[31] Therefore, although 2002 was a year of strong disinflation, the central bank raised interest rates. This conflict is all the more vivid as the MNB and the government had jointly set the inflation objectives in June 2001 for end 2002 and end 2003,[32] in the hope this would help the government support monetary policy objectives.

The conflict lessened in the first half of 2003 when the MNB lowered interest rates, not to support growth and competitiveness but to counter speculative attacks on the exchange rate.[33] But combined with an unexpected devaluation of the intervention band, this caused the exchange rate to drop very strongly, so the MNB increased rates again by six points in the second half of 2003 to maintain the exchange rate and combat inflation. Once again, this put pressure on the government to reduce the deficit and ran counter to its competitiveness policy.

The conflict flared up again in 2004 following the publication of the government's Convergence Programme in May and the nomination of a new government in October. The MNB criticized the Convergence Programme for relying more on growth than on cuts in public spending to reduce the budget deficit. Furthermore, the new government was very critical of monetary policy, 'accusing it of harming the Hungarian economy through inadequate economic policy co-ordination and monetary policy inflexibility'.[34] According to the MNB, its rate cuts could have been bolder if fiscal policy had been more restrained;[35] on the other hand, the government considered that 'under the tight monetary conditions, any greater fiscal austerity would jeopardize the strengthening export and investment driven growth'.[36] The further slippage in fiscal policy since 2004 has aggravated this conflict: as noted by the European Council, deficit targets have been revised upwards since 2004 while growth has not deteriorated, structural reforms have been delayed and tax cuts have been granted although the deficit targets were not met, contrary to recommendations. Fiscal policy failed to regain credibility before 2006.

With the government's first credible fiscal consolidation package in the summer 2006, the conflict has attenuated. The MNB has ceased to point out fiscal imbalances as a cause for a cautious policy.[37] However, the MNB considers the fiscal adjustment process as a source of potential inflation due to increases in taxes and regulated prices, so monetary policy has remained neutral-to-tight since 2006 to prevent a pick-up in inflation expectations.

In a last episode, the review of the long-term inflation target, scheduled for the summer 2008, was yet another occasion for conflict. The government argued that the current long-term objective, at 3%±1 point, was too ambitious considering fuel and food price inflation, and considering that an increase in interest rates, necessary to attain this target, would have adverse effects on the real economy, only just beginning to recover from the 2006 austerity programme. The MNB has remained strongly opposed to increasing the target, stating that it was necessary to maintain it to ensure the bank's credibility and anchor inflation expectations and thus achieve price stability, considering current inflation is well above targets. Furthermore, new rate increases (it had already increased rates by 100 basis points between January and May 2008) would strengthen the forint and protect the country against imported inflation. The MNB governor has said he was not willing to give up long-term benefits of low inflation in exchange for a short-term boost to the economy. Finally, in August both parties agreed to keep the long-term inflation target unchanged.

The conflict on the policy mix was paralleled by a conflict on the status of the central bank. In a first episode, after a new Act on the MNB was voted in 2001 to ensure compliance with EU regulations, the government submitted an amendment in June 2002 proposing to set up in the MNB a Board of Supervisors composed of four representatives of political parties appointed by the Parliament and two members appointed by the Minister of Finance. The governor of the MNB S. Jarai has stated (12 June 2002) that this amendment 'infringes on the Bank's operational independence' and that this type of committee does not exist in other EU countries. However, the amendment was voted and the Board of Supervisors was created in July 2002. Its scope of authority does not extend to the MNB's definition and implementation of monetary policy.[38] The nomination of Board of Supervisors members was modified[39] by the amendment to the Act on the central bank which came into force on 1 July 2007, but it still exists.

In a second episode, the government proposed in 2004 an amendment to the Act on the MNB threatening to undermine its independence. In particular, it proposed to increase the role of the government in the appointment of Monetary Council members: four were to be nominated by the MNB governor with the Prime Minister having a right of veto, the remaining three to five by the President of the Republic upon proposition of the Prime Minister without the governor having a right of veto.[40] Despite criticism from the ECB, who considered this to be contradictory with central bank independence, the amendment was voted in December 2004. The 2007 amendment to the Act on the MNB has reduced the number of Monetary Council members to seven without changing their mode of nomination.

Both changes were marginal in regard to the MNB's independence which was not affected, so their economic impact on the institutional design of macro-policies in Hungary was small, but they had a real political impact as they stemmed from the government's hostility to the MNB.

3.2. Conflicts in Poland

A conflict between the central bank and the government on macro-policies broke out in 1999–2001. Due to a more expansionary than expected fiscal policy, the NBP tightened its monetary policy, regretting that the short-term costs of reducing inflation were higher than they would have been with a tighter fiscal policy: 'an overly lax budgetary policy aggravated the unfavourable mix of monetary and fiscal policy'.[41] Conversely, the government (especially the left-wing government as of October 2001) criticized the scale and timing of this tightening, considering it unnecessarily reduced growth and it was maintained too long despite falling inflation, so that the 2001 inflation target was undershot.[42] The austerity programme in the first half of 2002 allowed the NBP to loosen its monetary policy, reducing the conflict and improving the policy mix. However, this conflict resumed in May 2002 when the government enlarged it due to disagreement on the exchange rate: it considered the high level of the parity was detrimental to competitiveness and growth.

The conflict was briefly attenuated in the second half of 2002 as Kolodko replaced Belka as Finance minister: he was more favourable to a fast EMU accession, implying greater support of the NBP's monetary policy, and the NBP pursued its rate cuts.[43]

The conflict resumed in 2003 when Kolodko renewed criticism on the NBP's exchange-rate policy and the fiscal deficit continued to rise. This occurred despite the Hausner plan and because of the political difficulties of its implementation and of the high political cost of fiscal adjustment. Therefore, the NBP considered that fiscal policy was neither sound nor credible, that it threatened price stability and crowded out private investment financing, narrowing the possibilities of further rate cuts. The NBP was particularly sceptical about the Hausner plan: it planned an increase in fiscal deficit in 2004 before its subsequent decrease and the far-reaching adjustment was only intended for 2005. It concluded that 'the unfavourable combination of fiscal and monetary policies raises the real costs of achieving and maintaining internal and external equilibrium'.[44] This conflict carried on into 2004 as the deficit remained high due to incomplete implementation of the Hausner plan. The NBP also criticized the government's delay in launching necessary structural reforms to increase potential GDP, such as property rights protection, labour market and tax reform, development of the financial system. This opposition subsided in 2005 as the deficit turned out to be lower than expected, which allowed further interest cuts. The government elected in November 2005 did not prove credible in pursuing fiscal consolidation, but unexpectedly strong growth allowed the fiscal deficit to improve in 2006, so as from 2006, the NBP has stopped indicating in its Annual report that it deems the macroeconomic policy mix unfavourable.

The conflict on the policy mix spilled over to the status of the NBP. First, at the end of 2001, the government proposed an amendment to the Act on the NBP to harmonize it with the Maastricht Treaty. However, it also aimed to reduce the independence of the NBP as its policy objectives would be fixed by the government[45] and would include growth and employment.[46] This amendment stood no chance of being voted, as it went against European rules and was eventually dropped. Second, further amendments to the Act on the NBP were proposed by members of Parliament in 2003 and then again in 2005,[47] considered unconstitutional and incompatible with EU regulations by the NBP. They were not voted either. These episodes are nonetheless significant of intense political conflicts between the government and the central bank, the government (or members of Parliament) using them – unsuccessfully – to try to bully the NBP into relaxing monetary policy.

3.3. Conflicts in the Czech Republic

The lack of coordination between fiscal and monetary policy in the Czech Republic was noted by observers in 1998–9.[48] Governments criticized the excessive speed of disinflation,[49] deemed too costly in terms of growth, considering the economy was only slowly recovering from the 1997 crisis and the inflation targets were repeatedly undershot. In the following years, the central bank did not criticize so strongly the government's fiscal policy, it only repeatedly pointed out that it was difficult to predict the size and timing of the fiscal impulse, making it more difficult to coordinate monetary and fiscal policies.[50] Conversely, the government strived to restrict fiscal policy as of 2003 to 'make room for a more accommodating monetary policy'.[51] The joint setting of the inflation targets for 2001–5 (see p. 15, below) also helped to attenuate the conflict. Fiscal policy has been easier to anticipate since 2004; in particular, the loosening of 2006 had been forecast and the CNB raised its rates in consequence in 2006.

The conflict on the policy mix led to legislative attempts to restrain the CNB's independence. The Act on the CNB was amended in 2000 to harmonize it with EU legislation (primary objective of price stability, non-financing of public institutions, etc). But some measures threatened the CNB's independence: the CNB and the government must agree on matters relating to the inflation target and the exchange rate regime, the Bank Board members are to be appointed by the President of the Republic at the proposal of the government. These changes, which entered into force on 1 January 2001, were considered incompatible with EU rules by the European Commission and the ECB. The Czech Constitutional Court repealed them in August 2001. The Constitution was then revised to change the CNB's primary objective to price stability. In May 2002, a second amendment to the Act on the CNB restored the CNB's independence. In the meantime, the yearly 2001 and the medium-term 2002–5 inflation targets had been set jointly with the government and although this was contrary to the CNB's independence, it was recognized that this helped to 'boost the credibility and effectiveness of the inflation target, as well as for forming the desired monetary and fiscal policy mix'.[52]

3.4. The Global Financial Crisis and Macroeconomic Policies

The autumn 2008 global financial crisis has also affected Central European countries and may have implications for the relations between governments and central banks. These countries have only been affected belatedly: the slowdown in Western European demand was compensated for by an increased intra-regional demand and relatively strong currencies; local banking sectors were relatively protected by stricter credit standards and loan provision criteria, high levels of liquidity and by financing of credits mainly through deposits which reduces dependence on foreign financial markets.[53]

But Central European countries were eventually caught up to differing degrees in the financial disturbances, as were other emerging markets, in September–October 2008. Due to their often large budget and current account deficits, especially in Hungary, which makes them dependent on private external finance, to the fact that most local banks are foreign owned and that the foreign parent banks have encountered difficulties, they have recently witnessed the beginning of a credit crunch, depreciation of their currencies[54] and strong contractions of their financial markets.[55]

These events could prove to be a new factor fuelling conflicts between governments and central banks. On one hand, central banks may find it necessary to increase interest rates to defend the exchange rate, which the government may criticize for harming the real economy; of course if the central bank reduces rates to supply liquidity to financial markets there is no cause for conflict. On the other hand, if governments implement anti-crisis packages to support consumption and investment or bail-out packages to support the banking sector, the central bank may criticize them for increasing public spending. However, in the case of the Euro zone countries, it is expected that higher deficits resulting from such packages will not be so harshly sanctioned as they would be in normal times as the exceptional circumstances clause may be invoked,[56] and this is likely to be the case in Central Europe too. But it seems that these conflicts have been avoided so far and each party supports the efforts of the other to restore confidence in the banking and financial sector.

In Hungary, the financial crisis has considerably changed the situation of public finances. Turmoil on international financial markets had put Hungary under strain as due to its high foreign debt and its creditworthiness was repeatedly downgraded by rating agencies in June 2006, April 2008 and November 2008. Hungary also incurred a strong depreciation of the forint in October–November 2008, and the banking sector developed liquidity problems and was touched by the global credit crunch.

So the Gyurcsany government introduced an anti-crisis package in mid-October based on further fiscal tightening (lower than previously targeted fiscal deficits for 2008 and 2009, a postponement of tax cuts initially planned for 2009, and a call for employers and trade unions to freeze wages until June 2009), help to SMEs financed from EU funds and the full guarantee on bank deposits (in parallel, the MNB has announced the full guarantee of interbank loans).[57] But then the government was forced to seek assistance from international financial institutions and, in October 2008, obtained $16 billion from the IMF, the World Bank and the EU. The conditions under which this help was extended further tightened the fiscal targets already tightened a few days earlier: the deficit must now be brought back from its initial target of 3.8% of GDP to 2.6% in 2009 thanks to drastic spending cuts and inflation must be brought back to 3% in 2010 (targets which were integrated in the December 2008 Updated Convergence Programme). This new context unexpectedly allowed the Parliament to pass a set of fiscal rules for 2010–11 that introduce a cap on public spending and on the speed of increase of real government debt, and create an independent budget council to monitor public spending. Many such drafts had been discussed for several months, but had remained unable to pass in Parliament up to now. Very strong new external constraints may thus finally allow Hungary to engage in a sustainable fiscal path. So it seems unlikely that this episode will fuel a renewed conflict between the government and the MNB, as 2009 opens with a tighter fiscal policy and a looser monetary policy.

In Poland, the financial crisis has not affected public finances to the same extent as in Hungary, for the moment at least. The exchange rate has weakened, the Warsaw stock exchange has plummeted and the liquidity crisis on the interbank market has also led to a credit crunch. But the situation did not deteriorate to the point where Poland had to seek for external help as did Hungary. Furthermore, the measures taken so far in response to the crisis[58] are more likely to foster good relations between the government and the NBP than to fuel conflicts. Indeed, on one hand the NBP has strived to maintain the liquidity of financial markets by providing additional open market facilities, in coordination with the ECB, to ensure access to foreign currencies, and guarantees of interbank loans. On the other hand, the government has increased the guarantees of private banking deposits, increased the capital of the National Economy Bank (BGK) for it to continue supplying credit to SMEs, and wishes to accelerate investments funded by EU structural funds. It has clearly stated that it is adamant about respecting its fiscal deficits targets.

The financial crisis has not greatly affected Czech public finances either, so far. The Czech financial sector has sounder fundamentals than in the other two countries, with less than 15% of loans in foreign currencies, and with an unusually high level of liquidity in the banking sector linked to painful memories of large-scale financial fraud in the early 1990s in the wake of the mass privatization programme. The credit crunch resulting from liquidity drying up has touched the Czech Republic later than the other two countries, and to a lesser extent (it is mainly a concern for the government, which is facing difficulties in issuing bonds to finance its debt). The koruna has also depreciated, but still maintained a positive appreciation over the year. As in Poland, the measures taken so far in response to the crisis[59] do not seem to risk deteriorating relations between the government and the CNB. The CNB has introduced a new facility in October aimed at providing more liquidity, and has strongly cut rates to loosen credit conditions. The government has increased the bank deposit guarantee and has pledged to cut public expenditure further if necessary to maintain the deficit on target. It has stated several times that for the moment, Czech banks do not need state assistance. Far from being in conflict, the government and the CNB have both criticized the EU-level fiscal actions they consider as too lax and putting the Stability and Growth pact at risk.

Conflicts of various duration and intensity on the policy mix and on the status of the central bank have been observed in the three countries, where governments criticized the speed of disinflation chosen by the central bank whereas the central bank criticized the excessive and often unpredictable fiscal policy of the government, these conflicts being shorter and milder in the Czech Republic. They do not seem to have been very profitable for either actor, as governments did not succeed in convincing the central banks to lower their rates. On the other hand, if governments have finally redressed public finances, this was not mainly due to pressure from central banks but also from European institutions or from financial markets (see below). Furthermore, the central bank sometimes lost popular support when it was perceived as trying to punish the government for its excessive fiscal policy rather than follow its monetary policy objectives, as in Poland in 1999–2001.[60] Globally, these conflicts risk reducing the efficiency of both policies: fiscal policy is hampered by high interest rates, monetary policy is constrained by loss of public support if it aims for too fast a disinflation. How can they be explained? We shall explore two successive explanations.

4. Can These Conflicts be Explained by Lack of Credibility of Monetary Policy?

Can they be explained, as suggested by Creel and Fayolle[61] in the case of EMU, by a lack of credibility of monetary policy? To explore this, we shall review two ways which allow to evaluate monetary policy credibility: central banks' ability to meet their targets and the capacity of private agents to anticipate monetary policy decisions.

4.1. Do Central Banks Meet Their Targets?

In Hungary, the inflation target was met in 2001 and 2002, overshot in 2003 and 2004, because of unexpected consumption growth related to the expansionary fiscal policy in 2003 and to indirect tax increases in 2004, then met again in 2005 and overshot in 2006 and 2007.[62] In Poland, the inflation target was overshot in 1999 and 2000, because of the unexpected fiscal expansion, then undershot since 2001 except in 2004, 2005 and 2007.[63] In the Czech Republic, the target was undershot in 1998 and 1999, essentially due to external factors such as plummeting raw materials and food prices, appreciation of the exchange rate and the continued restrictive fiscal policy containing demand in the wake of the Spring 1997 crisis. The target was then met in 2000 and 2001, then undershot again in 2002 and 2003 for the same reasons and met since.[64]

The results are thus mixed. Central banks usually worry more about overshooting than undershooting their objectives. These results point to some target overshooting in Hungary and Poland, but this was related to unexpectedly loose fiscal policies or tax changes and the target was never overshot in the Czech Republic, which indicates a rather high level of monetary policy credibility measured in terms of its capacity to achieve its objectives. Conversely, target undershooting may contribute to explaining the conflict on the policy mix as its cost is much greater for the government than for the central bank.

4.2. Are Monetary Policy Decisions Correctly Anticipated?

Another way to evaluate monetary policy credibility is to observe whether private agents anticipate it correctly. One way to measure this is to consider its impact on the yield curve. The idea is that monetary policy credibility reflects its ability to influence private agents' expectations regarding future inflation and future policy and that these expectations can be approached by observing the yield curve, which relates short-term interest rates, directly influenced by monetary policy and long-term interest rates, which are influenced by monetary policy to the extent it is correctly and credibly anticipated. Short-term interest rates should be smoother than central bank rates as they anticipate them, while long-term rates should not be affected by monetary policy if it is correctly anticipated. Another way to measure how well monetary policy is anticipated is to look at private inflation expectations.

In the Czech Republic, a study of the impact of monetary policy decisions on short-term and long-term interest rates from 1996 to 2002 shows that transparency of monetary policy has increased after 1997, as short-term interest rates were less 'surprised' by monetary policy decisions than before and long-term rates indicate monetary policy was credible throughout the period, its credibility increasing after the switch to inflation targeting.[65] Another study on the volatility of forward rates on 1999–2005 data qualifies this result by identifying phases of lesser credibility of the CNB, especially after the end of the first phase of disinflation in 2000, when private agents were not sure disinflation was definite.[66]

In Hungary, the MNB claims that the switch to inflation targeting has increased monetary policy credibility measured by its impact on long-term rates.[67] A study of the impact of monetary policy decisions on short-term and long-term interest rates from 2001 to 2005 qualifies this result: this impact is small for short-term rates (because of 'occasional inconsistencies of interest rate decisions and communication') and more important for long-term rates, implying greater long-term credibility.[68] Furthermore, it seems that monetary policy tightening is more credible than monetary policy easing.

In Poland, a recent study on the influence of the Polish Monetary Policy Council members' verbal comments on the yield curve between February 2004 and March 2007 shows that the MPC can influence expectations in an efficient manner.[69] A study on the comparison between inflation expectations of the private sector (consumers and commercial bank analysts) and the inflation target shows that monetary policy credibility has increased, especially for bank analysts, except in the period of fast disinflation in 2002–03 and of inflation in 2004.[70]

These fragmentary results indicate monetary policies were rather credible in Central Europe in the period under review. This is confirmed by several other studies, which tentatively conclude that the transmission from monetary policy to long-term interest rates is strongest in Poland, weakest in Hungary, with the Czech Republic in between.[71] Therefore, the explanation of conflicts between central banks and governments by lack of credibility of monetary policies does not seem to hold in this case and the source of the problem is probably related to lack of credibility of fiscal policies. We now propose to relate this lack of credibility of fiscal policies and the general conflict to the institutional framework governing macro policies in Central Europe.

5. Explaining These Conflicts by the Institutional Framework

5.1. Diverging Policy Objectives

At a first level, the conflicts between central banks and governments can be explained by their diverging policy objectives. We have seen that central banks pursue price stability to achieve disinflation in the short term and prepare EMU accession in the long term, whereas governments, while committed to EMU accession, also pursue real objectives such as growth and employment. This brings us back to two traditional questions of economic policy.

First, the confrontation of these objectives is related to the trade-off between nominal and real objectives: governments contest the speed of disinflation chosen by the central bank because of its negative effect on growth, especially when inflation targets are undershot. In this sense, both authorities support EMU accession as quickly as possible, but have diverging appreciations of what this horizon is. In the absence of an obvious optimal speed of disinflation and due to different distributional consequences of different choices, conflicts may be expected on this decision and are bound to be acute in cases of supply shocks, where prices and activity diverge.

Second, this opposition is related to the debate on economic policy instruments. Central European central banks are much more inclined than governments to consider that macroeconomic policies should be geared towards nominal adjustments, while stabilization of real variables should be obtained by spontaneous adjustments resulting from supply-side structural polices such as flexibilization of the labour market, completion of privatization, tax reform, competition policy, etc. Governments consider to a larger extent that macro policies can stabilize real variables. These conflicts may therefore also be interpreted in terms of the debate on the use of fiscal policy to stabilization ends.

5.2. Political Factors

At a second level, difficulties of coordinating fiscal and monetary policies may be political. Whereas in Western Europe, central bankers are generally technocrats, in Eastern Europe they are often former politicians (L. Balcerowicz, the governor of the NBP from 2001 to end 2006, and S. Jarai, the governor of the MNB from 2000 to 2007, are former Finance Ministers), or technocrats having ventured into politics (J. Tosovsky, the governor of the CNB in 1998–2000, briefly served as Prime Minister before going back to the CNB), which contributes to politicizing debates around monetary policy.

Furthermore, for a long time, the central bankers and the governments were of opposite political obedience: the former were all from or related to right-wing parties, while the latter were left-wing (in Hungary since 2002, in Poland from 2001 to 2005 and in the Czech Republic from 1998 to 2006).

5.3. *The 'Chicken Game'*

In a more economic framework, this conflict has been interpreted in terms of the 'chicken game', where each player seeks to convert the other to his own view, or failing that, to punish him and stick to his own convictions in order not to lose face (not to be the 'chicken').[72] In this setting, the policy mix is viewed as a non-cooperative game between the central bank and the government, where each player has a firm conviction on what the optimal policy mix is and these visions diverge. Thus, the optimal policy mix is a restrained fiscal policy and a neutral or accommodating monetary policy according to the central bank, as this minimizes the costs of a given disinflationary policy in terms of growth and employment; and a neutral or accommodating monetary policy and a neutral or accommodating fiscal policy according to the government, as this allows to pursue disinflation given a growth objective. Fitoussi applied this framework to the conflict between the ECB and national governments in the early years of EMU and it seems to fit the situation of Central European countries: Central European central banks as well as governments state very clearly that they have such a preference on the policy mix.[73]

The confrontation of these diverging conceptions of the optimal policy mix easily leads to a conflict hampering the emergence of either policy mix. The matrix of gains of the chicken game (Figure 7.1) illustrates how if each player pursues its objectives, the worst solution emerges (–1, –1). In dynamics, this situation worsens: monetary policy is all the more restrictive if fiscal policy is too lax, while fiscal policy is all the more lax as monetary policy is deemed too restrictive by the government. If either of the two players give in, both gain, but the one which gives in gains comparatively less. Two preferable equilibria exist (the 'conservative' and the 'social' solution) but because of non-cooperation and a wish not to lose face, they cannot be attained. This approach explains that in certain circumstances, central banks may have excessively tightened monetary policy in order to force the governments to revert to more fiscal restraint, while governments may have excessively loosed their fiscal policy to more than compensate for the restrictive monetary policy.

Figure 7.1: The matrix of gains of the 'chicken game'

		Governments	
		Restrictive fiscal policy	Expansionary fiscal policy
Central bank	Restrictive monetary policy	4 / 2 'Conservative solution'	−1 / −1
	Expansionary monetary policy	0 / 0	1 / 3 'Social solution'

Source: J-P. Fitoussi and J. Le Cacheux (eds), *Rapport sur l'Etat de l'Union* (Paris: Presses de Sciences Po, 1999).

5.4. Imperfections of the Institutional Framework of the Policy Mix

The chicken game approach usefully explains how the conflict can last but, taking non-cooperation as given, does not explain why the institutional framework of macro policies does not foster cooperation.[74]

The first step to understand this is to go back to the Kydland and Prescott model and the Rogoff model, at the foundation of the independence of central banks.[75] According to these models, the government pursues two partially conflicting objectives, price stability on one hand and growth and employment on the other, which implies a risk on inflation if the government tries to raise the level of output above its natural level to reduce unemployment. In order to render monetary policy credible – to make it able to achieve its objective of price stability and to convince agents of its credibility – the models recommend creating an independent central bank that will pursue the price stability objective while the government will pursue the real objectives. In this set up, there is no possibility of a trade-off between price stability and growth, since both objectives are not pursued by the same entity. It follows from this literature that central banks and governments necessarily have conflicting objectives, as the central bank's objective was precisely defined in opposition to the government's.

Furthermore, in the way these theoretical results were applied to EMU, the institutional architecture of EMU gives an explicit preference to the price stability objective. This is illustrated by the Stability and Growth Pact constraints imposed on fiscal policies to prevent them from interfering with the price stability objective. To the extent that Central European countries aim to integrate EMU and are submitted to these constraints, this also applies to them. This means that the fundamental trade-off between price stability and real objectives is no longer possible, the choice has been made once and for all. The choice of independent central banks is therefore much more than a technical choice, it also implies fundamental choices on the possible scope of economic policy objectives.

Even in this framework, conflicts are possible for two reasons. The first one is related to credibility. Creel and Fayolle suggested that the ECB pursued an excessively restrictive monetary policy in its first years in order to combat inflation and punish lax fiscal policies, thus doubly convincing agents of its determination to pursue price stability, in other words to quickly acquire credibility.[76] But we have seen that in Central Europe, monetary policy seems to have been rather credible, give or take a few exceptions, and if anything the conflicts were rather related to lack of credibility of fiscal policies.

The second reason is that conflicts may arise because the institutional safeguards intended to submit governments to the primacy of the price stability objective are not sufficient. In the case of EMU, the SGP has shown its limits, was suspended in November 2003 and reformed in March 2005. In the case of Central European countries, the excessive deficit procedure is even less effective because it is not constraining, which has allowed Hungary and Poland to delay the required fiscal adjustments. Therefore, a fundamental source of conflict lies in the imperfect coherence of the institutional architecture of macroeconomic policies, which leads to diverging objectives, the primacy of the central banks's objective, but more or less equal power of governments and central banks and no complete way to constrain the former to submit to this choice.

A contrario, the choice of the Hungarian and Czech independent central banks to set their inflation targets jointly with the government to make monetary policy more credible and to attenuate the conflict on the policy mix illustrates the fact that the trade-off between price stability and growth cannot without risk be entirely decided *ex ante* and that it may be helpful to re-examine this trade-off and to reintroduce political responsibility to the decision. However, if cooperation on inflation targets has seemed to work in the sense that this conflict was less severe in the Czech Republic than in the other two countries, it has not entirely solved the problem in Hungary and it is incompatible with EMU rules and will necessarily cease upon EMU accession, which means that the conflict may be revived then, in parallel to the ECB's first difficult years.

5.5. Resolving the Conflicts?

The conflicts between governments and central banks on fiscal and monetary policies have not been entirely resolved, as there are still no complete institutional safeguards against their reemergence. However, tensions have – at least temporarily – subsided as governments have launched credible fiscal consolidation programmes as of 2006–7 in Hungary, 2007 in Poland and 2004 and then 2007 in the Czech Republic. How can we account for this?

First, as disinflation is achieved (although less firmly in Hungary), the trade-off between nominal and real economic policy objectives is not so acute because monetary policy does not impose such high real costs. Further, disinflation has allowed monetary policies to be less restrictive and inflation targets were recently more often met (in the Czech Republic in 2006–7, in Poland in 2007) or over-shot (in Hungary in 2006–7) than undershot, attenuating a source of conflict.

Second, the change in central bank governors and political changeovers in governments have created a climate more favourable to cooperation between central banks and governments. The nomination of three rather politically-neu-tral personalities as new governors of the central banks (Z. Tuma in the Czech Republic in 2000, A. Simor in Hungary in March 2007 and S. Skrzypek in Poland in January 2007) has contributed to appeasing tensions. Furthermore, except in Hungary where the government has been left-wing since 2002, the accession to power of right-wing governments in Poland and the Czech Republic in 2005 and 2006 respectively has also reduced conflicts. The Polish right-wing govern-ment has thus not seriously criticized the undershooting of the inflation target in 2006 contrary to former left-wing governments in a similar situation.

Third, the attenuation of these conflicts can partially be explained by the evo-lution of economic constraints. In the three cases, fiscal consolidation has been easier for governments to decide and to achieve in a context of faster growth, as of 2004–5 in Poland and the Czech Republic (although as we have seen this consolidation was to a certain extent involuntary). Hungarian governments have also faced a strong constraint coming from financial markets: in 2005, Hungary's public long-term debt rating was downgraded several times and risks of further downgrading in the absence of fiscal consolidation, which could trigger a finan-cial crisis, have contributed to the government's resolution to seriously tackle fiscal imbalances as of summer 2006.

The current resolution of these conflicts thus does not seem to be explained by a good functioning of the institutional framework of macro-policies (as the necessary safeguards do not exist), neither by pressure from the European Union (as it was hardly credible), but rather by the better than expected growth and by the emergence of new economic constraints. Perhaps governments are also more committed to integrating EMU as they are under pressure from firms and finan-cial markets who stress that EMU membership is important to boost growth and catching-up and that other countries such as Slovenia and Slovakia have already adopted the euro in 2007 and 2009 respectively.

Finally, we can note that the financial crisis in September at least up to the end of 2008 did not lead to new conflicts between governments and central banks (at least up to now), which have importantly remained united in trying to restore confidence in the banking and financial sector. As this crisis may post-pone EMU entry for Central European countries by making their economic conditions more difficult, it might even contribute to defusing these conflicts (to a small extent) because the date at which the criteria must be fulfilled is thus pushed back.

Conclusion

Important conflicts were observed in Central Europe between monetary and fiscal policies in the 2000s. It seems that lack of coordination between the fiscal and monetary policy was less severe in the Czech Republic, where the CNB explicitly cooperated with the government in setting the inflation targets in 2000–1 and where fiscal policy was arguably more credible than in the other two countries. In this case, deviance from the inflation target seemed to result more from exogenous factors. On the contrary, this lack of coordination seemed more acute in Poland and Hungary, where deviance from the inflation target may be explained to a greater extent by the unsatisfactory macro-policy mix.

These conflicts are related to divergent policy objectives of central banks and governments and to the less-than-fully coherent institutional framework of macro policies in the preparation of EMU: central bank independence has not abolished the trade-off between nominal and real objectives and has not created good institutional conditions for this policy choice, especially in times of disinflation. These conflicts have lessened in recent years as central banks, having achieved disinflation, switched to more neutral monetary policies and as governments, under a weak pressure from European institutions and a stronger pressure from financial markets and thanks to better than expected growth, are more committed to EMU integration and have finally engaged in credible fiscal consolidation. As EMU countries themselves went through similar conflicts in the first years of the euro and as the institutional framework of EMU is also only imperfectly coherent, there is no reason to believe that EMU accession could entirely prevent the reappearance of this conflict, especially in times of slower growth (even more if this is the result of a strict monetary policy), especially if more spending-biased left-wing governments are in power.

Appendix 1: Inflation targets

In italics: medium-term inflation targets

Table 7.3a: Inflation targets in Hungary

Date adopted	Reference period	Target rates (consumer price inflation)
June 2001	December 2001	7% ±1 percentage point
June 2001	*December 2002*	*4.5% ±1 percentage point*
December 2001	December 2003	3.5% ±1 percentage point
Summer 2002	December 2003	Below 4.5%
October 2002	December 2004	3.5% ±1 percentage point
October 2003	*December 2005*	*4% ±1 percentage point*
November 2004	*December 2006*	*3.5% ±1 percentage point*
August 2005	As of January 2007 Continuous target	*3% ±1 percentage point*

November 2006   December 2007   3% ±1 percentage point
               Continuous target

Continuous inflation target: measured month to the corresponding month of the previous
year.

Table 7.3b: Inflation targets in Poland

Date adopted	Reference period	Target rates (consumer price inflation)
October 1996	December 1997	15%
October 1997	December 1998	9.5%
October 1998	*December 2004*	*4%*
October 1998	December 1999	8%–8.5%
Revised in March 1999	December 1999	6.6%–7.8%
October 1999	December 2000	5.4%–6.8%
October 2000	December 2001	6%–8%
August 2001	December 2002	5% ±1 percentage point
Revised June 2002		3% ±1
March 2003	*Continuous target since January 2004*	2.5% ±1 percentage point

Continuous inflation target: measured month to the corresponding month of the previous
year, until entry into ERM II or the end of term of office of the current Monetary Policy
Council.

Table 7.3c: Inflation targets in the Czech Republic

Date adopted	Reference period	Target rates (net inflation)
December 1997	December 1998	5.5%–6.5%
December 1997	*December 2000*	*3.5% –5.5%*
November 1998	December 1999	4%–5%
April 1999	*December 2005*	*1% –3%*
April 2000	December 2001	2%–4%
		Target rates (consumer price inflation)
April 2001	January 2002	3%–5%
April 2001	*December 2005*	*2% –4%*
		Target rates (consumer price inflation), permanent target
March 2004	As of January 2006	3% ±1 percentage point
March 2007	*As of January 2010*	*2% ±1 percentage point*

Net inflation excludes regulated prices.

Appendix 2: Cohesion Funds Expenditures Compared to SGP Sanctions

	(1) GDP 2004 million €	(2) 0.5% GDP million €	(3) Cohesion funds. 2007–13 million €	(4) Cohesion funds. yearly average million €	Ratio (4)/(2)
Czech Republic	87 205	436.0	8819	1259.9	2.9
Poland	203 952	1 019.8	22176	3168.0	3.1
Hungary	82 303	411.5	8642	1234.6	3.0

Source:
- GDP 2004: Eurostat
- Cohesion funds: Cohesion Policy 2007–2013, Commentaries and Official Texts, Guide, January 2007.

8 ECONOMIC AND ETHICAL ASPECTS OF DISCRIMINATION IN THE CONSUMER CREDIT MARKET

Ingrid Größl

It has become a widespread practice among banking institutions to charge higher interest rates on consumer loans extended to lower-income households. Typically this has been explained by a negative correlation between household income and risk. Größl[1] shows that this perspective may be flawed even from a purely economic viewpoint, and may hence lead to discrimination in the consumer credit market. In the following I take up this argument and discuss how income-dependent interest rates are valued from an *ethical* perspective. In doing so, I distinguish between teleological business ethics and integrative business ethics and explain why according to both strands of thought income-dependent interest rates are discriminating. However, I also clarify how both positions differ regarding their normative consequences for the behaviour of lending banks. Whereas teleological approaches shift responsibilities to the institutional environment, integrative ethics does not release banks from an ethical responsibility, irrespective of prevailing competitive pressures.

The discussion on how to price loans has become even more important against the background of the current financial crisis, which started as a subprime mortgage crisis in the US. Indeed, during the 1990s a process had started which should soon be named 'democratization of finance'. Underlying this process was the idea that financial markets were not only able to contribute to the efficient allocation of resources but that they could also contribute to increasing the fortune of lower-income households.[2] This was expected to be achieved by a process of generous lending to lower-income households. As the current financial crisis proves, banks had been too generous judging from the true risks. However, we should neither jump to the conclusion that lower-income households pose greater risks per se, nor to the conclusion that in fact the process of 'democratization of finance' in the US put an end to discrimination of lower-income households. The reason is that the observed generosity in lending was concentrated on mortgages which served to financing the purchase of real estate. The underlying motive to grant loans, therefore, was first and foremost based on the prospect of ever-rising prices for real estate which in the eyes of bank managers rendered mortgages as low risks – irrespective of borrowers' income situation. By contrast in this article we focus on unsecured consumer loans, and indeed against the background of the current financial crisis the issue of discrimination in this market has gained new interest. In order to recover, banks will try to remain on the safe side, thus avoiding risks which according to their view will be too high. Whether the discrimination of lower-income households as credit clients will continue depends to a high degree on whether banks decide to submit commonly used risk evaluating procedures to a thorough revision.

For the remainder of this article I proceed as follows: In the next section I briefly summarize an economic perspective explaining income-dependent interest rates as a discriminatory practice following Größl (2005). I then proceed to introduce the ethical standpoint by embedding teleological and integrative business ethics into utilitarianism and discourse ethics, respectively. I then show how income-dependent interest rates for consumer loans are treated in both ethical theories.

1. An Economic Perspective of Income-Dependent Interest Rates For Consumer Loans

In economics the term (improper) discrimination is used to describe unequal treatment of market participants leading to Pareto-inefficient results.[3] As major motives underlying discrimination thus defined, 'taste', statistical as well as 'profit motives', have been discussed in the literature.[4] Taste-based discrimination in the credit market denotes a situation where lenders claim higher interest rates from members of particular groups as a compensation for the higher psychic costs of lending.[5] Discrimination based on statistical reasons may ground in lenders' attempt to economize on screening costs thus using gender, race or income as indicators of quality.[6] Yinger and Größl add profit motives as a further reason form discrimination.[7] According to Yinger, profit-based discrimination describes a situation in which a lender charges higher interest rates from two borrowers – we will call them A and B – even if they both have the same quality, because other properties allow the lender to draw a higher profit from A than from B. The outcome is Pareto-inefficient if the bank simply redistributes profits (incomes) at the cost of others. However, his approach leaves unanswered the question why borrower B should accept the contract without first trying his luck with another bank. This question was taken by Größl, in 2005, who explains profit-based discrimination with a segmentation of the consumer credit market forcing lower-income borrowers to pay higher interest rates than justified by their risk position without having the opportunity to choose more favourable alternatives. Indeed by proving that lower-income borrowers are not necessarily a higher risk than higher-income borrowers, Größl also offers an explanation for what Arrow and Becker call 'statistical discrimination'. Her arguments are based on a microeconomic model of bank behaviour in which two types of banks are distinguished: A risk-neutral bank covers a borrower's demand for loans as long as he is willing to pay an interest rate which allows the bank to earn on average the rate of return of a riskless alternative. This interest rate then contains a mark-up over the riskless rate, which is determined by the borrower's expected default. With a given loans size, it is shown that the expected default depends on the borrower's worst-case income as well as on the size of the loan with the effect of a higher loan volume being stronger than the effect of a higher worst-case income. Hence it is the size of the loan and not the size of income which decides over the riskiness of a borrower. Of course, expected default also depends on the probability distribution of possible incomes, which in turn is affected by job security, health and other idiosyncratic risks, and also depends on the portfolio of invested wealth. With the exception of very low-income household with poorly qualified jobs, it appears rather far-fetched to assign higher income volatility to lower incomes than to higher incomes. Finally also a risk-averse bank is considered where risk aversion amounts to the extent to which a bank is willing to accept default, which explains why banks pose an upper limit to the loan volume they are willing to grant. It is shown that these credit lines depend on the maximum loss which a bank is willing to accept, average fixed costs, a mark-up due to imperfect competition and by the safe interest rate. Notably, expected default plays no role since borrowers are already charged for this by correspondingly higher interest rates. Again, no clear-cut correlation with lower-income households can be found. Rather, arguments like the loan size play a role. A further argument is given by the tolerated maximum loss. A main conclusion from this analysis is that income-dependent interest rates represent statistical discrimination in the sense that the 'wrong' indicator is chosen to estimate the borrower's quality.

The explanation of profit-dependent discrimination is more difficult. In Größl's 'The Poor Pay More' a necessary condition is given if banks seek to maximize the firm's value and in doing so, evaluate each customer according to his total contribution to this objective. Besides consumer loans, mortgages, financial investments and payment transactions are considered to play a role in this respect. Given that higher-income households allow the bank to realize cross-selling, then a particular bank will yield a higher average return from these clients. If this same bank takes this rate of return as a benchmark, then a household will only be accepted as a customer if the bank expects to earn this same return from him, too. If price differentiation poses no alternative, lower-return customers will be denied access. On the other hand access can be maintained if lower-income households pay higher prices for financial services thus becoming as profitable as high-income households, which also implies higher interest rates for consumer loans than higher-income households would have to pay. In order to provide both a necessary and a sufficient condition for profit-based discrimination, however, it must not be possible for the affected households to approach competing banks. Differently put, households affected by higher interest rates have to be locked into a particular contractual relation or market segment such that they can only decide between refraining from taking the loan or accept the unfavourable conditions. However, such a lock-in effect does not follow automatically. It has to be expected, especially if switching costs are high and if we have a large number of banking institutions which follow the practice of charging income-dependent interest rates. It is furthermore shown that free entry does not necessarily overcome this problem since as a consequence of lower interest rates 'old' lenders which follow a price discrimination strategy will leave the market thus causing a decline in the total supply of loans.

2. Income-Dependent Interest Rates and Discrimination in the Consumer Credit Market from and Ethical Perspective

Economics is concerned with the question of how the scarcity of resources can be overcome. Ethics, on the other hand, deals with moral principles, according to which individuals ought to decide and interact. That both issues are not unrelated is in particular shown by business ethics, which examines how moral principles and the economic principle of efficiency are connected.[8] However, both disciplines take different perspectives not only with respect to the desired importance of moral principles but already with respect to their understandings of the economic process as a tool to overcome the overall material scarcity. Economics interprets the economic process more or less as a *technical* relation between goods which serve to satisfying humans' needs, and required resources. In this respect, the focus of economics is efficiency, which in a static sense requires to avoiding any waste of resources, and in a dynamic sense requires the development of new technologies which enhance the availability of resources as such. Ethics, however, considers the economic process as a process of social interaction between a multitude of individuals, in which the existing interpersonal conflicts over the use and distribution of scarce resources ought to be solved in a morally justified manner. Point of departure is the insight that nature imposes material or physical constraints on human beings. No such physical constraint, however, guides human behaviour, which is entirely determined by individual will and the ability of choice. Morality implies that each individual has the right to self-determination but also the obligation to acknowledge that all other individuals are endowed with this same right.[9] The moral quality of an action taken by an individual thus depends on whether he does not only respect his own freedom but also that of all other people. In the context of economic decisions, this means that each human being has the right to augment his own welfare but also the obligation to concede this same right to all other human beings. This in turn requires that individual decisions should not only be evaluated according to their immediate personal advantages but also according to their *legitimacy*. Legitimate decisions are those which do not violate the moral rights of our fellow men.[10]

It was not until the beginning of the enlightenment that decisions over what should be considered as legitimate from a moral point of view were shifted from God to the human beings themselves. God was replaced by human reason according to which every subject is endowed with the same right to the same freedom of self-determination. Regarding the implications for what should be understood by 'legitimate' or 'moral', different strands of ethics with Kant's ethical theory and utilitarianism as the most important representatives can be distinguished. However, despite their differences, both share the insight that due to the universal right to self-determination, each human being has the obligation to take the position of impartiality saying that to each other individual is to assign the same right to the inviolability of dignity and the same right to self-determination, irrespective of sex, religion, colour, education, wealth and *weltanschauung*. Hence the principle of impartiality commands compliance with the principle of equal treatment. To put it in another way, discrimination is considered as immoral behaviour. This is true at least on principle, because both schools of thought concede that there might be legitimate deviations. However, both schools differ with respect to how deviations from the principle of equal treatment should be legitimated. Moreover, it can be found that both approaches differ with respect to the consequences to be drawn from observed discrimination.

In correspondence to utilitarianism and Kant's ethical theory, we can distinguish between teleological business ethics on the one hand and integrative business ethics on the other. In the following, we consider how income-dependent interest rates are considered, taking both schools of thought into account. Remember that from an economic point of view, income-dependent interest rates are discriminatory only to the extent that they lead to Pareto-inefficiency. This in turn requires that the concerned households are locked into their market segment and are thus exposed to the market power of their banks. By looking at income-dependent interest rates from an ethical perspective, we apply the principle of self-determination, which naturally implies that the individual decision-maker should take the right of others to the same self-determination into account. It will become evident, that both schools of business ethics consider income-dependent interest rates as discrimination. However, I will also show that they draw different consequences regarding a bank's duties towards its clients. In the next paragraph we consider teleological business ethics with utilitarianism as its foundation.[11]

3. Income-Dependent Interest Rates and Discrimination: The Perspective of Teleological Business Ethics

Teleological ethical theories are built on utilitarianism. Utilitarian ethical theories in their turn can be considered as the normative foundation of neoclassical economics. Utilitarianism holds that the moral legitimacy of actions has to be judged by their utility. In 'An Introduction to the Principles of Morales and Legislation', Jeremy Bentham,[12] one of the founding fathers of utilitarianism, proposes the principle of utility as a universal ethical criterion for individual actions. According to Ulrich, the utilitarian principle has four distinct aspects: First, the morality of each action should be judged by its consequences, which explains why utilitarianism belongs to the class of teleological ethical theories. Second, 'consequences' means the *moral* utility of an action. Third, the morality of an action is measured by the extent to which it promotes happiness. Fourth, of importance in this respect is not the individual utility but the utility of all affected individuals ('the greatest good for the greatest number'). Acknowledging that individuals are selfish, Bentham called for a legal order with an effective sanctioning mechanism which should set the egoist individuals incentives to take the impact of his own actions on all others into account.[13]

Utilitarianism has had a significant impact on neoclassical economics. Of importance in this respect is a focus on material needs which are satisfied by the use of scarce resources. The individual pursuit of the greatest happiness has been substantiated by the maximization of utility from the consumption of scarce resources. Taking this perspective, each opportunity to increase the aggregate production potential has to be valued as an essential prerequisite of the realization of individual freedom and thus self-determination. However, neoclassical economics is at odds with Bentham regarding the role of the law as a disciplining device for individual selfishness. Rather than by a legal order, according to neoclassical economics, this role should be taken by the market. Characterizing the market by the exchange of goods between large numbers of individuals arguably also acknowledges the market as a place where of social interaction. However, the social function of the marketplace has never been a focus of neoclassical economics. Assuming that markets are perfectly competitive, the General Equilibrium model proposes a solution for interpersonal conflicts of interests concerning the use of scarce resources, which does not rely on interpersonal bargaining processes and does nevertheless forbid personal enrichments at the cost of others. This Pareto-efficient outcome is achieved by a vector of generally accepted market prices brought about by some impartial auctioneer and by competition, which drives 'second-best' producers out of the market. Both the impartial auctioneer and competition release the individual market participant from examining the moral legitimacy of his own decisions. In this way the anonymous perfectly competitive market can be considered as a substitute for a critical reflection about the moral rightness of economic decisions. Indeed, within the framework of the General Equilibrium Model, it is shown that individual utility and profit maximization allow achievement of a maximum of individual and aggregate efficiency, given the properties of perfect competition and perfect specification of property rights (second theorem of welfare economics). This Pareto efficiency does not only allow production of a maximum of goods with a given quantity of resources, it also ensures that each individual achieves a maximum of utility in the sense that nobody in the economy can be made better without making at least one other person worse.[14] This has been considered as a specification of Bentham's claim for the greatest good for the greatest number.

We observe that in each general equilibrium the total quantity of produced goods is distributed among the members of the economy in a particular manner. Of crucial importance in this respect are initial individual endowments, which – together with the individual preference ordering – determine the individual willingness to pay. This reveals the limits of the market mechanism in solving the interpersonal conflict about the distribution of scarce resources.

A functioning market mechanism is only capable of ensuring that each market participant may use its initial endowment in a utility-maximizing manner but remains silent on whether initial endowments are distributed in the 'right' manner. On the other hand, utilitarianism, too, claims that the morality of an action ought to be evaluated according to both its contribution to efficiency as well as to distributive justice.[15] However, it is also in accordance with utilitarianism and hence teleological ethics that in the case of a conflicting relationship between these two principles, efficiency ought to have priority over distributive equity.[16] According to teleological ethics, human beings have a moral duty to use their individual capabilities, skills and talents as best as possible supported by a societal order which guarantees freedom of choice and self-determination. Since human beings are differently endowed with skills, talents and capabilities, the outcome of individual choices will of course be different as reflected in discrepancies between individual incomes and differences in wealth. The pursuit of a maximum of efficiency and implied by this, the pursuit of a maximum of profit or wealth is considered to be a supreme moral duty of the entrepreneur. In the same vein, the market as an institution as well as competition are assigned not only an economic but also an ethical legitimacy because perfectly competitive markets are considered to be the best way to realize solidarity among all human beings.[17]

If efficiency guides economic decisions, then of course the outcome does not rule out an ever-increasing gap between the rich and the poor with social conflicts following. In the absence of market power, externalities and information asymmetry, these discrepancies are exclusively the result of violations of equal opportunities in some imaginary initial situation determined by genetic factors as well as by inherited wealth and education. Unequal opportunities in some imaginary initial situation explain why different people are treated differently in the market. This different treatment, however, promotes economic efficiency. It does not violate the principle of impartiality because efficiency provides the material foundation for 'the greatest good for the greatest number'. The only way to increase the equality of income without impairing efficiency is to establish institutions which promote education for the poor or to tax bequests.[18] In the same vein, teleological ethics refutes the unequal treatment due to sex, race or religion as examples of discrimination, primarily because this implies that inefficient actions are preferred to efficient ones.

Teleological ethics grounds in utilitarianism and thus takes the principle of 'the greatest good for the greatest number' as the final measure of the morality of human behaviour. This also requires that a compromise between a maximum of efficiency and distributive justice has to be found, should the gap between rich and poor widen. In such a situation, advocates of teleological ethics favour institutions established by the state, over private solutions. In the absence of market power due to size or information asymmetry, the moral rightness of corporate decisions should be ensured by appropriate institutions, thus ensuring a maximum of individual and aggregate efficiency. This also implies that deviations from perfect competition which the state is unwilling or unable to remove by appropriate institutions claim for morality on the part of corporations. Indeed, how opportunistic behaviour on the part of corporations can be avoided through the establishment of good codes of conduct can be considered as a key research issue of utilitarian approaches to business ethics.[19]

What are the implications for income-dependent interest rates? As was already emphasized, utilitarianism, too, advocates the principle of equal treatment. Hence, if it is not necessarily true that a loan applicant with a low income has a low quality, but is nevertheless charged higher interest rates without further screening activities, then utilitarianism, too, considers this as statistical discrimination. However, if competition forces banks to maximize their profits, then this should have absolute priority. A bank is considered to be trapped in a prisoner's dilemma: Is the bank willing to undertake costly screening activities in order to reveal the true quality of lower-income borrowers? A bank that does this runs the risk of being squeezed out of the market. Hence the only way to get out of this trap is to establish rules which are binding for each market participant.

Statistical arguments are but one discussed explanation for income-dependent interest rates for consumer loans. A further argument rests on a strategy according to which a bank evaluates its customers according to their individual contribution to the bank's shareholder value. Does this represent discrimination if judged from the viewpoint of teleological ethics? In particular the question has to be answered as to why shareholders' interests should have more weight than the interests of other stakeholders. In economics shareholder value maximization has frequently been legitimated by its contribution to efficiency.[20] Following General Equilibrium Theory with complete markets, profits represent residual incomes which are distributed to shareholding households. It can be shown that given market completeness, all shareholders favour the maximization of the shareholder value (shareholders' unanimity) and that managers realize this preference (separation principle). In this model the maximization of shareholder value turns out to be a prerequisite for Pareto efficiency. This does not, however, rule out an ever-increasing gap between the rich and the poor. This increasing gap is in particular influenced by the fact that any initially given wealth position grows with positive savings which in their turn are also influenced by the growth of personal incomes. The growth rates of personal incomes, however, are also positively determined by the individual ability to participate in growing shareholder values and negatively by the servicing of loans. Income-dependent interest rates on consumer loans can thus promote increasing income and wealth inequalities. Since bank clients with higher income and wealth positions enjoy more favourable loan conditions, this development obviously violates the principle of unequal opportunities, which according to teleological ethics, too, represents discrimination.

This does not mean, however, that banks have to avoid these practices. Quite the contrary is the case if it can be shown that income-dependent interest rates promote aggregate efficiency. To the extent that this is the case, banks should be allowed to practise discrimination, thus contributing to a maximum of aggregate growth. Should the resulting distribution of incomes and wealth violate the society's ideals, then the government would have the task of taking corrective measures.

4. Income-Dependent Interest Rates and Discrimination: The Perspective of Integrative Business Ethics

Integrative Business Ethics derives from Habermas's discourse ethics, which has its roots in Kant's ethical theory, according to which the moral content of human actions ought to be determined by reason.[21] Rationality teaches human beings to concede to all other human beings the same right to self-determination and endows them with the capability of evaluating the consequences of their own actions on others. We are endowed with the capacity to put ourselves into the situation of others thus acknowledging the principle of reciprocity.[22] Human reason enables us to generalize our insight into the reciprocal structure of any particular situation and allows us to transform our role-taking into the universal role reversal. This is equivalent to saying that human reason guides us to honour the principle of impartiality, which of course forbids discriminating activities. Deviations are allowed only if they can be legitimated by the Kantian imperative: 'Act only according to that maxim by which you can and at the same time will that it should become a universal law'.[23]

According to Broad, Kant's ethical theory is deontological because, contrary to teleological approaches, the morality of an action according to Kant should not be evaluated by its consequences but rather by its properties as such.[24] Based on the insight that human beings are rational, Kant asked whether a particular action, for example lying, '...is something that a rational being could do and whether it shows respect for other persons'.[25]

However, a distinction between teleological and deontological approaches based on the role of the consequences of an action does not appear to be helpful. Indeed, deontological approaches, too, have a view to the consequence of an action. However, they emphasize that moral rules must be universal. Ulrich states that according to teleological ethical theories, the principle of reciprocity recommends that the actor take the consequences of one's actions into account because this is beneficial for oneself, at least in the long run.[26] However, reciprocity as a moral principle should not be restricted to the calculation of effects in favour of the long-run utility of those persons whose immediate concern is involved. Rather, reciprocity as a moral principle claims the unconditional priority of the right of self-determination assigned to every human being. Stated differently, whereas teleological ethical theory treats the principle of reciprocity as a (binding) constraint for an otherwise selfish individual, deontological ethical theory integrates the right of self-determination of alter into the utility function of ego.

According to Kantian ethics the moral value of an action can be found through experiments undertaken by individuals in isolation. This distinguishes Kantian ethics from discourse ethics.[27] Since moral rules guide social interaction, according to Habermas, the moral value of any particular action cannot be legitimated without taking recourse to a communicative process undertaken between the members of the society. By consequence, the moral rightness of an action depends on a mutual understanding that is achieved through a process of argumentation between the members of a society.

Ulrich applies the principles of discourse ethics to analyse the moral value of economic decisions.[28] He starts his analysis criticizing an ongoing process of 'economization' according to which society and social relations are increasingly treated as an adjunct of the market. He criticizes the way in which teleological ethical approaches even put the market logic, i.e., the normative logic of mutual advantage, on a par with the moral principle. The principle of mutual advantage cannot be used as a shortcut to ethical reason. To explain his point, Ulrich distinguishes between economic rationality and economic reason. Both have in common that they provide a measure of value creation. However, whereas economic rationality measures value exclusively by efficiency, economic reason goes beyond the efficient use of scarce material resources and in addition emphasizes the principle of a good life that each individual has a right to live. This pursuit of a good life is not only determined by the consumption of material goods, it also contains our search for meaning and our quest for fairness. Ulrich emphasizes that the economic management of scarce resources should serve this good life and not the other way round. More precisely, the efficient provision of scarce goods should enable individuals to realize their personal conception of a good life. According to Ulrich, personal freedom means the existence of an ample variety of options beyond material things. Of course for some individuals, a good life will certainly consist of maximizing the consumption of goods. However, this should not be generalized to be the only guiding principle of human life. Against this background, competition has to be viewed in another light, because unrestricted competition limits the set of feasible options which individuals may use in order to realize their own good life. Utilitarianism as well as teleological ethics emphasizes competition as a way to realize personal freedom. Integrative business ethics by contrast argues that this freedom is restricted to utility maximization with respect to material goods only.

It is important to note that according to integrative business ethics, the right to self-determination is not only limited to the realization of one's own good life. The right to self-determination includes the insight that this right is universal. This means that the moral value of an economic action depends on whether the actor respects other people's possibly differing concepts of a good life. Hence from an ethical point of view, a primacy of economic efficiency does not exist. Economic decisions have to take both principles into account without giving priority to economic efficiency as is recommended by teleological approaches.

In order to make this possible, Ulrich emphasizes the necessity of generally accepted principles of fairness. With respect to their development as well as with respect to their enforcement he appeals to the critical public. In this respect he distinguishes between civil society, the economic sphere and the legal order as places of the moral. In doing so, Ulrich departs from teleological ethical theories which consider the institutional framework established enforced by the government as the exclusive place of the moral. This also means that nobody in a society, irrespective of one's function, can be relieved from moral responsibility. It is not economic efficiency which should decide how moral responsibilities ought to be distributed among the members of a society, but the critical public where by means of the communicative power of a discourse, personal rights and duties have to be weighed against each other. By means of an ongoing discourse, a societal consensus concerning the morality of actions and their role in society should be possible, which also guides managerial decisions.

That banks as elements of the economic sphere are not only responsible for efficiency but also for the moral value of their decisions has crucial consequences for the treatment of unequal incomes. Since, according to business ethics, efficiency and profit maximization do not have priority, to charge lower-income households with higher interest rates for loans in order to increase profits, constitutes discrimination which, contrary to teleological approaches, should be avoided without having the appropriate legal norm in place. Ulrich states that competition does indeed restrict the set of feasible action which bank mangers have in order to realize their objectives. However, competition is just a procedural principle which ensures that the 'best' wins, leaving open what 'best' means. If a consensus existed that 'best' means the maximum of profits, then competition indeed ensures that less profitable banks have to leave the market. If on the other hand there is a consensus view which gives priority to fairness, then competition will exclude those banks which violate this principle. Again he points to the critical public as the appropriate place where this consensus could come about.

Ulrich emphasizes that it is by no means unimportant how a bank plans to realize profit maximization because the choice of a particular instrument decides whether and to what extent bank clients can achieve their personal objectives, and this in turn decides whether this same action is ethical or not. If the immorality of an action can be proved, then a bank ought to dispense with it, irrespective of its profit-maximizing effects. By consequence, Ulrich claims that the ethical legitimacy of an action takes priority over profit maximization as the ultimate goal.[29] Integrative business ethics represents the ethical foundation of the stakeholder principle which claims from firm managers that their decisions should take the interests of all stakeholders into account. With respect to lending practices, this means that bank managers should contribute to the utility enhancing consumption smoothing function of loan interest rates irrespective of bank clients' income situation.

Summary

Taking an economic point of view, income-dependent interest rates are not necessarily discriminating. This is the case even if different incomes do not signal differences in credit risk. Rather, for income-dependent interest rates to be discriminatory, it has to be proven that lower-income households become locked into a market segment. From an ethical point of view, the discriminatory content of income-dependent interest rates is generally accepted. However, opinions differ with respect to whether and how these practices should be avoided. Of importance in this respect are different views concerning the role of profit maximization. Whereas teleological approaches assign to profit maximization an ethical value as such, integrative business ethics states that profit maximization is ethical only if the actions taken to achieve this goal do not impair the well-being of concerned stakeholders. In particular, teleological approaches release bank managers from ethical responsibilities other than profit maximization and shift responsibilities for distributional fairness to the institutional framework which in its turn has to be established and made binding for all market participants. In the absence of such an institutional order, profit-maximizing bank managers should not be inhibited from charging income-dependent interest rates if this strengthens their competitive advantage. Integrative business ethics claims that firm managers should examine the morality of their actions to increase profits, which means taking into consideration the well-being of bank clients when deciding interest rates for loans. Ulrich appeals to an ongoing discourse between the members of the society (public discourse) in order to create an environment that does not punish other-regarding behaviour as inefficient. This, too, calls for an appropriate institutional order. Moreover, the teleological approach, too, supports discourses between corporations about their social responsibility. However, following teleological ethics, social responsibility should be proven to be in accordance with firms' profit objectives – at least in the long run. By contrast, according to integrative business ethics, a prevailing conflict between social responsibility and profit maximization should not be solved in favour of profit maximization.

9 BEYOND ETHICS: ALTERNATIVE BANKING IN SWITZERLAND

Elisabeth Paulet and Francesc Relano

'Ethics' has recently become a buzzword. One can no longer escape the ethical dimension in all domains: the action of politicians, the work of scientists, the impact of firms, even banks and financial institutions in general, are now fully concerned with the ethical impact of their transactions. The actual subprime crisis has even strengthened the obligation to moralize the international financial system. All over the world, banks have faced liquidity or solvency problems. Surprisingly, during the same period, ethical banks have faced this tumultuous episode relatively quietly, gaining clients from classical banking institutions. How can we characterize them? Among other factors, their use of financial markets is extremely reduced. Hence, in a context where investors' main preoccupation is to secure their savings, these ethical banks are actually capturing the clientele of commercial banks.

What are then the reactions of these traditional banks? In line with the fashionable perspective of sustainable development, and under the societal pressure, they all claim to integrate ethics within the financial sphere. Most banks, for instance, have developed new products and are now able to offer to their clients the possibility of investing in a wide range of 'ethical funds'. Likewise, most banks have special credit lines especially devoted to environmental or social issues. Some banks have even adopted, on the basis of voluntary commitment, the 'Equator' principles. In so doing, banks are engaged proactively with the stakeholders in assessing and managing the social and environmental impact of the projects they finance. And yet one can still wonder to what extent all these new policies and commitments to sustainability are strong enough for apprehending banks as ethical institutions. For instance, is a bank like HSBC 'ethical' in the same way as Triodos Bank? Surely not, and in order to illustrate the difference the present chapter will begin by characterizing the distinct nature of the so-called 'ethical banks', when compared with traditional banks. But one cannot say either that all ethical banks are the same. This paper will show that beyond the threshold of ethical or sustainable banking, still compliant to some degree with refined 'greenwash' or the superficial moralization of the economy, there are some few institutions which act as real alternative banks. We shall illustrate this point through an analysis of the WIR Bank and its specific counter-cyclical behaviour within the Swiss banking system as regards the credit policy. In a context, where access to credit for Small and Medium Enterprises (SME) is becoming more and more difficult, this counter-cyclical attitude is far beyond to be negligible. This could constitute a strong strategic advantage for these institutions to attract new clients only willing to pursue quietly their activity, without having to face continuously investment constraint. This is precisely what we intend to discuss now.

1. Ethical Banking in Switzerland

The European banking system has evolved considerably over the last thirty years. Changes have taken place in two main directions. On the one hand, a merger process has led to a relative homogenization of the banking sector.[1] On the other hand, the recent financial scandals have brought up the question of ethics.[2] Both issues are intimately related, since the ethical alignment is a way of getting differentiation within a rather standardized market. Dealing specifically with banks, this raises the following question: which model satisfies best the customer's simultaneous demands of profitability, transparency and ethics?

Since the mid-80s, a number of ethical banks have appeared. Their objective is to comply with these new demands of society. At the same time, 'traditional' banks have also tried to attract these new clients. They have thus stressed their commitment to sustainable development, for example by signing the Equator Principles or by issuing SRI products. Either way, at the first sight it is not easy to make the difference between the ethical/alternative banking born in the 80s and the traditional banks recently committed with a more social/environmental approach. And yet, they are not at all the same. A definition of the concept of ethical banking might give the first key for differentiation.

At the most basic level, ethical banking might simply designate the activities of banks concerned about the social and environmental use of its investments and loans. Therefore it refers to financial services that are designed to promote equity and sustainable development. The problem is that the instruments and mechanisms of ethical financing might eventually include many of the operations of traditional banks. Since virtually all financial institutions are committed to sustainable development in one form or another, proposing for instance SRI products or partnerships with microfinance institutions, it is very difficult to find difference between traditional banks and the new ethical banks that have appeared since the mid-80s. Further criteria are thus needed. In this sense, it is important to highlight that the so-called ethical banks believe that profitability should not be measured only in financial terms, but also in social terms. This means that for ethical banks the maximization of profit is not the only objective guiding their activities. Added social and environmental value should also be taken into consideration. Let us illustrate this point through one of the founding statements of the Alternative Bank ABS, one of the Swiss ethical banks which will be studied in this paper:

> The ABS Bank puts its ethical principles before profit maximization and conceives its activity as an alternative to the dominant economic logic, which is the principal responsible for the worsening of ecological problems and the increase of social and economic inequalities.[3]

This criterion seems indeed far more powerful for making the distinction between ethical and traditional banks. Whereas for the former the sustainable approach is an integral part of their overall strategy and, somehow, their 'raison d'être', for traditional banks the new ethical fashion is just an accessory instrument for attracting new clients and thus maximizing the benefits. This latter point is – as it has always been – their primary aim, the rest being subordinated to it. For the ethical banks, it is the other way round. So in order to make a distinction between traditional and ethical banks one should not focus on the volume or variety of SRI products (all banks issue them), but on other factors which really make the difference. Two of them seem particularly interesting:

- The financial activities, particularly as regards their participation in the financial market, their investment policy, the type of interests practised, the segment of clients to whom the banks are particularly addressed, the underneath strategy in the grating of loans etc.
- The internal functioning of the institution, particularly as regards the operational cost, the wage policy, transparency, gender equality etc.

The general presentation of three examples of Swiss ethical banks will allow us to make some of these differences more precise. For the time being, we would first like to make clear the reasons why we have chosen Switzerland for the study of these banking institutions. In that sense, it should be noted that this is a country with a well developed banking sector. The variety of financial institutions in Switzerland includes, among others, several examples of ethical/alternative banks. In addition, Switzerland is a relatively small country. It is thus easier to carry out a macro-economical analysis within the Swiss framework than within the general European context. Last but not least, the study of the Swiss banking system will allow us to present a very special bank which has no parallel with any other financial institution in the world.

The first Swiss bank which will be the object of analysis in the following chapters is the Freie Gemeinschaftsbank BCL.[4] Founded in 1984 in Donarch, near

Basel, by a group of anthroposophist members, the BCL Bank claimed since the very beginning that observing ethical principles takes precedence over maximizing profits. It is thus not surprising that, unlike most of traditional banks, the BCL Bank has refused to participate in the speculative operations of the financial market. Its main activities are therefore concentrated in the savings collection and credit distribution. Like most ethical banks, the BCL Bank privileges the social, ethical or environmental dimension of the projects financed. In that sense, particular attention is given to areas of social and ecological housing, biological agriculture, renewable energies, independent schools and kindergarten, social health care initiatives, communal living projects, small and medium-sized companies, etc. Solidarity is encouraged between depositors and borrowers to enable loans at reduced rates of interest for these particular activities. In addition, the BCL practises an active policy of transparency, since all loans are published. Another outstanding characteristic is that the BCL Bank has the juridical status of a Community bank. Cooperative members can subscribe for CHF 300, 500, 1000, 5000 or 10000 shares. This fact has at least two major consequences: on the organizational side, each of the cooperative members has, irrespectively of the capital invested, one vote; on the other hand, the cooperative status is also consistent with the BCL Bank general policy of restricting its activities to Switzerland. Finally, it should be noted that the cooperative members who have subscribed for shares renounce to the payments of interests. In fact, most of the benefits made by the institution are affected by the consolidation of the social capital (constitution of reserves), which today accounts for CHF 7 403 500.

Most of these characteristics, clearly at variance with the policy and organization of traditional banks, are shared by the second ethical bank which will be analysed in the present study: the Alternative Bank ABS.[5] Founded in 1990 with initial headquarters in Olten (midway between Berne and Zurich), its ethical approach to banking activities can be summarized in one of its own slogans: 'less profit, more sense'. Like the BCL Bank, the Alternative Bank ABS focuses on savings collection and loan granting. In 2002, the bank has began selling some sustainable investment funds, namely because of client demand. But the volume of these funds is quite insignificant, amounting at the end of 2005 to CHF 6.45 million and involving only 139 clients of 20,000. This modest incursion into the stock market products is not in contradiction with the expressed agenda of not participating in the international financial market. Like most ethical institutions of this type, its loans are granted to support ecological and social projects. Initially, the ABS Bank encouraged the domains of biological agriculture and renewable energies, but the reality has recently shown that the most active sector in the bank's present loan policy is cooperative and ecological housing (half of total loans and two-thirds of total volume). For these activities, reduced interest rates are eventually practised. Transparency is also part of the bank's explicit strategy. This policy is implemented in various ways: publication of all approved loans, inquiries about the origin of the money placed in the bank, suppression of the client confidentiality, etc. Particular emphasis is also given to ensure organizational equality at all levels, not only as far as equal opportunities for both sexes is concerned, but also as regards the distribution of posts according to regional, linguistic and personal experience criteria.

Both banks thus seem fairly comparable in their general values and banking activities, but there is also one outstanding difference between them. Unlike the BCL Bank, the Alternative Bank ABS has chosen the juridical status of a public limited company to carry out its banking activities. In so doing, the ABS Bank claims to be a less rigid structure than a cooperative bank without renouncing similar democratic requirements. Indeed, the internal organization is made so that no one can accumulate more than 3% of votes in a general assembly. In addition, the ABS Bank limits its clients to private individuals, organizations and companies domiciled in Switzerland. Therefore, the democratic and local development requirements of ethical banking are fulfilled. In order to make sure that this is indeed the case, the organizational chart of the ABS Bank has always provided for an Ethical Council. Since 2005, this Ethical Council has been externalized. It is now the institute of economic ethics at Saint Gall University that controls the general ethical positioning of the bank and the way it is put into practice. In so doing, not only is the independence of the bank's ethic policy guaranteed, but recurrent organizational problems concerning the role of the Ethical Council have been resolved.

In the end, one can easily notice that, despite their different juridical status, the two ethical banks presented so far have many things in common, particularly if compared with traditional banks. In the coming sections, we shall see that this fact is not contradicted by the econometric analysis of their impact within the Swiss economy. Nevertheless, it would be hasty from this to infer that all ethical banks are essentially the same. In the galaxy of ethical banks there is at least one institution which is a special case not only within the Swiss context but also at the world level. We thus need to introduce this bank in some more detail before carrying out the econometric analysis.

2. The WIR Bank

The WIR Bank is the modern name given to a cooperative organization founded in 1934: the WIR Economic Circle (*Wirtschaftsring-Genossenschaft*). It has become something quite unique in Switzerland – and in the world at large – because it is the sole financial institution, apart from the Swiss National Bank, to create its own money. This complementary currency system served initially as a means of payment and for granting loans among the members of the cooperative.

More recently, the WIR Bank has opened to a wider public and has diversified its activities, thus leaving the safe ground of a competition-free market niche to enter the fiercely competitive cash area of the Swiss banking industry. Why? What difference does it make? Which is still its distinct specificity?... In order to grasp the full significance of the WIR Bank in the context of ethical banking and its impact in the Swiss national economy, we need first to make a brief insight in its long developmental history.[6]

2.1. Ideals and founding of the WIR Economic Circle

The WIR Economic Circle was founded as a self-help organization by Werner Zimmermann and Paul Enz in 1934. At that time, Switzerland was still suffering the consequences of the global economic crisis following the stock market crash of October 1929. Far too little money was flowing into public demand for goods and services. Sales had thus receded dramatically and many employees had lost their jobs. But, paradoxically, Switzerland had not been particularly affected by the general shrink of bank deposits. Even if some citizens had lost their faith in the banking industry and preferred to store their money at home, the country did not really lack capital. The problem was just how to reintroduce the money hoarded in banks and outside the banking system back into economic circulation.

The efforts undertaken by the industrialized nations to manage this crisis differed in two opposing approaches: countries like the US and Germany chose an expansive strategy via state job creation programs, while accepting the inflationary tendency; others, like the UK and Belgium took the restrictive strategy of reducing state deficits and protecting a the domestic economy, leading to a deflationary tendency.[7] Seeing the collateral effects of both strategies, Switzerland was unable to choose a clearly-defined policy. The few concrete measures taken were predominantly of a restrictive nature, but the results were not visible in the short term. It was thus mostly through private initiatives that a new creative atmosphere emerged in Switzerland. Among them, there was Zimmermann's idea of applying Friederich Von Hayek's theory on the privatization of money and Silvio Gesell's doctrine on the free money in the context of a shelf-help organization.[8] This is how in October 1934 the WIR Economic Circle Cooperative was brought to life by 16 founding members and an initial capital of CHF 42,000.

In practical terms, the application of Gesell's theory took the following form: since the crucial question was how to increase turnover in the face of a scarcity of money, a complementary currency which functioned as a medium of exchange within the Circle was created: the WIR. Let it be noted that this complementary currency did not replace the national currency, but rather exercised a social function for which the national currency was not intended. In the case of WIR, the members support each other both by buying from one another and by gaining access to loans offered by the central office at more favourable rates than anywhere else. In addition, they equipped the new medium of exchange with a stimulus to spend it quickly, rather than holding on to it. Thus, as a rule, not only was no interest paid on accounts but, on the contrary, a 'storage fee' (a kind of negative interest) was charged. In so doing, the WIR became a powerful instrument for generating increased turnover. This arises from the fact that not only there is an additional economic activity which had never existed without the WIR, but also because the transactions remain at domestic level, thus favouring the local economy and in particular the small and medium-sized enterprises.

Under these conditions, the WIR organization grew at an amazing rate. By early 1935, it listed 1,700 account holders actively exchanging goods and services, and 3,000 by the end of the year. The members included not only small and medium business, but also public servants, farmers and even few large enterprises. WIR trade fairs also date from these earlier times. Already in the founding year, five Swiss cities witnessed the great success of these fairs. The first Christmas exhibition in Zürich in 1935 alone attracted 30,000 visitors. One year later, the Central Office of the Economic Circle, functioning as a clearing house, was subjected to the Swiss banking law. The fact of structuring the Circle with a credit-granting bank is surely one of the key milestones to the WIR's initial success. But the outbreak of the Second World War changed the contextual conditions. While in the founding period the main problem was the discrepancy between an abundant supply and limited buying power, the war years were characterized by a scarcity of goods and a relatively abundant money supply. Under these circumstances, the WIR clearing exchange lost a lot of its pre-war dynamism. But after the wartime turmoil, the WIR Economic Circle made a new start. Membership began again to grow rapidly, even if some reforms had to be imposed. In 1948, the demurrage feature that burdened accounts with storage fee was done away with. Such a strong stimulus for spending money rapidly would have been inappropriate to the fast-moving business climate of those days. But interest-free feature was maintained. Still today, WIR accounts earn no interest.

In the coming decades, the WIR witnessed other turbulent episodes but self-renewal allowed the Economic Circle not only to survive but to continue a near-constant growth with no major changes as far as the WIR credit clearing concept is concerned. Most importantly, the fact that the WIR has been able to develop a long-term sustainable entrepreneurial concept demonstrates that the basic currency idea is advantageous not only in times of economic crisis. But by the end of the 1980s, the WIR initiated an important diversification strategy which led us to the present-day situation.

2.2. The WIR Bank today

Seen in perspective, it might be said that for more than sixty years the WIR organization lived from a single package of services: the WIR credit-clearing exchange and the associated granting of WIR-denominated loans. This distinctive feature is in fact the main reason for its success. It began with just sixteen adherents and today the WIR Cooperative numbers over 62,000 members. Most of them are small and medium-sized enterprises (representing one-fifth of the Swiss firms of this type), which through the competitive advantage offered by the WIR clearing system could face the pressure from mass distributors. Transactions among themselves are worth of almost CHF two billion annually. Considering that payments on average are made only from 30–40% in WIR and the remainder in Swiss francs, the total value of goods and services traded can easily double that amount. Only about 1% of each transaction served to remunerate the functioning and services offered by the Central Clearing Office.

The WIR has thus filled its own market niche with practically no competition for more than half a century. But during the 1990s, it became increasingly apparent that the original concept of WIR credit-clearing was reaching its limits. The first steps towards diversification into cash transactions began in 1995, namely through the introduction of the 'Combi-Card'. Simultaneously, the concept of 'WIR Bank' began to replace the often misunderstood denomination of 'economic circle', even if this change was not made official until 1998. This very same year, the WIR Bank started offering its members attractive Swiss Franc interest rates on certain savings accounts. In 2000, the Bank opened its doors to the general public and introduced electronic banking. So current members and non-members alike can now carry their banking activities in Swiss francs with the WIR Bank. In so doing, the number of customers not participating in the WIR system has increased dramatically, now amounting to a total of around 15,000.

New classical bank products have been progressively introduced in recent years, thus completing the organization's transition to true bank status. On 25 May 2004, the General Assembly of the WIR Bank raised its social capital to CHF 14.4 million and broadened its capital-stakeholder base. Now, not only WIR-trading participants but all customer groups can purchase cooperative shares, thus sharing the bank's financial success. In this way, the integration of a complementary currency system into a classical bank has been completed, even if still retains its unique WIR cultural identity. Should one thus conclude from this introduction of the Bank into the cash arena and its expansion in the domain of classical banking services that the WIR Bank is now becoming a universal bank? The answer is clearly negative. Rather than becoming a conventional bank, the diversification of the WIR Bank into cash transactions has been accompanied by a new emphasis on its ethical dimension. Foreign exchange transactions, export financing, securities issuance, investment banking and rare metal transactions are not likely to be introduced among the new services offered in the future. Quite the reverse, its customer base is strongly anchored in the small/medium business sector and, like most ethical banks, the WIR is now offering them a new generation of 'green loans'. Most importantly, the WIR Bank preserves its most distinctive feature: the WIR complementary currency. As we shall see, the fact of still being able to create its own money for lending and spending endows the WIR Bank with a very special role within the Swiss national economy. A role which places the WIR Bank beyond ethical banking, mainly because of its counter-cyclical nature.

3. Identification of Swiss Business Cycles

In order to give evidence of the counter-cyclical nature of the WIR Bank, a clear connection between long term growth and credit cycle will be provided.[9] If the traditional credit cycle is significantly correlated to the economic Swiss trend, what could be said of this relation as regards the 'alternative' credit cycle of the WIR bank? What are then the consequences for the Swiss enterprises participating to this network?

3.1. Long-Term Business Cycle and Credit Trend

Our reference sample is 1983–2006. Between these two dates, our main objective is to focus on sub-samples in order to discuss the interrelation that growth and credit have. Our first observation based on gross data provided by central institutions enables us to identify three sub-samples that constitute complete long-term cycles: 1983–91, 1991–2001, and 2001–3. For all of them, long-term growth is synchronized at 60% (on the period 1985/2, 2006/2) to the credit trend.[10] For the whole period the interrelation between the two variables is bidirectional. What could be said on each period taken separately? For the period 1983–91, the credit cycle is highly correlated to growth (98.16% as shown in Table 9.1). The causality mentioned for the whole sample becomes unidirectional and seems to be exerted from the business cycle to the credit trend (the favourable economic situation could then incite banks to grant more credit or inversely). For the two last sub-samples these correlations between growth and credit based on a Markov chains provide no significant evidence (see Table 9.1).

Table 9.1: Correlation between business cycle and credit trend

Long-term cycles over the period	Correlation with the credit cycle
1983–91	**0,9816**
1991–2001	0,17
2001–03	0,02

Figure 9.1: Credit cycle and long-term cycle Switzerland

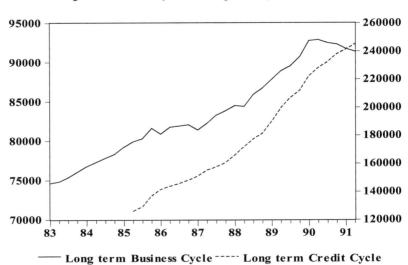

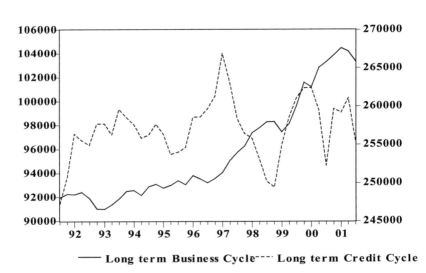

* The cycles presented here are growth cycles.

Figure 9.1 reinforces this argument. Weak correlations as regards the two trends on the period 1991–2003 could be explained by the fact that enterprises used other sources of liquidity to finance their investment project. Self-financing, credit claims among firms, or credit given by another European country could justify this result.

The specificity of the recent period gives us an interesting result. If 70% of the credit granted to enterprises between 2002 and 2006 has been in favour of small (or even very small) enterprises, the latter seem to have a particular trend (see Figure 9.2). Micro enterprises are very often the companies that need more banking credit to finance their investment project (they are also the privileged population to participate in the WIR network). For the period 2002–4, a significant decrease can be noticed as regards classical banking credit offer to these institutions. This inflexion is concomitant to a recession phase of the long term conjuncture.[11] The small enterprises (also good candidates for the WIR network) have not faced the same evolution: credit offer is remained stable over the same period.

Figure 9.2: Credit granted to enterprises, 2002–6

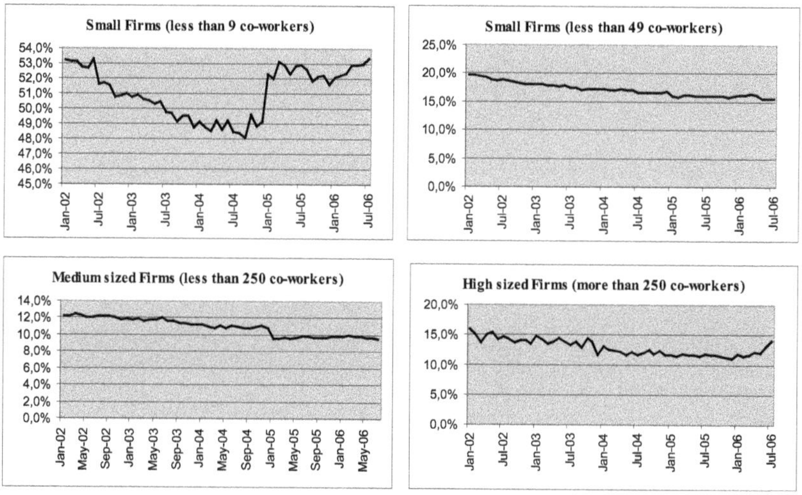

3.2. Inflation and Interest Rate Structure Curve

Other factors that can reinforce our argument could be interest rate (long term and short term), synchronized unemployment, inflation rate (expressed in annual sliding factor). These variables exhibit a mitigated correlation with the long term growth cycle (see Table 9.2).

Table 9.2: Correlations among GDP, inflation and interest rate structure curve

Variable :	Correlation with long term cycle:
Short-term interest rate	56.53%
Long-term interest rate	54.33%
Unemployment rate	19.48%
Annual sliding inflation rate	−50.37%

In particular, inflation seems to be negatively correlated to the long-term growth rate. J. M. Keynes qualifies this situation as a Gibson paradox (observed during the Gold Standard period in England between 1717 and 1931). This empirical evidence is verified at 83% in the Swiss case for the period 1980–2006.[12]

If the presence of this paradox lends more complexity to the interpretation of the correlation existing between credit and business cycles (largely based on the Austrian theory), factors other than inflation reinforce this position.

The yield structure curve is negatively correlated to the long term growth cycle (at 63%).[13] Moreover, Granger's unidirectional causality test is relevant (with a lag of one quarter). This seems to prove that the interest rate evolution (long- and short-term) determines the orientation of business activity on the period under consideration (1980–2006). The estimated regression presented in table 9.3 confirms this hypothesis.

The tested regression is following:

$$y_t = a y_{t-1} + b Yield_{r-1} + cst \ (1)$$

Where y_t corresponds to the long-term growth cycle (10 years), Yield is the structure curve defined by

$$Yield_t \ \frac{1 + tc_t}{1 + tl_t}$$

(where 'tc' is short-term interest and 'tl' the long term interest rate)

Table 9.3: Yield structure curve and long term cycle (1980–2006)

Estimating Method used :	A	b	c	R^2	DW
OLS	0.99	−406.75	Not significant	0.9968	1.49
	139.36 (0.00)	−1.67 (0.09)			
GMM	0.98	−1136.26	Not significant	0.9962	1.35
	122.75 (0.00)	−3.70 (0.00)			

For Keeler, the yield curve is a relevant indicator of economic fluctuations. He has applied this methodology to the American context during the period 1950–91. The results he has obtained (causality test of Granger, correlation tests and Phillips-Perron tests), confirm the Austrian hypothesis according to which monetary shocks (constituting the basis of business cycles) induce distortions in relative price structures. Our results seem to confirm this hypothesis in the Swiss case.

Having thus clearly identified the business cycles existing over the period (1980–2006), the next step of our argument will be to discuss the counter-cyclical nature of alternative/ethical banks in the Swiss context.

4. Are Ethical Banks Counter-Cyclical?

The WIR system offers to enterprises the opportunity of acceding to credit for financing their project. The fact of being able to issue a complementary currency constitutes for this institution a way of promoting not only the creation of small enterprises, especially in the building sector, but also a way of ensuring the economic growth of more mature companies. The essential question which could be asked in this regard is: Does this alternative solution to traditional financing sources provide a real advantage for enterprises whose access to conventional credit is quite difficult? Is the evolution of this credit connected with GDP fluctuations? If not, could the argument of support to SME during recession periods be defended? And in which measures could this hypothesis be confirmed?

To build up our argument, a comparison among three ethical Swiss banking institutions will be provided (the WIR Bank, the Freie GemeinschaftsBank, and the Alternative Bank ABS). Two steps can be distinguished to describe our methodology. In a first time, we shall try to connect the classical evolution of the GDP to the credit offer (in alternative money for the WIR, in the traditional liquidity for the two other institutions). In a second stage, we shall correlate the classical cycle of the GDP to the mortgage credit (in alternative and traditional money). The basic hypothesis is then the following: if the traditional credit offer is strongly pro-cyclical, our aim is to demonstrate that the credit offer in alternative money could be, in certain cases, counter-cyclical. A global vision for the whole system is also given in order to correlate the evolution of the credit offer to the trend of the GDP. The graphs below intend to provide a first glance of this fact that have to be deepened through empirical analysis.

Figure 9.3: ABS credits and GDP

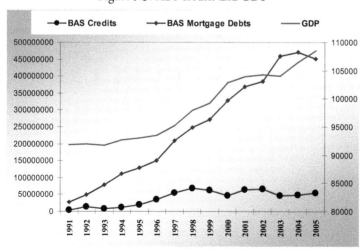

Figure 9.4: Gemeinschaftsbank credits and GDP

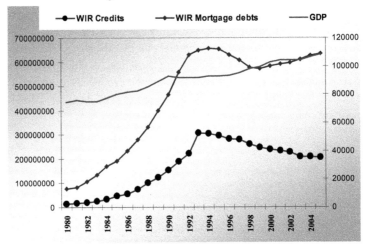

Figure 9.5: WIR credits and GDP

Figure 9.6: Credit and mortgage debts offered by all 'traditional' banks of Switzerland

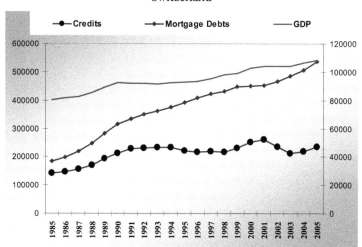

The credit in alternative money proposed by the WIR Bank is heterogeneous and seems not to follow the same evolution of the GDP.[14] A similar argument can be defended for the Freie Gemeinschaftbank, but to a lesser extent. This point is definitively false for the Alternative Bank ABS. This evidence is confirmed by the following table.

Table 9.4: Correlation Credit – GDP

Correlations	ABS Credit	GDP
ABS Credit		0.7467
WIR Credit	−0.2533	−0.5797
Gemeinschaftsbank Credit	0.06096	−0.0038

As shown in this table, the alternative credit offer fluctuates differently from the classical credit. Its evolution is clearly counter-cyclical because the coefficient obtained by the regression is negative.[15] On the contrary, the classical credit of the ABS Bank is strongly pro-cyclical with a coefficient of correlation of 75%

In addition, Table 9.5 proves that, despite a weak correlation 24% of credit offer for the whole banking system (122 institutions) over the period (1985–2005), this latter variable constitutes a significant explanatory parameter of the trend followed by the business cycle.

Table 9.5: Correlations between traditional credit offer and specific ones

Correlations with :	All traditional Banks	GDP
All 'Traditional' banks		0.24
WIR Credits	−0.10	−0.57

| Gemeinschaftsbank Credits | 0.18 | −0.003 |
| ABS Credits | 0.10 | 0.74 |

The use of a Granger's test for causality provides further evidence that the conjuncture does not motivate the banks, alternative or not, to distribute their credit.

Table 9.6: Classical business cycle – Credit cycle – Alternative credit business cycle

$$GDP_t = a.CBAS_t + b.CWIR_t + cCG_t + d\,(1)$$

	a	b	c	d	R^2	DW
OLS[16]	3.93	−2.56	−0.40	10.12	0.7247	0.80
	(0.00)[17]	(0.02)	(0.69)	(0.00)		
GMM[18]	2.011	−15.52	−0.48	41.82	**0.9443**	**1.75**
	(0.07)	(0.00)	(0.64)	(0.00)		

$$GDP_t = a.PIB_{t-1} + bCBAS_t + cCWIR_t + dCG_t + e\,(2)$$

	a	b	c	d	e	R^2	DW
OLS	9.66	1.71	0.40	0.28	−0.14	0.97	2.09
	(0.00)	(0.11)	(0.69)	(0.78)	(0.88)		
GMM	0.32	3.36	−3.82	0.23	2.93	**0.95**	**1.88**
	(0.75)	(0.00)	(0.00)	(0.81)	(0.01)		

The classical credit offer constitutes a relevant pro-cyclical indicator of the trend followed by the Swiss business cycle. Expansion phases coincide with a significant increase of the ABS Bank credit offers. The alternative credit offer of the WIR Bank is the only one to exhibit a clear counter-cyclical behaviour. The number of transactions tends to increase in recession phases and decrease otherwise.

Table 9.7: Classical business cycle – Credit cycle – Alternative credit business cycle

$$GDP_t = a.CBAS_t + b.CWIR_t + cCG_t + dCA_t + e\,(3)$$

	a	b	c	d	e	R^2	DW
OLS	3.83	−2.46	−0.55	0.94	4.99	0.74	0.81
	(0.00)	(0.03)	(0.58)	(0.36)	(0.00)		
GMM	−1.68	−16.88	0.52	8.90	41.52	**0.97**	**1.98**
	(0.10)	(0.00)	(0.61)	(0.00)	(0.00)		

$$GDP_t = a.GDP_{t-1} + bCBAS_t + cCWIR_t + dCG_t + e.CA_t + f\,(4)$$

	a	B	c	d	e	F	R^2	DW
OLS	–	–	–	–	–	–	–	–
GMM	4.09	1.22	−10.49	−1.48	6.05	9.01	**0.96**	**1.62**
	(0.00)	(0.26)	(0.00)	(0.18)	(0.00)	(0.00)		

The consideration of the whole sample improves and confirms the preceding results. As shown in Table 9.7 (regression 1 and 2, coefficient d and c significantly different from zero), the Durbin Watson and R^2 are better in the second case.

Up to now we have discussed the behaviour of the normal credit cycle for all institutions. Could these results be extended to mortgage credits? This would be our next point. In order to begin our discussion, we first present the results for the whole banking system.

Table 9.8: Correlations between traditional mortgage debts and specific ones

Correlations with :	Traditional Mortgage Debts	GDP
Traditional Mortgage Debts		0,95
WIR Mortgage Debts	−0,07	−0,21
Gemeinschaftsbank Mortgage Debts	0,9622	0,96
ABS Mortgage Debts	0,9694	0,97

Table 9.9: Classical business cycle – Mortgage debts cycle

$$GDP_t = a.MBAS_t + b.MWIR_t + cMG_t + dMA_t + e\,(5)$$

	A	B	c	d	e	R^2	DW
OLS	2.10	−0.73	0.18	0.44	8.34	0.95	0.97
	(0.06)	(0.47)	(0.85)	(0.66)	(0.00)		
GMM	−2.63	−8.26	13.97	0.34	19.06	0.96	1.009
	(0.02)	(0.00)	(0.00)	(0.73)	(0.00)		

$$GDP_t = a.GDP_{t-1} + bMBAS_t + cMWIR_t + MCG_t + eMA_t + f\,(6)$$

	A	B	c	d	e	f	R^2	DW
OLS	–	–	–	–	–	–	–	–
GMM	6.52	−3.02	−1.23	−1.05	1.30	5.47	0.95	1.49
	(0.00)	(0.01)	(0.25)	(0.32)	(0.23)	(0.00)		

The mortgage credit distributed by Swiss banking institutions is strongly correlated to the business activity fluctuations (95%, Table 9.9). It constitutes, therefore, a good indicator of the economic cycle (coefficient d, regression 6, Table 9.9). These results enable us to confirm the pro-cyclical character of the traditional mortgage credit as shown by figure 9.6.

What could be said for the three specific institutions? As shown in the table below, the mortgage credit of the Freie Gemeinschaftsbank are much correlated to the ones of the ABS Bank and the GDP (more than 95%).

Table 9.10: Correlation between mortgage credit and the GDP

Correlations	Mortgage Credit ABS	GDP
Mortgage credit ABS		0,9756
Mortgage credit WIR	−0,1579	−0,2170
Mortgage credit Gemeinschaftsbank	0,9760	0,9655

The WIR Bank maintains its specificity. Even if the correlations are lower, the coefficients are still negative. Hence for this type of credit also, the WIR could be considered as counter-cyclical.

Table 9.11: Classical business cycle – Mortgage debts cycle

$$GDP_t = a.MBAS_t + b.MWIR_t + cMG_t + d \ (7)$$

	a	b	c	D	R^2	DW
OLS	2.44	−0.60	0.53	9.74	**0.9570**	**0.96**
	(0.03)	(0.55)	(0.60)	(0.00)		
GMM	2.09	−0.72	1.00	2.82	0.87	1.67
	(0.06)	(0.48)	(0.34)	(0.02)		

$$GDP_t = a.GDP_{t-1} + bMBAS_t + cMWIR_t + MCG_t + e \ (8)$$

	a	b	c	D	e	R^2	DW
OLS	4.00	0.20	−0.06	1.63	1.72	0.98	1.88
	(0.00)	(0.84)	(0.95)	(0.13)	(0.11)		
GMM	5.32	−2.31	−0.79	2.39	−1.36	**0.94**	**2.13**
	(0.00)	(0.04)	(0.44)	(0.04)	(0.20)		

The regressions of this last table confirm that the mortgage credit of the ABS Bank and the Freie Gemeinschaftsbank is pro-cyclical. The mortgage credit of the WIR does not constitute however a relevant indicator of business activity fluctuations. The main coefficient (b in regression (7) and c in regression (8)) are significantly different from zero. Moreover, the credit strategy of the three institutions is very different. As mentioned in the preceding figures (Figures 9.3 and 9.4) the mortgage credit offers from the ABS Bank and the Freie Gemein-schaft Bank follows the same trend (smoothly increasing). For the WIR, the same observation cannot be made (see graph below). Between 1994 and 2000, the number of credit granted decreases in comparison to the other institutions. After direct verification with the WIR Bank, it does not come from a disaffection of the clientele, which would have implied a reduced efficiency of this alterna-tive credit. As the WIR functions as a normal banking institution, it reflects a reorientation of the global strategy and does not prevent us to conclude towards a counter-cyclical attitude.

Conclusion

All banks claim to be ethical but, when analysing their activities in depth, it is quite clear that their overall approach and concrete practice of ethical banking is quite different. In that sense, a first major distinction to be made is to set apart the strategies of 'traditional banks' and 'ethical banks'. For the former, the new ethical fashion is just an instrument for attracting new clients and thus maximiz-ing their benefits. In order to comply with this demand, their primary strategy is to issue a wide variety of SRI products. Unfortunately, recent studies show that

Figure 9.7: WIR credits and mortgage debts

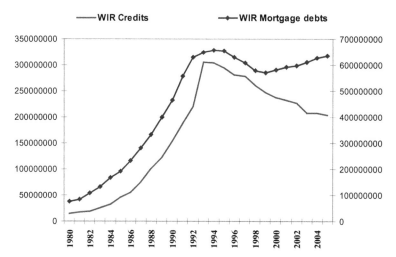

this is more a form of 'greenwashing' or ethical marketing than a real commitment.

Quite the reverse, for the so-called 'ethical banks' the sustainable approach is an integral part of their overall strategy. First and foremost, the maximization of profits is not their primary purpose, at least if only measured in financial terms. For them, the social and environmental added value should also be taken into consideration. In order to comply with this commitment, ethical banks tend to dismiss their participation on the speculative operations of the international financial market and to focus their banking activities in the savings collection and credit distribution. This allows them to support the local/regional economy and to privilege the social, ethical or environmental dimension of the projects they finance. The Alternative Bank ABS and the Freie Gemeinschaftsbank BCL are two outstanding examples of this kind of approach.

The problem is that, as the present study has shown, the impact of these two ethical banks on the Swiss economy does not differ substantially from that of traditional banks. So even if all ethical banks claim in their foundational charts to offer an alternative banking practice in order to change the dominant economic logic which is responsible for the worsening of ecological problems and social inequalities, the reality is that they are still far from being able to change the world. As the present paper has pointed out, the credit policy of the Freie Gemeinshaftsbank and the ABS Bank follow roughly the same trend as that the traditional banks. Up to now, ethical banks were thus an interesting instrument for 'moralizing' the economy, but an inefficient tool for a real change. The actual context of the subprime crisis could be a strong factor for change. The question is yet not only to moralize the system but also to find the basis for the founding of a new financial paradigm. In that respect, ethical banks could constitute a model for traditional banks as regards their functioning and their allocation of credit to enterprises.

In the context of the Swiss banking system, the present study has demonstrated that only the WIR Bank has a counter-cyclical behaviour as regards all types of credits. This fact illustrates that, beyond ethical banking, only the WIR Bank can be seen as a real alternative to the dominant financial practice. This is why the extreme originality of the WIR Bank deserves further consideration. Could it be an example to be implemented outside Switzerland? Can its capacity to comply with present-day regulation (Basel II) inspire the banking strategies of other ethical banks? Should Central Banks allow the competition of other financial institutions in issuing complementary currencies (Austrian theory)? These and other questions will be the object of further research in the future. One could expect that, in our fluctuating financial context, these interrogations could be the issues of the current debate to regulate and to propose alternative behaviour for banking institutions as regards their core business: the optimal allocation of liquidity to economic system.

CONCLUSION

The different arguments presented in the book cannot be disconnected from the context of global crisis. In the United States, the last decade was characterized by a combination of low interest rates and large inflows of foreign funds which helped to create easy credit conditions leading up to the actual situation. Speculation in real estate and financial innovations, which enable the banks to sell rights to the mortgage payments and related credit risk to investors, through a process called securization, have led to a considerable increase of systemic risk. As a consequence, the crisis caused panic in financial markets and encouraged investors to take their money out of risky mortgage bonds and put them into commodities. This trend contributes to the food price crisis causing problems in countries which rarely faced such difficulties, such as Egypt. This was not without influence on oil prices: financial speculators seeking returns removed their money from equities and mortgage bonds and reinvested their liquidity into raw materials. Europe was also touched by the financial crisis and price increase of food and raw materials. Europe's stock exchange places suffered declines in share prices for European corporations, and its banking system was affected by securitization process. However, the banking model privileged in our European countries seems to be more accurate to resist the actual turbulences. As a whole, the last decade has created the optimal conditions:

- first, to a general increasing level of risk both for financial markets and banking institutions at over the world
- second, for a transfer of financial problems to the real sphere at the origin of the actual recession
- third, for a complete re-consideration of our capitalism model: strong pressures are put on governments and regulators to give more importance to transparency and ethics in the business world.

What are the lessons of the last events? Despite the warnings of economists and central bankers about the dangers of our global finance over the last few years, investors and markets have benefited from the real estate bubble until the downturn point. Many financial institutions borrowed huge amounts of liquidity during 2004–7 and made investments in mortgage-backed securities, essentially betting on the continuous appreciation of home values and sustained mortgage payments. Of course these same institutions suffered enormous losses during the crisis period. Everything seems to point out that capitalism is no longer capable of controlling the financial sphere. Three main factors could explain this. First, the banks are not playing their role of lenders any longer. In the 90s, they gave an enormous amount of credit to enterprises. The present subprime crisis reflects the attitudes of these financial institutions. Borrowers cannot repay their credit on the basis of higher interest rates (comparing to their level at the moment of the negotiation contract). Their indebtedness has hence increased.

Second, contemporary finance is confronted with the phenomenon of securitization. Banks do not keep their credit in balance sheets but transform it into assets. With the advent of securitization, banks transfer credit risk to investors through mortgage-backed securities. Hence, the level of debt has increased tremendously for all actors: households, enterprises, states. This shows that the subprime crisis has led to collateral consequences such as a decrease in consumption for the population, a contraction of credit for the enterprises and more deficit for states willing to rescue their financial markets.

Last, but nor least, the third problem with our finance is the short-term vision. Investments amd the new approach of reporting for firms and financial institutions based on market value (IFRS) reinforce the situation. Instead of leading to more stability, this contributes to more fluctuations as regards the evaluation of corporation performance.

What were the reactions of our governments in front of such a situation? Considering these alarming events, what are the attitudes of central bankers? Two opposing reactions must be discussed. Let us first consider the case of the United States. The Fed, conscious of its portion of responsibility in the actual situation, intends to react. During recent years, with its accommodating monetary policy (partly led by Alan Greenspan), the Fed has contributed to the expansion of credit and to the emergence of the building speculative bubble. From 2000 to 2003 the Federal Reserve lowered the federal funds rate targeted from 6.5% to 1.0%. The increase of interest rates in 2004 has intensified the trend towards speculation and contributed to the crisis. The central bank now attempts to limit the effects of the crisis on the real sector, control inflation and re-establish confidence in financial markets.

On the other side, for the European Central Bank, the situation is less dramatic as regards interest rate fluctuations. The risk seems to be more a smoothed rate of growth, even a recession than a sudden increase of inflation. In a context where inflation never overshoots 3.2%, its monetary policy remains prudent.

As regards the rescue plan for the banking system, both Europe and the United States have adopted a common attitudes to inject liquidity in the economic system to prevent banking runs, to buy a large amount of non-performing loans to restore confidence in the financial sector. However, American authorities adopted a 'case by case' principle for solvency problems of banks. Lehmann Brothers declared bankruptcy on 15 September 2008, AIG was rescued by a government intervention according to the 'too big to fail' principle. Europeans have chosen, in the first stage, to give to support to all institutions and in the second stage, to examine the causes of the difficulties.

The last observation as regards the differences between Europe and the United States concerns banking structures. In response to the crisis, the last independent investment banks, Goldman Sachs and Morgan Stanley elected to become bank holding companies in order to gain access to additional liquidity. Such a change is not necessary in Europe as the main structures in the banking system are universal. An interesting common trend is worth mentioning: the banking system is likely to be more and more integrated in the near future.

Is there, anyway, any positive aspect in the actual situation? The strongest point to bear in mind is the will of our governments to coordinate their intervention. The United States, Europe and China intend to discuss the resolution to the current crisis together. What are the main issues of this debate? First the capitalist system has to redefine its main goals. Over the last year, it seems that financial questions were prevalently towards economic and social factors. The demand to introduce more ethic and social values in the business world corresponds to the preoccupations of individual economic agents, who are waiting for a real change in the global world. First, they want to substitute short-term attitudes with long-term perspectives. An alternative model to our capitalism is necessary and possible. If the concept of profit is not questionable, its use is a matter of discussion. More transparency and more protection as regards financial investments are required. Productive participation should replace speculative assets. Even banking institutions have to improve their strategy to become more sustainable. Some of them have already done so; they have excluded from their activities any participation on the financial markets. This book has tried to give some insight as regards these different elements.

One could wonder if this evolution corresponds to a circumstantial attitude which will disappear as soon as the economic trend becomes more stable. The multiplicity of collective initiative in the real and the financial world enables us to refute this argument. The emphasis put on local levels to create economic and social wealth (that emerged from associations or from alternative banks like in Switzerland) and the social responsibility given to the different actors present on the economic market stress the new orientation for our global world. Entrance into a sustainable strategy means renewing the definition of capitalism by introducing profitability criteria not strictly focused on financial performance but also on economic and social conditions, guaranteeing a better repartition of wealth for people.

At least, historical evidences prove that the markets and the individual actions do not prevent crises from occurring. The regulation, both on a national and international level should integrate mechanisms to prevent such situations and not reduce their role to the resolutions of crises a posteriori. To do so, they should identify problems in the evolutions of economies and sources of risks in the financing of productive projects. Growth, inflation, and credit trends and financial markets functioning should be considered to enable nations to really undertake a sustainable development strategy. This was precisely the goal of this book. Far from giving all the answers to the actual situation, it intends to lead to further research for improving our global world.

NOTES

1 Aglietta, Towards a New Model of Long-Term Finance

1. The conditions for the optimal portfolio to be time invariant have been disclosed by Merton and Samuelson as early as 1973.
2. Empirical evidence on mean-reverting processes in financial markets is reported in C. Campbell and L. M. Viceira 'The Term Structure of the Risk-Return Trade-Off', *Financial Analysts Journal*, 61 (2005).
3. 1, pp. 34–44.
4. An estimate of long-run return on US stock market, using co-integration technique has been made by M. Aglietta, L. Berrebi, A. Cohen-Benamran and J. J. Jacob, 'Marchés boursiers américains, cycles réels, cycles monétaires', *Groupama-AM, Expertises*, 4 (2005). Another econometric study on the US bond market by the first three authors of the former study is forthcoming.
5. See C. Campbell and L. M. Viceira, 'Strategic Asset Allocation' (Oxford: Oxford University Press, 2002).
6. Ibid.
7. O. Davanne and T. Pujol, 'Allocation d'actifs, variation de primes de risque et benchmarks', *Revue d'Economie Financière*, 79 (2005), pp. 95–110.
8. W. Sharpe and L. Tint 'Liabilities: a New Approach', *Journal of Portfolio Management* (Winter 1990), pp. 5–10.
9. D. Blake, A. Cairns and K. Dowd, 'Turning Pension Plans into Pension Planes: What Investment Strategy Designers of Defined Contribution Plans Can Learn from Commercial Aircraft Designers', Pensions Institute Discussion Paper, PI-0806 (April 2008).
10. The four databases are: Hedge Fund Research (HFR), Morgan Stanley Capital Indices (MSCI), TASS and CISDM
11. F. S. Lhabitant estimates that only 3% of the funds are accounted for simultaneously in the four databases, see 'Les indices de hedge funds doivent-ils être éligibles ou non aux fonds grand public?', *Les cahiers scientifiques*, 2 (September 2006).
12. N. Amenc, P. Malaise and L. Martinelli 'Benefits and Risks of Alternative Investment Strategies', *Journal of Asset Management*, 4:2 (2003) found that the indices computed on the long short equity strategy had discrepancies in performance as large as 22% according to the data providers.
13. 'Capital Funds: A Critical Analysis', Draft Report presented by Ieke Van Den Burg, and Nyrup Rasmussen, PSE, *European Parliament* (March 2007).

14. See 'HF Returns are Vastly Overstated', *The Times* online, accessed 28 February 2006.

2 Chane and Boyer, IFRS and the Need for Non-financial Information

1. IAS: International Accounting Standards ; IFRS: International Financial Reporting Standards.
2. B. Colmant and G. Hubner, 2005. 'L'impact économique des intérêts notionnels – Première partie: Références à la théorie financière classique'. *Forum Financier – Revue Bancaire et Financière – Bank en Financiewezen*, 69:8, p. 499.
3. IASB: International Accounting Standards Board.
4. J. L. Beffa, R. Boyer R. and J-P. Touffut, 'Les relations salariales en France: Etat, entreprises, marchés financiers', *Notes de la fondation Saint-Simon*, 107 (1999).
5. M. Aglietta, *Régulation et crises du capitalisme*, 2nd edn (Paris: Odile Jacob, 1997).
6. R. Boyer, 'Is a Financed-Led Growth Regime a Viable Alternative to fordism? A Preliminary Analysis', Economy and Society, 29:1 (2000), pp. 111–45.
7. A. Orlean, *Le pouvoir de la finance* (Paris: Odile Jacob, 1999).
8. Hampel Report, *The Final Report* (London: The Committee on Corporate Governance and Gee professional Publishing, 1999).
9. J. Bourdin, *Information Report n°367* (French Senate Delegation for Planification: 2003).
10. C. Hill and T. M. Jones, 'Stakeholder-Agency Theory', *Journal of Management Studies*, 29 (1992), pp. 134–54. R. A. G. Monks, *The New Global Investors: How Shareholders can Unlock Sustainable Prosperity Worldwide* (Oxford: Capstone Publishing, 2001).
11. J. Solomon, *Corporate Governance and Accountability* (New York: Wiley, 2007).
12. M. Blair, *Ownership and Control, Rethinking Corporate Governance for the Twenty First Century* (Massachusetts: Washington Brookings Institution, 1995). K. E. Montgomery, *Market Shift – the Role of Institutional Investors in Corporate Governance*.
13. J. Solomon, *Corporate Governance and Accountability* (London: Wiley, 2007).
14. N. Minow and R. A. G. Monks, *Corporate Governance*, 2nd edn (Oxford: Blackwell, 2001).
15. K. E. Montgomery, 'Survey of Institutional Shareholders', *Corporate Governance Review*, 5 (1992).
16. R. Bushman and A. J. Smith, 'Financial Accounting Information and Corporate Governance', *Journal of Accounting and Economics*, 32 (2001), pp. 237–333.
17. J. Hendry, P. Sanderson, R. Baker and J. Roberts, 'Responsible Ownership, Shareholder Value and the New Shareholder Activism', *ESRC, Centre for Business Research, University of Cambridge* (Working Paper, 2004), p. 297.
18. J. C. Coffee, 'The SEC and the Institutional Investor: an Half Time Report' (1994), p. 906.
19. R. Crete and S. Rousseau, 'De la passivité à l'activisme des investisseurs ', *MacGill Law Journal*, 42 (1997), pp. 864–959.
20. T. A. Thompson and G. F. Davis, 'The Politics of Corporate Control and the Future of Shareholders' Activism in the United States', *Corporate Governance*, 3:3 (1997).
21. G. P. Stapeldon, 'Exercise of Voting rights by Institutional Investors in the UK', *Corporate Governance: an International Review*, 3 (1995), pp. 144–55.
22. Montgomery, 'Survey of Institutional Shareholders'.

23. C. A. Mallin, 'The Voting Framework: a Comparative Study of Voting Behaviour of Institutional Investors in the US and in the UK', *Corporate Governance: an International Review*, 4:2 (April 1996), pp. 107–22.

24. Crete and Rousseau, 'De la passivité à l'activisme des investisseurs'.

25. W. M. O'Barr and J. M. Conley, *Fortune and Folly: the Wealth and Power of Institutional Investing* (Howewood, IL: Business One Irvin, 1992).

26. M. Amblard, *Comptabilité et conventions* (Paris:L'Harmattan, 2002).

27. IASC: International Accounting Standards Committee.

28. IASC, 1989, Framework for the preparation and presentation of financial statements.

29. Most of them were (former) Commonwealth countries e.g., India and New Zealand in 1974, South Africa in 1979...

30. International Organization of Securities Commissions. This organization groups the most important securities regulators in the world and consequently is able to set world standards for companies intending to raise funds.

31. FASB: Financial Accounting Standards Board.

32. Concerning fair-value application and accounting for hedges.

33. It should be noted that brokers are generally remunerated by the movements effected on titles

34. J-O. Charron, 'L'idéologie de la transparence dans l'audit ', *Comptabilité contrôle Audit*, 6 (2004), pp. 105–31.

35. Orlean, *Le pouvoir de la finance*.

36. W. Lazonick and M. O'Sullivan, *Corporate Governance and Sustainable Prosperity* (Basingstoke: Palgrave Macmillan, 2001).

37. The market efficiency hypothesis. According to the economical model used, it is considered either as strong or semi-strong. It is the cornerstone of fundamentalist evaluation, but its very existence is heavily disputed. See R. Cobbaut'Pour tenter de conclure: à la croisée des chemin', *Reflets et perspectives de la vie économique – L'efficience des marchés financiers*, 43:2 (2004).

38. These methods are described in depth by L. Batsch in *Finance et stratégie* (Paris: Economica, Collection gestion, série Politique générale, finance et marketing 1999), chapter on 'comparative and patrimonial methods '.

39. Y. Taddjedine, *Décisions financières, risques, politique prudentielle, mémoire mineur de DEA* (Paris: Université Paris X, 1996).

40. *Le modèle français de détention et de gestion du capital*, Lecture at the Ministre de l'Économie, des Finances et de l'Industrie, Les éditions de Bercy.

41. 'These remarks will prompt us to highlight the autoreferential dimension of financial markets. An autoreferential system is characterized by the fact that the norm of evaluation of its different constitutive elements is not an external one, as in a hetero-referential structure, but the very product of the interaction of basic strategies. As a consequence, this norm of evaluation is defined circularly. The average opinion is [...] then simultaneously the result of individual anticipations and the object on which these expectations are based. ' (Orléan, *Le pouvoir de la finance*).

42. S. Galanti, 'Les analystes financiers comme intermédiaires en information' (Thesis in economic science published 26 September 2006 at Paris X University, Nanterre).

43. F. Morin, Le modèle français de détention et de gestion du capital, Rapport de François Morin au Ministre de l'Économie, des Finances et de l'Industrie, Les éditions de Bercy 1999.

44. S. Mavrinac and T. Siesfeld, 'Measures that Matter: an Exploratory Investigation of Investor's Information Needs and Value Priorities ', *Actes du colloque 'Measuring Intangible Investment* ', OCDE (December 1998).

45. D. Greene, 'Measures that Matter, The Path of Intangible Value', Your Brand & the Bottom Line Conference, The Ernst & Young Center For Business Innovation, 25 February 1999.

46. M. Andrieu and P. Frotiée, 'Valeur actionnariale et immatériels', *Analyse financière*, 116 (1998).

47. T. Boyer, 'Corporate Governance et emploi: les attentes des marchés financiers ', *Gérer et Comprendre* (September 2002; rpt *Problèmes économiques*, 2789 (18 December 2002)).

48. G. Clinch and J. Magliolo, 'Market Perceptions of Reserve Disclosures Under SFAS No. 69', Accounting Review, 57:4 (October 1992), pp. 843–61; K. Lajili and D. Zéghal, 'A Content Analysis of Risk Management Disclosures in Canadian Annual Reports', *Canadian Journal of Administrative Sciences*, 22:2 (2005), pp. 124–42; S. Bryan, 'Incremental Information Content of Required Disclosures Contained in Management Discussion and Analysis', *Accounting Review*, 72:2 (April 1997), pp. 285–301; C. Cole, 'The Usefulness of MD&A Disclosures in the Retail Industry', Journal of Accounting, Auditing and Finance, pp. 361–88.

3 Turquey, The Lessons of Luxembourg's Financial Centre: Towards a Certification to Ethics for Financial Centres to Replace Current Assessments

1. See Press release, ABBL (27 July 2004).

2. Parliamentary question 1076 (10 May 2006), to Luc Frieden, Ministy of Justice, Treasury and Budget; answer dated 15 June 2006.

3. IMF/World Bank Group, Joint Annual Discussion, Press Release 8 (29 September 2002).

4. 'Luxembourg has in place a solid criminal legal framework and supervisory system to address the significant challenge of money laundering faced by this important international financial center' (Report dated 1 November 2004, p. 1).

5. For instance, see www.luxembourgforfinance.lu.

6. C. Maréchal, *Meurtres à l'ombre de la qualité* (Paris: INSEP, 2002), p. 49.

7. 'Virtue is in the middle'

8. See P. Majerus, *Les institutions du Grand-Duché de Luxembourg*, Service Information et Presse (S.I.P.) of the Luxembourg government, p. 120 and brochure 'About political institutions ' from the S.I.P. of the Luxembourg government (February 2004).

9. Source: GRECO, *Evaluation Report on Luxembourg* (11–15 June 2001), p. 12.

10. Merrill Lynch, *Capgemini et Vontobel Equity Research*. Quoted by *Le Temps* on (14 September 2005). According to the same study, the UK gathers 14% of offshore assets and Switzerland 26%.

11. STATEC, Portrait économique et social du Luxembourg, www.portrait.public.lu (March 2003).

12. This is true as well for other financial centres.

13. Paperjam TV (20 October 2008): available on www.paperjam.lu

14. A. Dumont, 'L'interférence entre le secret fiscal et la lutte contre le blanchiment de capitaux. Une étude comparative entre le Luxembourg, la Suisse et l'Angleterre'. *Annales du droit luxembourgeois*, 12 (2002) (Bruxelles, Bruylant, 2003), pp. 191–315.

15. Article 41 al. 2 of law of 5 April 1993.

16. See J. Kauffman, 'Le secret bancaire en droit luxembourgeois. Actualité et perspectives ', in: *Droit bancaire et financier au Grand-Duché de Luxembourg* (Bruxelles, 1994), p. 521. See, A. Steichen, *Le secret bancaire face aux autorités publiques, nationales et étrangères*, Conference dated 9 June 1995.

17. Kik Schneider, director at Fortis Banque Luxembourg (former BGL), is responsible for the network of agencies since 2006 (www.fortisbanque.lu).

18. Source: site of the DP (www.dp.lu).

19. M. Zwick, *Banking Secrecy and Money Laundering* (Paris: Promoculture, 2003): although the book is based on the normative framework former to the law of 12 November 2004, it preserves all its relevance in particular for its SWOT analysis of the financial centre.

20. See UN General Assembly Twentieth Special Session (8–10 June 1998).

21. French MPs who wrote a report about Luxembourg, which was circulated on 22 January 2002.

22. Article '10e anniversaire du Fonds national de lutte contre le trafic des stupéfiants' dated 30 January 2003, on the website of the Luxembourg government.

23. 'Luxembourg's contribution to UNDCP's work and programmes is a tangible sign of the commitment of the country in the field of drug control' stated UNDCP Executive Director Pino Arlacchi. 'I hope that other countries will follow Luxembourg's example' he added (See press release UNIS/NAR/682 dated 14 March 2000).

24. Chambre d'accusation, 23 Juillet 2002, 8G.80/2002 /rod ; Cour de cassation pénale suisse, 24 février 2006, 6S.293/2005 /fzc and 6S.298/2005 /fzc and Cour de cassation pénale suisse, arrêt du 5 mai 2006, 6S.160/2006 /rod.

25. *Practices and Recommendations Aimed at Reducing the Risk of Money Laundering and Terrorist Financing in the Luxembourg Fund Industry* (December 2006).

26. See OECD Working Group on Bribery, report of 28 May 2004 on Phase 2, pp. 14, 21 and 22.

27. AFP 7 March 2006.

28. Dirección General de la Policía y de la Guardia Civil, press release (3 November 2006).

29. *Le Soir*, 17 January 2007. Nine chargings were decided by the judge (*Le Soir*, 9 June 2008) including one for a Luxembourg-based company.

30. 'Redressement fiscal pour AOL France ', *Les Echos* (28 February 2007).

31. See for example the information published by Transparence Internationale France (www.transparence-france.org): 'Les commissions occultes de la DCN allaient toutes aux paradis ' (15 September 2008).

32. See GRECO, report on Luxembourg (14 May 2004), p. 13 and see OECD Working Group on Bribery, report of 28 May 2004 on Phase 2, pp. 5–6.

33. Opinion Chamber of Commerce/ABBL dated 19 September 2003 in parliamentary sources.

34. European directive 2001/97/CE (4 December 2001) on prevention of the use of the financial system for the purpose of money laundering.

35. Opinon of the prosecuting authorities dated 15 December 2003 in parliamentary sources.

36. N. Pons, *Cols blancs et mains sales* (Paris, Odile Jacob, 2006).

37. See www.bourse.lu.
38. To be accurate the word 'integrity' is quoted twice in the preamble.
39. Articles 61 and 62.
40. See, for example, the opinion of the ABBL on the draft law relating to corruption 5262 (17 March 2004).
41. Opinion dated 13 February 2007.
42. Judgement 447/2006 (26 January 2006), p. 29.
43. J-N. Schaus, Director General of the Commission de Surveillance du Secteur Financier, report 2004, p. 5.
44. This is the wording that was on the website
45. 'The financial centre of Luxembourg as a centre of competence', *Börsen-Zeitung* (19 April 2006).
46. See PwC brochures: 'Luxembourg a prime location for doing business' (2006) and ' Why Luxembourg: VAT advantages for commercial companies'.
47. See Annual Report 2005, pp. 19 and 22, and Annual Report 2006 p. 22.
48. Parliamentary sources are available on www.chd.lu.
49. Kik Schneider was appointed member of the Conseil d'Etat on April 8, 2000 (Source: www.ce.etat.lu).
50. The draft law wanted to increase the amount of fines, which would have put Luxembourg at the level of the UK. Regulary the FSA in the UK publishes the detail of fines. Press releases are detailed and state who was fined, what was the fine for, and the amount of the fine. The average of fines in the UK is £ 760,000.
51. *Financial Havens, Banking Secrecy and Money Laundering.* Issued as: Double issue 34 and 35 of the *Crime Prevention and Criminal Justice Newsletter*, Issue 8 of the UNDCP Technical Series.
52. Olivier Gallet underlines that financial directors are naturally exposed to the fraud because they often cumulate important functions in the companies and are in contact with the accountancy and the means of payment. he raises moreover the implication of the financial directors when a company do not respect accounting rules. See O. Gallet, *Halte aux fraudes* (Paris: Dunod), p. 36. This was verified in the scandals of past years, when financial directors were in question.
53. He took the company car to go on vacation with his family, abused signature power for expenses and used the company credit card for private expenses. See pp. 6 and 8 of the Exempt-appel, R°30422, 12 October 2006.
54. Judgement 1873/2005 (25 April 2005).
55. Judgement N° 2594/2004 (26 May 2004).
56. The court demonstrated a contradiction in the wording.
57. See p. 5 of the Exempt-appeal in Labour Law, R°30422 (12 October 2006).
58. See articles 4 and 5 of Law of 10 June 1999 on chartered accountants.
59. In spite of this public lack of competence, it was not dismissed by the Company, which made a simple corrigendum, thereby showing its deliberated choice and support for such a professional (Mémorial C, N° 104, 3 February 2003). The corrigendum is evidence that quality of 'chartered accountant' was not legitimate.
60. See Belgian doctrine in *IEC-Info*, N° 6/2002 – May 2002.
61. See Mémorial C, N°677, 9 September 1999, R. C. Luxembourg B 65.477.
62. See for example Mémorial C, N° 1146, Décembre 12, 2001.
63. He is a partner (See Mémorial C Ñ° 916, 18 December 1998) in the auditing firm he joined in 1983 (See press release dated 28 January 2003): he was chairman of the Insti-

tute of registered auditors (Institut des Réviseurs d'Entreprises) and was a partner of the auditing firm when the financial director was an employee.

64. *Paperjam*, interview (14 January 2002).
65. See Mémorial C, N° 771 (23 October 1998).
66. *Paperjam* (8 February 2002).
67. For example: *Roundtable on Entrepreneurship in Luxembourg* (15 February 2006).
68. The Big four and the Company are two of the six founding members of the Societal Movement Institute in Luxembourg (See *Paperjam*, December 2006 and February 2007).
69. Press release (15 February 2008).
70. Press release (28 May 2008).
71. See 'Irregularities (including Fraud) Checklist' on www.auditnet.org: questions 'Has there been a high turnover of management?' and 'Has the client unrealistically aggressive sales?'
72. Major leaders of the financial sector also regularly contribute.
73. See *Fundlook* (July–September 2004), p. 3.
74. The managing director who hired and knowingly supported the financial director and but also made by imprudence o inaccurate declarations easy to check for the tribunal was pleased as well with the 'clear and pragmatic laws and regulation' (See *Fundlook*, July – September 2004, p. 1).
75. See advertisements published in December 2006.
76. See Mémorial C, R.C.S. Luxembourg B 85.224, 781 (1 April 2008); see as well Memorial C, R. C. S. Luxembourg B 50.539 and R.C.S. Luxembourg B 74.360.
77. Greco Eval III Rep (2007) 6E, theme I (13 June 2008, published on 25 August 2008). The full quotation of p. 18, n. 10 to explain the small number of cases coming before the courts is: 'Limited police access in law and/or practice to administrative and financial information at the preliminary inquiries stage, tax data base scattered over several local authorities, lack of staff in the investigating authorities, who concentrate on important and priority cases, no "whistle blowing" arrangements and in some cases reporting hindered by professional confidentiality, excessively strict rules on the burden of proof in criminal law, room for improvement in relations between the prosecution service and investigating judges, and so on. There are currently proposals for improving cooperation between the police and the administrative authorities, facilitating police access to on-line information and resolving the problem of relations between the prosecution service and investigating judges. A prosecutor has stated that even though banking confidentiality has been relaxed in recent years, the non-banking financial sector and financial institutions such as trust funds were still very reluctant to impart information. Certain lawyers stressed the importance of relationships and networks of persons in Luxembourg society, the difficulties faced by the police in dealing with complex economic and financial crime, particularly because of lack of legal and other resources, and the ease with which companies can be established in Luxembourg.'
78. International Narcotics Control Strategy Report (March 2008).
79. The managing director was among the six candidates for the Entrepreneur of the Year (EOY) competition that was organized by Ernst & Young following a strict selection process (See press release dated 29 September 2006). He did not win.
80. GRECO, report on Luxembourg, 14 May 2004, p. 13.
81. See *L'essentiel*, 27 February 2008.
82. Paragraph 54, p. 17 of the FATF Annual Report 2006–7.

83. We are exactly in the situation of a judge receiving with public satisfaction a 'generous grant' from a litigant he/she is about to judge or a bank receiving with public satisfaction a 'generous grant' from a client it is about to assess in the framework of AML procedures. The list of examples is not exhaustive. By accepting, the judge or the bank or the auditor would definitely compromise their *ability to address issues freely, thoroughly and objectively* (Transparancy International words). Additionally, in many companies such 'generous grants' to employees are a reason for dismissal. Anyway such grants are not a financing of the FATF: as explained paragraph 55 '*Funding for the FATF is provided by its members on an annual basis and in accordance with the scale of contribution to the OECD. The cost of the secretariat and other services is met by the FATF budget, using the OECD as the channel for these operations. This scale is based on a formula related to the size of the country's economy. Non-OECD members' contributions are calculated using the same scale of OECD members. The two member organizations also make contributions to the FATF budget*'.

84. See www.luxembourgforfinance.lu.

4 Levratto, Is Economic Efficiency a Meaningful Device with which to Assess Insolvency Laws?

1. P. Bravard-Veyrieres, *Manuel de Droit Commercial*, 2nd edn (Paris: Joubert, Libraire-Editeur, 1840).
2. Ibid.
3. R. La Porta, F. Lopez-de-Silanes, A. Shleifer and R. W. Vishny 'Law and Finance', *Journal of Political Economy* 106:6 (1998), pp. 1113–55.
4. E. L. Glaeser and A. Shleifer, 'Legal Origins', *Quarterly Journal of Economics*, 117:4, pp. 1193–229.
5. S. Djankov, C. McLiesh and A. Shleifer, *Private Credit in 129 Countries* (NBER Working Paper, W11078, 2005).
6. *Doing Business: Understanding Regulation. A Copublication of the World Bank, the International Finance Corporation, and Oxford University Press* Washington DC: The World Bank, 2004), p. 72.
7. F. Cabrillo, and B. W. F. Depoorter 'Bankruptcy Proceedings', in B. Bouckaert, and G. De Geest (eds), *Encyclopedia of Law and Economics, Volume V: The Economics of Crime and Litigation* (Cheltenham: Edward Elgar, 1999), p. 261.
8. T. Kirat, 'Introduction Générale', in T. Kirat (ed), *Les mondes du droit de la responsabilité: regards sur le droit en action* (Paris: LGDJ, 2003).
9. We would recall that for Commons, economics is 'a practical science of the coordination of individual and collective actions based on rules, which integrates conflicts of interest and power relationships between social groups, for the rules are largely produced within the scope of settling disputes'. See L. Bazzoli, and T. Kirat, 'À Propos du Réalisme en Economie des Institutions et ses Implications sur l'Analyse des Fondements Juridiques des Transactions Economiques: Commons versus Williamson', *Economie et Sociétés: Institutions et Évolution*, 3 (2003), pp. 31–56.
10. P-C. Hautcoeur and N. Levratto, *Les Défaillances d'Entreprises au XIXème Siècle en France: du Droit à la Pratique* (Working Paper, Paris School of Economics, 2006).

11. Here we find implicitly imposed Locke's idea according to which contractual freedom is a natural human right, an institution of natural law which exists independently of the consent or sanction of society and therefore of the legal system.

12. S. Djankov, R. La Porta, F. Lopez-de-Silanes, and A. Shleifer, 'Courts', *Quarterly Journal of Economics* 118:3 (2003), p. 455.

13. C. L. Backer, 'Toiletter notre Droit', *La Lettre de Presaje*, 14 (2006), p. 2.

14. On this topic, see S. A. Davydenko and J. R. Franks, *Do Bankruptcy Codes Matter? A Study of Defaults in France, Germany and the UK* (Working Paper, London Business School, 2005).

15. S. L. Bufford, 'What's Right about Bankruptcy and Wrong about its Critics', *Washington University Law Quarterly*, 72 (1994), pp. 829–48.

16. M. M. Siems, 'Numerical Comparative Law: Do We Need Statistical Evidence in Order to Reduce Complexity', *Cardozo Journal of International and Comparative Law*, 13 (2005), pp. 521–40.

17. Ibid, p. 529.

18. P. R. Milgrom, D. C. North and B.R. Weingast, 'The Role of Institutions in the. Revival of Trade', *Economics and Politics*, 2:1 (1990), pp. 1–23.

19. This is indeed the case of R. Saleilles, 'Préface', in F. Gény (ed.), *Méthode d'Interprétation et Sources en Droit Privé Positif-Essai Critique* (Paris: Bibliothèque de jurisprudence civile contemporaine, 1899).

20. Saleilles, 'Préface', in Gény (ed.) *Méthode d'Interprétation*, p. v.

21. *Doing Business: Creating Jobs. A Copublication of the World Bank and the International Finance Corporation. Washington DC* (The World Bank, 2006). p. 67.

22. See P.-C. Hautcoeur and N. Levratto 'Faillite', in A. Stanziani (ed.), *Dictionnaire du Droit/Economie* (Paris: LGDJ, 2007), for a presentation of these two tendencies in French law in the nineteenth century.

23. R. Tartarin, 'La Théorie des Droits de Propriété: vers un Historicisme Libéral?', in W. Andreff, A. Cot, R. Frydman, L. Gillard, F. Michon, R. Tartarin (eds), *L'économie-Fiction* (Paris: François Maspéro, 1982).

24. See the OECD reports on this issue, particularly the Bologna charter.

25. Assemblée Nationale, *Compte Rendu n° 21 de la Commission des Lois Constitutionnelles de la Législation et de l'Administration Générale de la République* (Tuesday 2 February 2005, meeting at 1:30).

26. D. Kaufmann, *Rethinking Governance: Empirical Lessons Challenge Orthodoxy* (Working Paper, World Bank, 2003), p. 20 (http://ssrn.com/abstract=386904).

27. See Davydenko and Franks, *Do Bankruptcy Codes Matter?* and S. Djankov, O. Hart, C. McLiesh and A. Shleifer, *Debt Enforcement around the World* (NBER Working Paper, 12807, 2006).

28. B. Milan and C. Poutet. 'L'activité des Juridictions Commerciales en 2005' (Paris: Infostat justice, 2006), p. 91.

29. An example of the application of this method to bankruptcies is proposed by Hautcoeur and. Levratto, 'Les Défaillances d'Entreprises au XIXème Siècle'.

30. R. Gertner and D. Scharfstein, 'A Theory of Workouts and the Effects of Reorganization Law', *Journal of Finance*, 46:4 (1991), pp. 1189–22.

31. This law introduced a negotiation process within the framework of an amicable settlement procedure between creditors and debtors. It yielded mediocre results due to the delayed activation of the provision, the opportunistic behaviour of some company directors aimed at obtaining sacrifices on the part of the creditors to increase their profits and

the free-riding attitude of some creditors who refused to reduce their demands, counting on company recovery resulting from payment deferments granted by others.

32. This law, oriented towards continuing company activity, actually improved the situation of secured creditors, while seeking to encourage the commencement of an amicable settlement and increase the weight of creditors in negotiations.

33. This law provides for three different procedures of amicable company management prior to actual cessation of payments: an ad hoc mandate that does not require validation by a judge in which creditors take part voluntarily in possible waivers of debt, an amicable settlement that allows confidential renegotiation of the debt with the creditors with approval of the agreement by a judge and a protection procedure that authorizes the managing director to request that its liabilities be frozen in order to renegotiate the debt.

34. A. Shleifer and S. W. Vishny (1992), 'Liquidation Values and Debt Capacity: a Market Equilibrium Approach', *Journal of Finance*, 57:4, pp. 1343–66.

35. In a case of financial distress, the managing director may be tempted to reduce expenditures and investment or, on the contrary, to take more risks and over-invest. A strict bankruptcy law might pressure management to adopt the first approach, whereas a mild one should encourage taking more risks to try and save the business. See A. C. Eberhart and L. W. Senbet, 'Absolute Priority Rule Violations and Risk Incentives for Financially Distressed Firms', *Financial Management*, 22:3 (1993), pp. 101–6.

36. See R. Blazy, *La Faillite: Eléments d'Analyse Economique* (Paris: Economica, 2000), p. 53 and *passim*.

37. P. Aghion, O. Hart and J. Moore, 'The Economics of Bankruptcy Reform', *Journal of Law, Economics and Organization*, 8:3 (1992), 523–46.

38. The model foresees the problems of company valuation raised by this procedure and solves them through the Bebchuk procedure (1988) which, by organizing a system of attribution of property rights through successive, orderly share buyouts by creditors, guarantees the transfer of control under good conditions. Obviously, this manner of proceeding is quite difficult to put into practice. See L. Bebchuck, 'A New Approach to Corporate Reorganization', *Harvard Law Review*, 101 (1988), pp. 775–804.

39. The term 'floating charge' designates a special pledge of the whole estate of the debtor business. The value of the estate may change over time (e.g. the inventory) and the company may freely dispose of this property with the consent of the protected creditor until the moment when the claim 'crystallizes'. This 'crystallization' may take place, for example, when an administrative receiver is appointed, at the time of company liquidation, or in the cases provided for in the contract that created the claim.

40. C. Pochet, 'Traitement Légal de la Défaillance et Gouvernance: une Comparaison Internationale', *Revue Internationale de Droit Economique*, 4 (2001), pp. 465–88.

41. M. A. Armstrong and A. Cerfontaine, 'Echecs Economiques et Dérive du Pragmatisme Juridique: l'Expérience Anglaise du Droit de la Faillite', *Droit et Société*, 46 (2000), 547–48, p. 563.

42. Ibid., p. 564.

43. M. J. White, 'The Cost of Corporate Bankruptcy: a U.S.-European Comparison', in J. S. Bhandari (ed.), *Bankruptcy: Economic and Legal Perspectives* (Cambridge: Cambridge University Press, 1994).

44. It is distinct from a Type I error which consists in restructuring the debt or the assets of an inefficient company.

45. E. Berkovitch, R. Israel and J. F. Zender, *The Design of Bankruptcy Law: A Case for Management Bias in Bankruptcy* (Working Paper, University of Utah, 1994).
46. It is almost the case for Davydenko and Franks, *Do Bankruptcy Codes Matter?*, Pochet, 'Traitement Légal de la Défaillance et Gouvernance'; J. W. Bowers, 'Security Interests, Creditors' Priorities and Bankruptcy', in B. Bouckaert and G. De Geest (eds), *Encyclopedia of Law and Economics, Volume II: Civil Law and Economics* (Cheltenham: Edward Elgar, 2000); G. Recasens, 'Faut-il Adopter un Système Pro-Créanciers de Défaillances ? Une Revue de la Littérature', *Finance, Contrôle, Stratégie*, 6:1 (2003), pp. 119–53.
47. Chapter 11 procedure may be compared to the French receivership system. In most cases, the company itself decides to file for bankruptcy. This procedure results in suspending any collection effort on the part of unpaid creditors (this is the Automatic Stay which corresponds in France to temporary suspension of individual proceedings). Failure to comply with the suspension of proceedings (e.g. lawsuits as well as letters and telephone calls to the debtor) may incur the payment of damages on the part of the creditor. The period of protection offered to the debtor is used to negotiate and draw up a restructuring plan that must be approved by the majority of creditors and the judge.
48. It provides for, in particular:
    a. The substitution of the conciliation procedure for the amicable procedure. In cases of financial distress, it will allow entrepreneurs to engage in amicable renegotiation of their debt with the main creditors as confidentially as possible without suspending the proceedings. The firm must give evidence of its legal, economic or financial problem, either actual or foreseeable, without being in a state of cessation of payment. The agreement may be approved by the commercial court. The managing director retains control of its management.
    b. The creation of a rehabilitation procedure. This is a system of negotiation enabling the suspension of proceedings prior to cessation of payment. The aim is to arrive at a rescue plan negotiated with the creditors and approved by a qualified majority. This is a prevention procedure and not a reorganization procedure. The managing director remains in charge of the company and is merely assisted by an administrator for the negotiations. He or she may set up two committees: one bringing together banking institutions and the other, suppliers. The managing director presents them with a draft of the plan and must obtain a majority vote in favour of it (two-thirds of the votes and one-half of voters). The court takes official note of the agreement.
    c. A period of forty-five days, instead of the former fifteen-day period, as of the date of cessation of payments, to request the commencement of reorganization or liquidation proceedings.
    d. The reorganization or liquidation proceedings may henceforth be commenced after the cessation of professional activity if it is the source of all or part of the debts.
49. They are proposed by Alary and Gollier, Chopard and Langlais and Recasens. D. Alary and C. Gollier, 'Debt Contract, Strategic Default and Optimal Penalties with Judgment Errors', *Annals of Economics and Finance*, 5 (2004), pp. 357–72; B. Chopard, and E. Langlais, 'Répudiation Opportuniste de la Dette, Risque Juridique et Risque Comptable'. Unpublished manuscript. EconomiX-University of Paris 10 Nanterre, 2007); G. Recasens, 'Aléa Moral, Financement par Dette Bancaire et Clémence de la Loi sur les Défaillances d'Entreprises', *Finance*, 22:1 (2001), pp. 64–86.

50. R. Blazy and B. Chopard, 'Bankruptcy Law: a Mechanism of Governance for Financially Distressed Firms' (first Workshop on Bankruptcy EconomiX-University of Paris 10 Nanterre, 2006).
51. Davydenko and Franks, *Do Bankruptcy Codes Matter?*, Djankov et al., *Private Credit in 129 Countries*.
52. Ibid., p. 5.
53. J. Franks and O. Sussman, 'Financial Distress and Bank Restructuring of Small to Medium Size UK Companies', *Review of Finance*, 9:1 (2005), pp. 65–96.
54. Davydenko and Franks, *Do Bankruptcy Codes Matter?*, pp. 23–4.
55. T. Beck, A. Demirguc-Kunt and R. Levine, *Law and Finance: Why Does Legal Origin Matter?* (Working Paper 9379. National Bureau of Economic Research, Inc, 2002).
56. The rules drawn up by the courts do not necessarily constitute Common Law rules in the strict sense, because only the rules accepted and applied by the Royal Courts of Westminster establish Common Law. In the fifteenth century, however, the Court of Chancery enriched English law with rules of equity. Dual jurisdiction was abolished in England by the Judicature Acts of 1873–5 when the new High Court of Justice was created. While all courts can apply both the rules of Common law and of equity, equitable remedies (e.g. the right of injunction) are still opposed to Common law remedies (e.g. the right to damages) today. In the event of a conflict, the rules of equity prevail.
57. Siems, *Law Legal Origins, Reconciling Law & Finance and Comparative* (Working Paper, University of Cambridge, 2006).
58. P. P. Lele and M. M. Siems, *Shareholder Protection: a Leximetric Approach* (Working Paper 2006).
59. Djankov et al., in *Private Credit in 129 Countries*, distinguish the countries of English, German, Nordic and socialist legal origin.
60. Siems gives highly representative examples of debatable groupings. Siems, *Law Legal Origins*, pp. 9 and 10.
61. Ibid, p. 22.
62. J-G. Locré, *La Législation Civile et Commerciale de la France: tome 19, Code de commerce* (Paris: Treuttel et Würtz, 1827–32).
63. J-C. Colfavru, Le Droit Commercial Comparé de la France et de l'Angleterre (Paris: Imprimerie et Librairie Générale de Jurisprudence, 1863), p. iv and P. Santella, *Le Droit des Faillites d'un Point de Vue Historique. Communication, Faculté de Droit de l'Université catholique de Louvain et Centre Jean Renauld. Louvain-la-Neuve* (2002).
64. J. Sgard, *The Liberalization of Bankruptcy Law in Europe* (Working paper, CEPII, 2005).
65. On this subject, one may consult the special 2003 issue of the Revue Juridique Thémis devoted to the harmonization of bankruptcy law with Quebec civil law.
66. To prevent the initiation of a different insolvency procedure in each Member State of the European Union where a company in a group is represented, the EU regulation of 29 May 2000 introduced a single procedure for reorganization or liquidation effective in all Member States. The legislation of the Member State in which the company has its main interests is to be applied, even if the company's head office is not located in that country. The 'Isa Daisytek' decree of the Versailles Court of Appeals, dated 4 September 2003, applied the provisions of this Regulation in France for the first time.
67. In eighteenth-century France, the Third Estate contested the immunity to personal bankruptcy enjoyed by the nobles and the clergy, which spared them imprisonment for debt. In 1789, traders and financiers demanded tighter rules, which were granted for a

while by the Commercial Code of 1807, in a society that had become bourgeois and individualist, where the estates had been abolished (Hilaire, 1986).

68. For the French case, see L. Marco, *La Montée des Faillites en France, 19e–20e siècles* (Paris: L'Harmattanm, 1992). About Italy and England, refer to P. Di Martino, 'Approaching Disaster, a Comparison between Personal Bankruptcy Legislation in Italy and England, 1880–1930', *Business History*, 45:1 (2005), pp. 23–43.

69. 'Faillite' article, in Y. Guyot and A. Raffalovitch, *Dictionnaire du Commerce, de l'Industrie et de la Banque, Tome II* (Paris: Guillaumin et Cie, 1901).

70. Ibid, '*Déconfiture*' article.

71. E. Dalloz and C. Vergé, *Les Codes Annotés. Code de Commerce Annoté et Expliqué d'après la Jurisprudence et la Doctrine* (Paris: Bureau de la Jurisprudence générale, 1877), pp. 547–9.

72. L. Tripier, *Les Codes Français Collationnés sur les Editions Officielles* (Paris: Librairie de Jurisprudence de Cotillon, 1902), pp. 640–1.

73. See Sgard, *The Liberalization of Bankruptcy Law in Europe*.

74. H-F. Mascret, *Dictionnaire des Faillites, 1848–1913* (Paris: Chez l'auteur, 1863), p. xxiii.

75. M. A. F. Lainné, *Commentaire Analytique de la Loi du 8 Juin 1838 sur les Faillites et Banqueroutes* (Corbeil: Imprimerie de Crété, 1839).

76. Bravard-Veyrieres, *Manuel de Droit Commercial*, p. 617.

77. D. Desurvire, *Histoire de la Banqueroute et Faillite Contemporaine* (Paris: L'Harmattan, 1992), p. 39.

78. Colfavru, *Le Droit Commercial Comparé de la France*, p. 433.

79. Filing for bankruptcy marks the entry into the procedural order: the bankruptcy is made public and all management actions – buying, paying, hiring, investing and repaying – are subject to restrictions and close supervision. From a formal standpoint, it is no longer the same agent. But the judges' capacity to set the date of the beginning of cessation of payments also confers upon decisions prior to the formal commencement of the procedure an eminently suspect character: they can also be cancelled retrospectively.

80. See T. H. Jackson, *The Logic and Limits of Bankruptcy Law* (Cambridge, MA: Harvard University Press, 1986).

81. On this topic, see also K. Ayotte, 'Bankruptcy and Entrepreneurship: The Value of a Fresh Start', *Journal of Law, Economics, and Organization*, 23:1 (2007), pp. 161–85.

82. F. Goré, 'The Administrative Autonomy of Creditors and French Legislation on Bankruptcy', *American Journal of Comparative Law*, 17:1 (1969), pp. 5–23.

83. Traditionally, later creditors known as 'article 40 creditors' (art. L. 631-32 of the Commercial Code) benefited from favourable treatment in so far as their so-called 'later' claims had to be paid at due date by the debtors, as opposed to 'earlier' claims that were frozen until the end of the observation period and then settled, if possible, either within the scope of a continuation plan or a sale plan.

84. T. Noël, 'La Pratique du Droit de la Faillite dans le Ressort de la Cour d'Appel de Rennes au XIXe siècle – Les Prémices du Droit Economique' (Doctoral Thesis University of Rennes I, 2003).

85. These trends were also perceptible abroad. Starting in the nineteenth century, bankruptcy law in the United States gradually detached itself from English legislation. Throughout the century, economic crises encouraged the adoption of laws favourable to debtors, which allowed the sale of residual property to creditors and sometimes recognized the right to be freed from unpaid debts without the consent of the creditors, which were

repealed several years later under pressure from creditors. At the same time, the practice of amicable agreements between creditors and debtors became more widespread, even though it was impeded by the power of any creditor to denounce these agreements by requesting the commencement of bankruptcy proceedings. In Italy, the same demands were expressed by the Prodi law and several other extraordinary laws introduced between the end of the 1960s and the beginning of the 1980s to limit the social effects of industrial crises.

86. The use of out-of-court modes of payment by companies in financial distress guaranteeing wide latitude for negotiation with stakeholders appeared as early as the Ancien Régime and was quickly denounced due to the high costs they engendered. G. Michel, 'Faillites', in L. Say and J. Chailley (eds), *Nouveau Dictionnaire d'Economie Politique* (A-H. Paris: Guillaumin et Cie 1900), vol. 1; H. de Balzac, *Code des gens honnêtes ou L'art de ne pas être dupe des fripons* (Paris: Editions du Trait, 1948); P. Bertholet, *Etudes et Notaires Parisiens en 1803, au Moment de la Loi du 25 Ventôse An XI* (Paris: Edition de l'Association des Notaires du Châtelet, 2004).

87. B. Soinne, *Traité des Procédures Collectives* (Paris: LGDJ, 1995).

5 Parnaudeau, Financialization of European Economies

1. S. Avouyi-Dovi, R. Kierzenkowski and C. Lubochinsky, 'Cycles réels et cycles du crédit: Convergence ou divergence ?', *Revue Economique*, 57:4 (2006), pp. 851–80.

2. H. P. Minsky, 'A Theory of Systemic Fragility', in E. Altman and A. Samaets, *Financial Crisis-Institutions and markets in a Fragil Environment* (New York: Wiley, 1977); H. P. Misky, *Can it Happen Again?: Essays on Instability and Finance* (Armonk, NY: M.E. Sharpe, 1982); H. P. Minsky, *Stabilizing an Unstable Economy* (New Haven, CT and London: Yale University Press, 1986).

3. C. Aubin, J. P. Berdot and J. Leonard, 'Banques Centrales, liquidité et prix d'actifs: une mise en perspective théorique', *Economies et Sociétés, Série Monnaie*, 5 (2006).

4. The bubble 'is not the result of investor behaviour, victims of irrational exuberance or excessive confidence in the ability of their assets to generate future profit'.

5. M. Parnaudeau, 'Natural Interest Rate and European Business Cycles: An Austrian Approach', *Economie Appliquee*, 40:2 (June 2007), pp. 5–28.

6. This analysis is partially consistent with the work of J. H. de Soto, according to whom the reversal is first announced by a reduction of sectoral profit rates. Banks respond to this by increasing their nominal interest rates, thus plunging the economy into crisis. See J. H. De Soto, *Money, Bank Credit and Economic Cycles* (Auburn: Mises Institute, AL 2005).

7. To be differentiated from rationality in the sense of the new classics.

8. See in particular P. Honohan and P. R. Lane, 'Divergent inflation rates in EMU', *Economic Policy*, 37 (October 2003), pp. 357–94; M. Duarte, 'The Euro and Inflation Divergence in Europe', *Federal Reserve Bank of Richmond, Economic Quarterly*, 89:3 (2003), pp. 53–70, and I. J. M. Arnold and C. J. M Kool, 'The Role of Inflation Differentials in Regional Adjustment: Evidence from the United States', Utrecht School of Economics, Tjalling C. Koopmans research Institute, Discussion Paper 04–13 (2003).

9. With a view to showing that Central Bank control over the price of assets or credit would have the same stabilizing effects today as inflation control, see P. Artus, 'Stabilisation de

la valeur des actifs ou de l'endettement: un substitut parfait à la stabilisation de l'inflation si celle-ci a disparu', *Doctoriales MACROFI, Poitiers* (April 2006).

10. According to Artus, in 'Stabilisation de la valeur', the expression (3) results from equality between the real return on assets (corrected for inflation) *pa* and the real interest rate $(i - \pi)$. The income from assets (in real terms) is assumed to depend on the profit made (linked to production), which is the source of the term σy.

11. This shows the idea that, when entrepreneurs make a profit, they do not necessarily reinvest it in assets. This hypothesis can be contested if entrepreneurs are involved in cumulative asset purchasing strategies which, according to Aubin, Berdot and Leonard, are strategies which have now become a standard form of searching for profitability.

12. If the stability conditions of the model are verified, in this case sufficiently low values of σ (the effect of the profits on the appreciation of assets) and γ (effect of debt on the production of entrepreneurs).

13. Regardless of the system (Figure 5.2) used by the author (simplified or complete), it is difficult accurately to define the impact on production.

14. With a view to simplifying, we have assumed here that A=B=D=1.

15. M. Aglietta, 'Inflation Targeting and Financial Stability', *Communication aux 21ᵉᵐᵉˢ Journées d'Economie Monétaire et Bancaire* (June 2004).

16. Corrected for risks linked to launching the investment project.

17. The author considers that Von Hayek was clearly aware of these mechanisms and that Keynes had also reached this conclusion, but not for identical reasons. In the case of Keynes, it is the instability of the expected return on capital, due to the radical uncertainty facing the agents that impedes all reference to exogenous benchmarks.

18. In order to prove that Central Bank control over the price of assets or credit would have the same stabilizing effects today as inflation control. See Artus, 'Stabilisation de la valeur'.

19. We do not have quarterly data on debt, and this variable was therefore left out of the impulses.

20. The long-term growth cycle is obtained with the help of a Hodrick-Prescott filter. For precisions on dating and on the value of the chosen adjustment criteria, cf. M. Parnaudeau, 'European Business Fluctuations in the Austrian Framework', *Quarterly Journal of Austrian Economics*, 11:2 (2008), pp. 94–105.

21. The long-term growth cycle (average duration of around 10 years) is calculated as the long-term trend in GNP deviation (GNP filtered with an adjustment coefficient $\lambda = 7000$), having previously removed the short-term disruptions (GNP filtered with an adjustment coefficient $\lambda = 100$).

22. We have used a weight matrix compatible with the presence of heteroskedasticity and self-correlation calculated with a Bartlett Kernel and a fixed bandwidth equal to 3 (automatic selection resulting from the conclusions of Newey, Whitney and West).

23. The explanatory variable is significant (s), the best results are shown in bold.

6 von Mettenheim, European Banking: A Review of Trends and Policies for Reassessment of Bank Reform and Development in Brazil and Latin America

1. W. O. Douglas, *Democracy and Finance: the Addresses and Public Statements of William O. Douglas as Member and Chairman of the Securities and Exchange Commission* (New Haven, CT: Yale University Press, 1941).
2. G. Ardant, 'Financial Policy and Economic Infrastructure of Modern States and Nations', in C. Tilly (ed.), *The Formation of National States in Western Europe* (Princeton, NJ: Princeton University Press, 1975), pp. 164–242.
3. Ibid, p. 241, along with previous sentence.
4. A. C. Pinheiro, 'Uma Agenda Pós-Liberal de Desenvolvimento para o Brasil', IPEA Discussion Paper, 989 (October 2003).
5. L. C. Bresser-Pereira, *Developing Brazil: Overcoming the Failure of the Washington Consensus* (Boulder, CO: Lynne Rienner, forthcoming, 2009).
6. G. A. Cornia (ed.), *Inequality Growth and Poverty in an Era of Liberalization and Globalization* (Oxford: Oxford University Press, 2004).
7. A. Amsden, 'Editorial: Bringing Production Back In: Understanding Government's Economic Role in Late Industrialization', *World Development*, 25:4 (2003), pp. 469–80 and A. Amsden, *The Rise of the Rest: Challenges to the West from Late Industrializing Economies* (Oxford: Oxford University Press, 2001).
8. H. J. Chang, *Kicking Away the Ladder? Policies and Institutions for Economic Development in Historical Perspective*. London: Anthem Press, 2002; Evans, Peter. *Embedded Autonomy: States and Industrial Transformation* (Princeton, NJ: Princeton University Press, 1995).
9. B. Stallings and R. Studart. *Finance for Development* (Washington, DC: Brookings Institution, 2006).
10. On development banks, see: B. Aghion, 'Development Banking'. *Journal of Development Economics*, 58 (1999), pp. 83–100. In Latin America, see: Alcas, R.C. 'La banca de desarrollo en América Latina y el Caribe' (United Nations Economic comisión on Latin America, Development Finance Series (LC/L.2330–P), 2005).
11. See: R. Sylla, 'The Role of Banks', in R. Sylla and G. Toniolo (eds). *Patterns of European Industrialization in the 19ʰ Century* (London: Routledge, 1991), pp. 45–63. Aghion notes: 'The oldest government-sponsored institution for industrial development is the Societe General pour Favoriser l'Industrie National which was created in the Netherlands in 1822. However, it was in France that some of the most significant developments in long-term state-sponsored finance occurred. In this respect, the creation in 1848–1852 of institutions such as the Credit Foncier, the Comptoir d'Escompte, and the Credit Mobilier, was particularly important'. Aghion, 'Development Banking', p. 3.
12. Cameron notes: 'Of even greater importance than the outcome of the operations of the Credit Mobilier were the intangible benefits such as the imitated skills of the engineers and technicians which it sentabroad, the efficiency of its administrators, and the organizational banking techniques which were so widely copied'. Cameron, E., 'The credit mobilier and the economic development of Europe'. *The Journal of Political Economy*, 53: 6 (1953), p. 486 (cited in Aghion, 'Development Banking', p. 86).
13. W. Diamond, *Development Banks* (Baltimore, MD: Johns Hopkins University Press, 1957).

14. Aghion cites: Societe National de Credit a l'Industrie (Belgium, 1919), Credit National (France, 1919), 1928, National Bank, Poland, 1928), 1928, Industrial Mortgage Bank (Finland, 1928), Industrial Mortgage Institute (Hungary, 1928), 1933, Instituto Mobiliare Italiano (Italy, 1933), Instituto per la Reconstructione Industriale (Italy, 1933).

15. The planned privatization of the Japan Development Bank is of special interest in terms of combining access to financial markets and modernizing development banking with social, environmmental, and public policy mandates.

16. C. Johnson, *MITI and the Japanese Miracle: The Growth of Industrial Policy, 1925–1975* (Stanford, CA: Stanford University Press, 1982).

17. J. E. Woo, *Race to the Swift: State and Finance in Korean Industrialization* (New York: Columbia University Press, 1991).

18. M. Woo-Cumings (ed.), *The Developmental State* (Ithaca, NY: Cornell University Press, 1999).

19. However, for Hall, competing paradigms dispute causal interpretations of the Asian financial crisis. R. B. Hall, 'The Discursive Demolition of the Asian Development Model', *International Studies Quarterly*, 47:1 (2003), pp. 71–99.

20. See: R. C. Alcas, 'La Banca de Desarrolo en América Latina e el Caribe' (Santiago: ECLA Special Studies, 2005).

21. Caixa Econômica Federal, 'Demonstrações Contabeis' (June 2004), p. 2.

22. See M. Neri, 'Miséria, Desigualdade e Políticas de Renda: O Real do Lula' (Rio de Janeiro: Centro de Política Social, FGV, 2008)

23. J. M. M. Mena and E.L. Errázuriz. 'The Chilean BancoEstado: Inclusive Finance, Expanding Borders' in K. Mettenheim and M. A. T. Lins (eds). *Government Banking: New Perspectives on Sustainable Development and Social Inclusion from Europe and South America* (São Paulo: Konrad Adenauer Foundation Press, 2008), pp. 135–54.

24. J. Amyx, H. Takenaka and A. M. Toyoda, 'The Politics of Postal Savings Reform in Japan'. *Asian Perspective*, 29:1 (2005), pp. 23–48.

25. P. Hall and D. Soskice (eds), *Varieties of Capitalism: The Institutional Foundations of Comparative Advantage* (Oxford: Oxford University Press, 2001).

26. J. M. Sellers, 'National Local Political Economies and Varieties of Capitalism: A Classification and Analysis of Twenty-One OECD Countries'. Paper presented to the APSA Meeting, Philadelphia, PA, 2003, Hopkin, J. 'How Many Varieties of Capitalism? Structural Reform and Inequality in Western Europe'. Paper presented at the the Annual Meeting of the APSA, Chicago, Illinois, 1–5 September 2004.

27. Y. Tiberghien, 'Global Forces, Political Mediation, and the Fragmentation of Corporate Governance Patterns: The Cases of France, Japan, and Korea'. Paper presented to the APSA Meeting, Chicago, IL, 2004 and Y. Tiberghien, 'EU Mediation of Global Finance vs National Corporate-Labor Coalitions: The Mighty Battle over the Takeover Directive, 1989–2003'. Paper presented to the APSA Meeting, Philadelphia, PA, 2003, Gourevitch, P. & J. Shinn. 'Explaining Corporate Governance: the Role of Politics' Paper presented to the APSA Meeting, Philadelphia, PA, August 27–31, 2003, G. Jackson, 'Toward a Comparative Perspective on Corporate Governance and Labour Management' (RIETI Discussion Paper Series 04–E–023).

28. R. Deeg, 'Measuring Institutional Complementarity and Change in Capitalist Systems'. Paper Presented at the Annual Meeting of the APSA,Chicago, IL, 2004.

29. S. Lütz, 'Convergence within national diversity – a comparative perspective on the regulatory state in finance'. Paper presented at the Meeting of the APSA, Chicago, Illinois, 1–5 September 2004.

30. B. R. Schneider, 'Varieties of Semi-Articulated Capitalism in Latin America'. Paper presented to the APSA, Philadelphia, PA August 27–31, 2003.

31. 'We concentrate here on economies at relatively high levels of development because we know them best and think the framework applies well to many problems there. However, the basic approach should also have relevance for understanding developing economies as well. Hall and Soskice, *Varieties of Capitalism*, p. 2.

32. C. Conaghan and J. Malloy, *Unsettling Statecraft: Democracy and Neoliberalism in the Central Andes* (Pittsburgh, PA: University of Pittsburgh Press, 1994).

33. J. Nelson (ed.), *A Precarious Balance: Democracy and Economic Reforms in Latin America* (Washington, DC: Overseas Development Council, 1994).

34. On bank centered and market centered financial systems, see: R. Rajan and L. Zingales. 'Banks and Markets: The Changing Character of European Finance' (NBER Working Paper 9595, March 2003), F. Allen and D. Gale, *Comparing Financial Systems* (Cambridge: MIT Press, 2000), Levine, R. & Zervos, S. 'Stock markets, banks, and economic growth. *American Economic Review*, 88:3 (1998), pp. 537–58.

35. '... where investors are linked to the firms they fund through networks that allow for the development of reputations based on extensive access to information about the internal operations of the firm, ... investors will be more willing to supply capital to firms on terms that do not depend entirely on their balance sheets'. Hall & Soskice, op.cit., p. 10.

36. We differ with this description of banking in Germany because of the importance of a large number of small credit institutions such as savings banks and cooperative banks.

37. Allen and Gale, *Comparing Financial Systems*. p. 3.

38. Hall and Soskice, *Varieties of Capitalism*, pp. 21–23.

39. R. C. Smith and I. Walter, *Global Banking* (Oxford: Oxford University Press, 2003).

40. M. P. Hampton and J. Christensen. 'Offshore Pariahs? Small Island Economies, Tax Havens, and the Re-configuration of Global Finance', *World Development*, 30:9, pp. 1657–73.

41. J. Caporaso and D. Levine, *Theories of Political Economy* (Camberidge: Cambridge University Press, 1992).

42. Hall and Soskice note: '(...varieties of capitalism) tend to discribute income and employment differently... In liberal market economies, the adult population tends to be engaged more extensively in paid employment and levels of income inequality are high. In coordenated market economies, working hours tend to be shorter for more of the population and incomes more equal. With regard to the distribution of well-being, of course, these differences are important'. Hall and Soskice, *Varieties of Capitalism*, p. 21.

43. Gini coefficients for market-centred financial systems: Australia (1994) 0.311, Ireland (1995) 0.336, UK (1995) 0.344, US (1994) 0.355. Gini coefficients for bank-centered financial systems: Austria (1995) 0.277, Denmark (1995) 0.263, Finland (1995) 0.217, Germany (1994) 0.261, Netherlands (1994) 0.253, Sweden (1995) 0.221. From Luxembourg Income Study Key Figures.

44. L. Guiso, et al (eds). *Household Portfolios* (Cambridge, MA:. MIT Press, 2002).

45. G. A. Dymski, *The Bank Merger Wave: The Economic Causes and Social Consequences of Financial Consolidation in the United States* (Armonk, NY: M.E. Sharpe, Inc. 1999).

46. See A. Turner and I. Grossle. 'Community Banking Networks and Financial Exclusion: How Savings Banks and Cooperative Banks Contribute to Financial Inclusion in Germany'. In von Mettenheim and Lins (Eds). *Government Banking: New Perspectives on Sustainable Development and Social Inclusion from Europe and South America* (Rio de Janeiro: Konrad Adenauer Foundation Press, 2008), pp. 41–64.

47. S. Vitols, 'Modernizing Capital: Financial Regulation and Long-Term Finance in the Postwar U.S. and Germany' (Ph.D. Dissertation, Department of Sociology, University of Wisconsin, Madison, WI, 1996).

48. G. Jackson and S. Vitols. 'Between Financial Commitment, Market Liquidity and Corporate Governance: Occupational Pensions in Britain, Germany, Japan and the USA', in B. Ebbinghaus and P. Manow (eds), *Comparing Welfare Capitalism* (London: Routledge, 2001).

49. Ibid., p. 177.

50. On foreign bank entry, see: L. F. R. Paula, *The Recent Wave of European Banks in Brazil: Determinants and Impacts* (Oxford: Centre for Brazilian Studies, 2001).

51. On PROER, see: W. Baer and N. Nazmi, 'Privatization and Restructuring of Banks in Brazil', *Quarterly Review of Economics and Finance*, 40:1 (2000), pp. 3–24, E. McQuerry, 'Managed Care for Brazilian Banks'. *Federal Reserve Bank of Atlanta Review*, 86:2 (2001), pp. 27–44.

52. On PROES, see: T. Beck, et al., 'State Bank Transformation in Brazil: Choices and Consequences', *Journal of Banking and Finance* 29:8–9 (2005), pp. 2223–57 and D. Samuels, 'Fiscal Straightjacket: The Political Economy of Macroeconomic Reform in Brazil, 1995–2002', *Journal of Latin American Studies*, 35 (2003), pp. 1–25.

53. On the Central Bank of Brazil, see: L. Whitehead and L. Sola (eds), *Statecrafting Monetary Authority: Democracy and Financial Order in Brazil* (Oxford: University of Oxford Center for Brazilian Studies, 2006).

54. A. Kumar, *Access to financial services in Brazil* (Washington, DC: World Bank, 2005).

55. I. Goldfajn, et al. 'Brazil's Financial System: Resilience to Shocks, no Currency Substitution, but Struggling to Promote Growth' (Central Bank of Brazil Working Paper 75, June 2003, p. 5). Stallings and Studart, *Finance for Development*, p. 30.

56. Central Bank of Brazil, *Financial Stability Report*, 2003, p. 51.

57. Central Bank of Brazil, *Financial Stability Report*, 2002, p. 50.

58. Source: Pesquisa FAPESP 'A Construção da Autoridade Monetária e Democracia: A Experiência Brasileira no Contexto da Integração Econômica em Escala Global' 2002 Survey

59. See FGV *Sondagem Industrial*, available on www.fgv.br

60. J. Zysman, *Governments, Markets and Growth: Financial Systems and the Politics of Industrial Change* (Oxford: Robertson, 1983).

7 Vincensini, Monetary and Fiscal Policy Conflicts in Central Europe: How Credible are Macro Policies in the Phase of Preparation for EMU?

1. In 2001, Hungary aimed to integrate EMU in 2006–7, Poland in 2008 and the Czech Republic in 2010.

2. J. Creel and J. Fayolle, 'La Banque centrale et l'Union monétaire européennes: les tribulations de la crédibilité', Revue de l'OFCE, Hors-série 'La mondialisation et l'Europe' (2002), pp. 211–44.

3. For example, the CNB has decided to disclose the votes cast by individual Board members in interest rates changes to increase transparency of monetary policy as of 2008, whereas the NBP has published this information since January 2001 and the MNB since October 2005.

4.   See J. Jonas and F. Mishkin, 'Inflation Targeting in Transition Countries: Experience and Prospects', in B. Bernanke and M. Woodford (eds), *The Inflation-Targeting Debate, National Bureau of Economic Research Studies in Business Cycles* (Chicago, IL: University of Chicago Press, 2004), pp. 353–413; M. Jarmuzek, L. Orlowki and A. Radziwill, 'Monetary Policy Transparency in Inflation Targeting Countries: the Czech Republic, Hungary and Poland', Studies and Analyses, 281 (Warsaw: CASE, 2004); T. Lyziak, J. Mackiewicz and E. Stanislawska, 'Central Bank Transparency and Credibility: The Case of Poland 1998–2004', European Journal of Political Economy, 23:1(2007), pp. 67–87.

5.   MNB, Annual Report (Budapest: Magyar Nemzeti Bank, various years).

6.   NBP, Annual Report (Warsaw: Narodowy Bank Polski, various dates).

7.   CNBc, Inflation Report (Prague: Ceska Narodni Banka, various dates).

8.   NBP, Annual Report (2002).

9.   NBP, Annual Report (2007).

10. MNB, Annual Report (2001).

11. MNB, Annual Report (2004).

12. MNB, Annual Report (2008).

13. For criticism of the double pillar strategy of the ECB, see P. Artus and C. Wyplosz, *La Banque centrale européenne* (Paris: Rapport du Conseil d'Analyse Economique, 2002).

14. European Council, Council Regulation No 1084/2006 of 11 July 2006 establishing a Cohesion Fund (Brussels: European Council, 2006).

15. Hungarian Ministry of Finance, Pre-Accession Economic Programme (PEP) (Budapest: Hungarian Ministry of Finance, 2003).

16. Polish Ministry of Finance, Pre-Accession Economic Programme (PEP) (Warsaw: Polish Ministry of Finance, 2002).

17. Czech Ministry of Finance, Convergence Programme (CP) (Prague: Czech Ministry of Finance, 2004).

18. Hungarian Ministry of Finance, PEP (2002).

19. Hungarian Ministry of Finance, PEP (2003).

20. Ibid.

21. Hungarian Ministry of Finance, Convergence Programme (CP) (Budapest: Hungarian Ministry of Finance, May 2004).

22. EIU, Hungary Country Report (London: The Economist Intelligence Unit, 4Q2005).

23. Hungarian Ministry of Finance, CP (September 2006).

24. Hungarian Ministry of Finance, CP (December 2006).

25. An amendment to the Act on public finances in July 2006 is designed to strengthen fiscal discipline and transparency; it states that the government must submit a budget that assures primary surplus of the Maastricht balance indicator of the government sector. A draft bill submitted by the government in November 2007 seeks to prevent the increase of the real value of public debt and to set up a legislative budget office to control government policy (Hungarian Ministry of Finance, CP (November 2007)).

26. Polish Ministry of Finance, Convergence Programme (CP) (Warsaw: Polish Ministry of Finance, April 2004).

27. Polish Ministry of Finance, CP (January 2006).

28. Polish Ministry of Finance, CP (November 2006).

29. I. Matalik and M. Slavik, 'Fiscal Issues and Central Bank Policy in the Czech Republic', BIS Papers, 'Fiscal issues and central banking in emerging economies', 20 (Basel: BIS, 2003), pp. 122–30.

30. Czech Ministry of Finance, Pre-Accession Economic Programme (PEP) (Prague: Czech Ministry of Finance, 2003).
31. MNB, Annual Report (2002).
32. MNB, Annual Report (2002).
33. see G. Kiss, 'Monetary Policy Issues in Hungary on the Eve of EU Membership', BIS Papers, 'Globalisation and monetary policy in emerging markets', 23 (Basel: BIS, 2005), pp. 156–60.
34. CNBb, Central Bank Monitoring, December (Prague: Ceska Narodni Banka, 2004).
35. MNB, Annual Report (2005).
36. Hungarian Ministry of Finance, CP (December 2004).
37. MNB, Annual Report (2006).
38. MNB, Annual Report (2002).
39. Now, the ruling party nominates the chairman and half the members, the opposition nominates the other half. Their term of office coincides with the Parliament's mandate.
40. CNBc, Inflation Report (2004).
41. NBP, Annual Report (2001).
42. Jonas and Mishkin, 'Inflation Targeting in Transition Countries: Experience and Prospects'.
43. EIU, Poland Country Report (London: The Economist Intelligence Unit, 4Q2002).
44. NBP, Annual Report (2003).
45. NBP, Annual Report (2002).
46. Jonas and Mishkin, 'Inflation Targeting in Transition Countries: Experience and Prospects'.
47. Submitted by members of Sambroona (Self-Defense, a populist right-wing group), this draft bill sought to amend the Act on the NBP by changing, among others, the objectives of the NBP (to include growth) and the rules of nomination of its president and monetary policy council members. Deemed incompatible with the Constitution and the European Treaty, the bill was rejected in January 2007 (NBP, Annual Report (2007)).
48. European Commission, Report on the Czech Republic's Progress Towards EU Accession (Brussels: European Commission, 1998).
49. Jonas and Mishkin, 'Inflation Targeting in Transition Countries: Experience and Prospects'.
50. CNBa, Annual Report (Prague: Ceska Narodni Banka, 2000, 2001, 2002).
51. Czech Ministry of Finance, CP (May 2004).
52. CNBd, The Setting of the Inflation Target for 2001 (Prague: Ceska Narodni Banka, 2000).
53. CNBe, Press release of 30 September (Prague: Ceska Narodni Banka, 2008).
54. All three currencies have lost between 16% and 34% against the US dollar in September and October 2008.
55. In September and October 2008, their stock exchanges have respectively lost 48% in Budapest, 38% in Warsaw and 52% in Prague.
56. The European Council has stated on 16 October 2008 that 'budget policies must continue to be in line with the revised Stability and Growth Pact, which should also be applied in a manner which reflects the current exceptional circumstances, as provided for in its rules'.
57. See EIU, Hungary Country Report (4Q2008).
58. See EIU, Poland Country Report (4Q2008).

59. See EIU, Czech Republic Country Report (London: The Economist Intelligence Unit, 4Q2008).

60. Jonas and Mishkin, 'Inflation Targeting in Transition Countries: Experience and Prospects'.

61. Creel and Fayolle, 'La Banque centrale et l'Union monétaire européennes: les tribulations de la crédibilité'.

62. MNB, Annual Report (various years).

63. NBP, Annual Report (various years).

64. CNBa, Annual Report (various years).

65. R. Matousek and A. Taci, 'Direct Inflation Targeting and Nominal Convergence: The Czech Case', *Open Economies Review*, 14:3 (2003), pp. 269–83.

66. K. Bruna, 'Disinflationary Monetary Strategy and Instability of the Forward Yield Curve: The Case of the Czech Republic, 1999–2005', *Post-Communist Economies*, 18:4 (2006), pp. 459–78.

67. MNB, Annual Report (2001).

68. P. Gabriel and K. Pinter, 'The Effect of the MNB's Communication on Financial Markets', *MNB Working Papers*, 9 (Budapest: Magyar Nemzeti Bank, 2006).

69. T. Wlodarczyk, 'The Influence of Polish Monetary Policy Council Members' Verbal Comments on the Yield Curve. The Analysis of the Semi-Strong Form Informational Efficiency of FRA and IRS Markets', *Bank and Credit*, 2 (2008), pp. 43–59.

70. Lyziak, et al., 'Central Bank Transparency and Credibility: The Case of Poland 1998–2004'.

71. P. Arestis and K. Mouratidis, 'Credibility of Monetary Policy in Four Accession Countries: a Markov Regime-Switching Approach', *International Journal of Finance and Economics*, 10:1 (2005), pp. 81–9; Z. Darvas, 'Monetary Transmission in the New EU Member States: Evidence from Time-Varying Coefficient Vector Autoregression', *Focus on European Economic Integration*, 1 (Vienna: Oesterreichische Nationalbank, 2006), pp. 140–57; J. Crespo-Cuaresma, B. Egert and T. Reininger, 'Interest Rate Pass-Through in Central and Eastern Europe: Reborn from Ashes Merely to Pass Away?', *Journal of Policy Modelling*, 29:2 (2007), pp. 209–25.

72. J-P. Fitoussi and J. Le Cacheux (eds), *Rapport sur l'Etat de l'Union* (Paris: Presses de Sciences Po, 1999).

73. According to the CNB (Central Bank Monitoring (December 1999)), 'the general trend should not be one of a tight monetary policy subsequently offsetting or counterbalancing excessively relaxed wage-income or fiscal dimensions. On the contrary, the conditions of the Czech economy should normally require a prudent wage-income policy combined, as far as possible, with a more relaxed monetary policy'. According to the NBP (Annual Report (2004)), 'the non-optimal macroeconomic policy mix which couples a restrictive monetary policy with a loose fiscal policy increases the cost of price stability maintenance in the form of lower GDP growth (in relation to the optimal mix)'. For the governments' preferences, see above (Fiscal policy objectives).

74. According to Fitoussi and Le Cacheux (eds), *Rapport sur l'Etat de l'Union*, the situation is non-cooperative in EMU countries because the Stability and Growth Pact, which could have been a coordination device favouring the 'conservative' solution, is not constraining enough on fiscal policies.

75. F. Kydland and E. Prescott, 'Rules Rather than Discretion: The Inconsistency of Optimal Plans', *Journal of Political Economy*, 85:3 (1977), pp. 473–91; K. Rogoff, 'The Optimal

Degree of Commitment to an Intermediate Monetary Target', *Quarterly Journal of Economics*, 100:4 (1985), pp. 1169–89.

76. Creel and Fayolle, 'La Banque centrale et l'Union monétaire européennes: les tribulations de la crédibilité'.

8 Größl, Economic and Ethical Aspects of Discrimination in the Consumer Credit Market

1. I. Größl, 'The Poor Pay More': Another Case of Discrimination in the consumer Credit Market? Homo Oeconomicus, 2005, 22:3, pp. 381–400.
2. J. Shiller, *The Subprime Solution. How Today's Global Financial Crisis Happened, and What to Do about it* (Princeton, NJ and Oxford: Princeton University Press, 2008).
3. G. S. Becker, 'The Economics of Discrimination' (Chicago, IL: University of Chicago Press, 1957).
4. K. J. Arrow, 'The Theory of Discrimination', in O. Ashenfelter and A. Rees (eds) '*Discrimination in Labor Markets*' (Princeton, NJ: Princeton University Press, 1973), pp. 3–33 and J. Yinger, 'Evidence on Discrimination in Consumer Markets', *Journal of Economic Perspectives*, 12:2 (1998), pp. 23–40.
5. G. S. Becker, 'The Evidence against Banks doesn't Prove Bias' (Business Week, 1993); S. Han, *On the Economics of Discrimination in Credit Markets* (Washington, DC: Federal Reserve Board, 2001) and R. L. Peterson, 'An Investigation of Sex Discrimination in Commercial Banks' Direct Consumer Lending', *Bell Journal of Economics*, 12:2 (1981), pp. 547–61.
6. Arrow, 'The Theory of Discrimination', and E. S. Phelps, 'The Statistical Theory of Racism and Sexism', *American Economic Review* 62:4 (1972), pp. 659–61.
7. Yinger, 'Evidence on Discrimination in Consumer Markets' and Größl, 'The Poor Pay More'.
8. P. Ulrich, *Transformation der ökonomischen Vernunft. Fortschrittsperspektiven der modernen Industriegesellschaft* (Stuttgart, Wien, 3. Aufl.: Haupt Verlag, 1993), p. 174.
9. J. Hagel, *Effizienz und Gerechtigkeit. Ein Beitrag zur Diskussion der ethischen Aspekte in der neoklassischen Wohlfahrtstheorie* (Baden-Baden: Nomos Verlagsgesellschaft, 1993), p. 73.
10. P. Ulrich, *Integrative Wirtschaftsethik. Grundlagen einer lebensdienlichen Ökonomie* (Stuttgart, Wien: Haupt Verlag, 1997), p. 32.
11. Hagel, *Effizienz und Gerechtigkeit*, p. 165; C. D. Broad, *Five Types of Ethical Theory* (New York: Harcourt, Brace and Co, 1930), distinguishes between teleological and deontological ethical approaches depending on whether they evaluate the morality of an action according to their consequences (teleological view) or whether the action as such is considered (deontological view).
12. Jeremy Bentham (1748–1832) and John Stuart Mill (1806–73) are considered as the founding fathers of utilitarianism.
13. Ulrich, *Transformation der ökonomischen Vernunft*, pp. 191–93.
14. K. W. Rothschild, *Ethik und Wirtschaftstheorie* (Tübingen: Verlag JCB, 1992).
15. Hagel, *Effizienz und Gerechtigkeit*, p. 33.
16. Ibid., p. 254.

17. R. Wagner, *Unternehmensführung, Ethik und Umwelt* (Wiesbaden, 1999), p. 47.
18. Hagel, *Effizienz und Gerechtigkeit.*
19. Wagner, *Unternehmensführung, Ethik und Umwelt.*
20. A. Shleifer and R. W. Vishny, 'A Survey of Corporate Governance', *Journal of Finance*, 52 (1997), pp. 737–83.
21. J. Habermas, *Moralbewusstsein und kommunikatives Handeln* (Frankfurt: A. M., 1983).
22. Ulrich, *Integrative Wirtschaftsethik.*
23. J. R. Boatright, *Ethics in Finance* (Oxford: Blackwell Publishers, 1999), p. 56.
24. Broad, *Five Types of Ethical Theory.*
25. Boatright, *Ethics in Finance.*
26. Ulrich, *Integrative Wirtschaftsethik.*
27. K. O. Apel, *Diskurs und Verantwortung. Das Problem des Übergangs zur postkonvetionellen Moral* (Frankfurt: A. M., 1988); Habermas, *Moralbewusstsein und kommunikatives Handeln.*
28. Ulrich, *Integrative Wirtschaftsethik.*
29. Ibid., p. 428.

9 Paulet and Relano, Beyond Ethics: Alternative Banking in Switzerland

1. O. Pastré: 'Industrie bancaire: les espoirs des Davids face aux Goliaths ', *Revue d'Economie Financière*, 61 (2001), pp. 53–62.
2. W. Buiter, 'Lessons from the 2007 Crisis', *CEPR Policy Insight*, 18 (December 2007), pp. 1–17.
3. M. König and A. Wespe, *L'histoire d'une banque extraordinaire: L'Alternative* (Zurich: Banque Alternative BAS, 2005), pp. 47–8.
4. Information about this bank taken from personal communications and from the bank's we b site: www.gemeinschaftsbank.ch
5. For a more detailed presentation of this bank, see König and Wespe, *L'histoire d'une banque extraordinaire.*
6. For a general overview, see T. Studer, *Wir and the Swiss National Economy*, trans. P. H. Beard (Basel: Wir Bank, 1998).
7. For an overall picture, see H. P. Minsky, *Can 'It' Happen Again? Essays on Instability and Finance* (Amonk, NY: M.E. Sharpe, 1982). See also, H. James, *The End of Globalization: Lessons from the Great Depression* (Cambridge, MA: Harvard University Press, 2001).
8. See, respectively, F. A. Von Hayek, 'Toward a Free Market Monetary System', *Journal of Libertarian Studies*, 3:1 (1979), pp. 1–8. S. Gesell, *The Natural Economic Order*, trans. P. Pye (London: Peter Owen Ltd., 1958).
9. For a pioneer but incomplete study on this issue, see J. Stodder, 'Reciprocal Exchange Networks: Implications for Macroeconomic Stability', Working Paper (Albuquerque, August 2000, available on line at www.appropriate-economics.org/materials/reciprocal_exchange_networks.pdf).
10. Short term growth trend is not relevant for our analysis as only variations due to short fluctuations are provided by the sample. It is therefore excluded from our analysis
11. A recession has been observed between the third quarter of 2002 and the third quarter of 2004. This period could a good reference to give evidence of the contra-cyclical behaviour of the WIR (see section 3).

12. According to Friedman, 'Another empirical regularity, which was predominant not many years ago, exists not between money and interest rates, but between prices and interest rates. The Gibson Paradox is the observed tendency of prices and interest rates to move together'. M. Friedman, 'The Optimum Quantity of Money' (Chicago, IL: Aldine, 1969).

13. This curve shows the relation between return rates and duration for specified assets. The returns chosen here are fixed. A negative yield curve exists when short term rate exceed long term rate. This situation is observed on periods corresponding to credit restrictions. A positive yield curve corresponds to the reverse situation. Long-term investments benefit from higher returns than short-term investments.

14. Data Adjusted for seasonal variations, constant prices. Source National bank of Switzerland

15. The weak value obtained for the Freie Gemeinschaftbank (–0,0038) prevents us from determining with precision if the credit offer is really contra-cyclical.

16. Ordinary Least Squares.

17. Statistics, with probability in parenthesis.

18. Generalized moment method. The retained instruments are lagged values of explanatory variables. Using annual data, we apply two lags by variables.

WORKS CITED

Aghion, B., 'Development Banking', *Journal of Development Economics*, 58 (1999), pp. 83–100.

Aglietta, M., *Régulation et crises du capitalisme*, 2nd edn (Paris: Odile Jacob, 1997).

—, 'Inflation Targeting and Financial Stability', *Communication aux 21ᵉᵐᵉˢ Journées d'Economie Monétaire et Bancaire* (June 2004).

Aglietta, M., L. Berrebi, A. Cohen-Benamran and J. J. Jacob, 'Marchés boursiers américains, cycles réels, cycles monétaires', *Groupama-AM, Expertises*, 4 (2005).

Aglietta, M. and Rigot, S., 'The regulation of hedge funds under the prism of the financial crisis. Policy implications', *Louvain Economic Review*, forthcoming, (2008).

Allen, F., and D. Gale, *Comparing Financial Systems* (Cambridge: MIT Press, 2000).

Amblard, M. *Comptabilité et conventions* (Paris: L'Harmattan, 2002).

Amenc N., Martellini L. and Vaissié M., 'Benefits and Risks of Alternative Investment Strategies', *Journal of Asset Management*, 4:2, (2003).

Amenc N., Malaise P., Martellini L. and Vaissié M., 'Fund of hedge Funds reporting', discussion Paper, EDHEC Risk and Asset Management research Centre Publication, (2004).

Amsden, A., 'Editorial: Bringing Production Back In: Understanding Government's Economic Role in Late Industrialization', *World Development*, 25:4 (2003), pp. 469–80.

—, *The Rise of the Rest: Challenges to the West from Late Industrializing Economies.* (Oxford: Oxford University Press, 2001).

Amyx, H. Takenaka and A. M. Toyoda, 'The Politics of Postal Savings Reform in Japan'. *Asian Perspective*, 29:1 (2005), pp. 23–48.

Andrieu M., Frotiée P., 1998, 'Valeur actionnariale et immatériels', *Analyse financière*, 116.

Apel, K. O., *Diskurs und Verantwortung. Das Problem des Übergangs zur postkonventionellen Moral* (Frankfurt: A. M., 1988).

Ardant, G., 'Financial Policy and Economic Infrastructure of Modern States and Nations', in C. Tilly (ed.), *The Formation of National States in Western Europe* (Princeton, NJ: Princeton University Press, 1975), pp. 164–242.

Arestis, P., and K. Mouratidis, 'Credibility of Monetary Policy in Four Accession Countries: a Markov Regime-Switching Approach', *International Journal of Finance and Economics*, 10:1 (2005), pp. 81–9.

Armstrong, M-A., and A. Cerfontaine, 'Echecs Economiques et Dérive du Pragmatisme Juridique: l'Expérience Anglaise du Droit de la Faillite', *Droit et Société*, 46 (2000), pp. 547–48.

Arnold, I. J. M., and C. J. M. Kool, 'The Role of Inflation Differentials in Regional Adjustment: Evidence from the United States', Utrecht School of Economics, Tjalling C. Koopmans research Institute, Discussion Paper 04–13 (2003).

Artus, P., 'Stabilisation de la valeur des actifs ou de l'endettement: un substitut parfait à la stabilisation de l'inflation si celle-ci a disparu', *Doctoriales MACROFI, Poitiers* (April 2006).

Arrow, K. J., 'The Theory of Discrimination.' in O. Ashenfelter and A. Rees, eds. '*Discrimination in Labor Markets*' (Princeton, NJ: Princeton University Press, 1973), pp. 3–33.

Aubin, C., J. P. Berdot and J. Leonard, 'Banques Centrales, liquidité et prix d'actifs: une mise en perspective théorique', *Economies et Sociétés, Série Monnaie*, 5 (2006).

Avouyi-Dovi, S., R. Kierzenkowski and C. Lubochinsky, 'Cycles réels et cycles du crédit : Convergence ou divergence ?', *Revue Economique*, 57:4, (2006), pp. 851–80.

Ayotte, K., 'Bankruptcy and Entrepreneurship: The Value of a Fresh Start', *Journal of Law, Economics, and Organization*, 23:1 (2007), pp. 161–85.

Backer, C. L., 'Toiletter notre Droit', *La Lettre de Presaje*, 14 (2006), p. 2.

Baer, W., and N. Nazmi, 'Privatization and Restructuring of Banks in Brazil', *Quarterly Review of Economics and Finance*, 40:1 (2000), pp. 3–24.

Balzac, H. de, *Code des gens honnêtes ou L'art de ne pas être dupe des fripons* (Paris: Editions du Trait, 1948).

Batsch L., *Finance et stratégie* (Paris: Economica, Collection gestion, série Politique générale, finance et marketing 1999).

Bazzoli, L., and T. Kirat, 'À Propos du Réalisme en Economie des Institutions et ses Implications sur l'Analyse des Fondements Juridiques des Transactions Economiques: Commons versus Williamson', *Economie et Sociétés: Institutions et Évolution*, 3 (2003), pp. 31–56.

Beck, T., A. Demirguc-Kunt and R. Levine, *Law and Finance: Why Does Legal Origin Matter?* (Working Paper 9379. National Bureau of Economic Research, Inc, 2002).

Beck, T., et al., 'State Bank Transformation in Brazil: Choices and Consequences', *Journal of Banking and Finance* 29:8–9 (2005), pp. 2223–57.

Becker, G. S., 'The Economics of Discrimination' (Chicago, IL: University of Chicago Press, 1957).

—, 'The Evidence against Banks doesn't Prove Bias' *Business Week* (1993).

Beffa, J-L., R. Boyer and J-P. Touffut, 'Les relations salariales en France : Etat, entreprises, marchés financiers', *Notes de la fondation Saint-Simon*, 107 (1999).

Berkovitch, E., R. Israel and J. F. Zender, *The Design of Bankruptcy Law: A Case for Management Bias in Bankruptcy* (Working Paper, University of Utah, 1994).

Bertholet, P., *Etudes et Notaires Parisiens en 1803, au Moment de la Loi du 25 Ventôse An XI* (Paris: Edition de l'Association des Notaires du Châtelet, 2004).

Blake D., A. Cairns and K. Dowd, 'Turning Pension Plans into Pension Planes: What Investment Strategy Designers of Defined Contribution Plans Can learn from Commercial Aircraft Designers', Pensions Institute Discussion Paper, PI-0806 (April 2008).

Blazy A., P. Court and V. Plagnol, 'Fonds souverains: l'émergence d'un nouveau capitalisme', ESN, CM-CIC Securities (9 November 2007).

Blazy, R., *La Faillite : Eléments d'Analyse Economique* (Paris : Economica, 2000).

Boatright, J. R., *Ethics in Finance* (Oxford: Blackwell Publishers, 1999).

Borio, C., 'The crisis of 2007–?, preliminary assessment and some policy considerations', BIS Economic Papers, 251 (March 2008).

Bourdin, J., *Information Report n°367* (French Senate Delegation for Planification: 2003).

Bowers, J. W., 'Security Interests, Creditors' Priorities and Bankruptcy', in B. Bouckaert and G. De Geest. (eds), *Encyclopedia of Law and Economics, Volume II: Civil Law and Economics* (Cheltenham: Edward Elgar, 2000).

Boyer, R., 'Is a Financed-Led Growth Regime a Viable Alternative to fordism? A Preliminary Analysis', Economy and Society, 29:1, (2000), pp. 111–45.

Boyer, T., 'Corporate Governance et emploi: les attentes des marchés financiers', *Gérer et Comprendre* (September 2002; rpt *Problèmes économiques*, 2789 (18 December 2002)).

Bravard-Veyrieres, P., *Manuel de Droit Commercial*, 2nd edn (Paris: Joubert, Libraire-Editeur, 1840).

Bresser-Pereira, L. C., *Developing Brazil: Overcoming the Failure of the Washington Consensus* (Boulder, CO: Lynne Rienner, forthcoming, 2009).

Broad, C. D., *Five Types of Ethical Theory* (Harcourt, Brace and Co), New York 1930.

Bruna, K., 'Disinflationary Monetary Strategy and Instability of the Forward Yield Curve: The Case of the Czech Republic, 1999–2005', *Post-Communist Economies*, 18:4 (2006), pp. 459–78.

Bryan S., 'Incremental Information Content of Required Disclosures Contained in Management Discussion and Analysis', *Accounting Review*, 72:2 (April 1997), pp. 285–301.

Bufford, S. L., 'What's Right about Bankruptcy and Wrong about its Critics', *Washington University Law Quarterly*, 72 (1994), pp. 829–48.

Buiter, W., 'Lessons from the 2007 crisis', *CEPR Policy Insight*, 18 (December 2007), pp. 1–17.

Buiter, W., 'Lessons from the 2007 financial crisis', *CEPR Policy Insight*, 18 (December 2007), pp. 1–17.

Bushman, R. and A. J. Smith, 'Financial Accounting Information and Corporate Governance', *Journal of Accounting and Economics*, 32 (2001), pp. 237–333.

Cabrillo, F., and B. W. F. Depoorter 'Bankruptcy Proceedings', in B. Bouckaert, and G. De Geest (eds), *Encyclopedia of Law and Economics, Volume V: The Economics of Crime and Litigation* (Cheltenham: Edward Elgar, 1999), p. 261.

Campbell, C. and L. M. Viceira, *Strategic Asset Allocation* (Oxford: Oxford University Press 2002).

—, 'The Term Structure of the Risk-Return Trade-Off', *Financial Analysts Journal*, 61:1 (2005), pp. 34–44.

Chang, H. J., *Kicking Away the Ladder? Policies and Institutions for Economic Development in Historical Perspective*. London: Anthem Press, 2002; Evans, Peter. *Embedded Autonomy: States and Industrial Transformation*. (Princeton, NJ: Princeton University Press, 1995).

Charron J.-O., 'L'idéologie de la transparence dans l'audit', *Comptabilité contrôle Audit*, 6 (2004), pp. 105–31.

Clinch, G., and J. Magliolo, 'Market Perceptions of Reserve Disclosures Under SFAS No. 69', Accounting Review, 57:4 (October 1992), pp. 843–61.

CNBa, *Annual Report* (Prague: Ceska Narodni Banka, various years).

CNBb, *Central Bank Monitoring*, December (Prague: Ceska Narodni Banka, various years).

CNBc, *Inflation Report* (Prague: Ceska Narodni Banka, various dates).

CNBd, *The Setting of the Inflation Target for 2001* (Prague: Ceska Narodni Banka, 2000).

CNBe, Press release of 30 September (Prague: Ceska Narodni Banka, 2008).

Cobbaut, R., 'Pour tenter de conclure: à la croisée des chemin', *Reflets et perspectives de la vie économique – L'efficience des marchés financiers*, 43:2 (2004).

Coffee, J. C., 'The SEC and the Institutional Investor: an Half Time Report' (1994), p. 906.

Cole, C., 'The Usefulness of MD&A Disclosures in the Retail Industry', Journal of Accounting, Auditing and Finance, pp. 361–88.

Colmant, B., and G. Hubner, 'L'impact économique des intérêts notionnels – Première partie: Références à la théorie financière classique'. *Forum Financier – Revue Bancaire et Financière – Bank en Financiewezen*, 69:8, p. 499.

Conaghan, C., and J. Malloy, *Unsettling statecraft: democracy and neoliberalism in the Central Andes*. (Pittsburgh, PA: University of Pittsburgh Press, 1994).

Cornia, G. A. (ed.), *Inequality Growth and Poverty in an Era of Liberalization and Globalization* (Oxford: Oxford University Press, 2004).

Creel, J. and J. Fayolle, 'La Banque centrale et l'Union monétaire européennes : les tribulations de la crédibilité', *Revue de l'OFCE*, Hors-série « La mondialisation et l'Europe », (2002), pp. 211–44.

Crespo-Cuaresma, J., B. Egert and T. Reininger, 'Interest Rate Pass-Through in Central and Eastern Europe: Reborn from Ashes Merely to Pass Away?', *Journal of Policy Modelling*, 29:2 (2007), pp. 209–25.

Crete, R. and S. Rousseau, 'De la passivité à l'activisme des investisseurs', *MacGill Law Journal*, 42 (1997), pp. 864–959.

Czech Ministry of Finance, *Convergence Programme* (CP) (Prague: Czech Ministry of Finance, various dates).

Czech Ministry of Finance, *Pre-Accession Economic Programme* (PEP) (Prague: Czech Ministry of Finance, 2003).

Dalloz, E., and C. Vergé, *Les Codes Annotés. Code de Commerce Annoté et Expliqué d'après la Jurisprudence et la Doctrine* (Paris: Bureau de la Jurisprudence générale, 1877).

Darvas, Z., 'Monetary Transmission in the New EU Member States: Evidence from Time-Varying Coefficient Vector Autoregression', *Focus on European Economic Integration*, 1 (Vienna: Oesterreichische Nationalbank, 2006), pp. 140–57.

Davanne, O. and T. Pujol, 'Allocation d'actifs, variation de primes de risque et benchmarks', *Revue d'Economie Financière*, 79 (2005), pp. 95–110.

Davis, S., Lannoo K., 1997, 'Shareholder voting in Europe', *Corporate Governance – Les perspectives internationales*, Alice Pézard et Jean-Marie Thiveaud ed., Finance et Société, Montchrestien.

Davis, E. and Steil B., *Institutional Investors* (MIT Press, 2001).

European Central Bank, *Hedge funds: developments and policy implications*, Monthly Bulletin, January (2006).

Davydenko, S. A., and J. R. Franks, *Do Bankruptcy Codes Matter? A Study of Defaults in France, Germany and the UK* (Working Paper, London Business School, 2005).

De Soto, J. H, *Money, Bank Credit and Economic Cycles* (Auburn: Mises Institute, AL 2005).

Diamond, W., *Development Banks* (Baltimore, MD: Johns Hopkins University Press, 1957).

Di Martino, P., 'Approaching Disaster, a Comparison between Personal Bankruptcy Legislation in Italy and England, 1880–1930', *Business History*, 45:1 (2005), pp 23–43.

Djankov, R. La Porta, F. Lopez-de-Silanes, and A. Shleifer, 'Courts', *Quarterly Journal of Economics* 118:3 (2003), p. 455.

Djankov, S., C. McLiesh and A. Shleifer, *Private Credit in 129 Countries* (NBER Working Paper, W11078, 2005).

Douglas, W. O., *Democracy and Finance: the Addresses and Public Statements of William O. Douglas as Member and Chairman of the Securities and Exchange Commission* (New Haven, CT: Yale University Press, 1941).

Duarte, M., 'The Euro and Inflation Divergence in Europe', *Federal Reserve Bank of Richmond, Economic Quarterly*, 89:3 (2003), pp. 53–70.

Dumont, A. 'L'interférence entre le secret fiscal et la lutte contre le blanchiment de capitaux. Une étude comparative entre le Luxembourg, la Suisse et l'Angleterre'. *Annales du droit luxembourgeois*, 12 (2002), pp. 191–315.

Dymski, G. A., The Bank Merger Wave: The Economic Causes and Social Consequences of Financial Consolidation in the United States (Armonk, NY: M.E. Sharpe, Inc. 1999).

Eberhart, A. C., and L. W. Senbet, 'Absolute Priority Rule Violations and Risk Incentives for Financially Distressed Firms', *Financial Management*, 22:3 (1993), pp. 101–6.

EIU, *Poland Country Report*, (London: The Economist Intelligence Unit, various dates).

Ernst& and Young LLP, 1997, 'Measures that matter', *Étude Ernst&Young* (1997).

Escaffre L., 2002, 'Contribution à l'analyse de l'offre d'information sur le capital intellectuel', *Thèse en sciences de gestion soutenue publiquement le 28 novembre 2002 à l'université Paris IX Dauphine*.

European Commission, *Report on the Czech Republic's Progress Towards EU Accession* (Brussels: European Commission, 1998).

European Commission, *European SMEs and Social and Environmental Responsibility*, (Luxembourg, Office for Official publications of the European Communities, 2002).

European Council, Council Regulation No 1084/2006 of 11 July 2006 establishing a Cohesion Fund (Brussels: European Council, 2006).

Fitoussi, J-P. and J. Le Cacheux (eds), *Rapport sur l'Etat de l'Union*, (Paris: Presses de Sciences Po, 1999).

Franks, J., and O. Sussman, 'Financial Distress and Bank Restructuring of Small to Medium Size UK Companies', *Review of Finance*, 9:1 (2005), pp. 65–96.

Friedman, M., *'The Optimum Quantity of Money'* (Chicago, IL: Aldine, 1969).

Gabriel, P. and K. Pinter, 'The Effect of the MNB's Communication on Financial Markets', *MNB Working Papers*, 9 (Budapest: Magyar Nemzeti Bank, 2006).

Galanti S., 'Les analystes financiers comme intermédiaires en information' (Thesis in economic science published 26 September 2006 at Paris X University, Nanterre).

Garbaravicius T. and Dierick F., 'Hedge Funds and their implication in financial stability', *ECB Occasional Paper*, n°34, (August 2005).

Gertner, R., and D. Scharfstein, 'A Theory of Workouts and the Effects of Reorganization Law', *Journal of Finance*, 46:4 (1991), pp. 1189–22.

Gesell, S., *The Natural Economic Order*, trans. P. Pye, (London: Peter Owen Ltd., 1958).

Glaeser, E. L., and A. Shleifer, 'Legal Origins', *Quarterly Journal of Economics*, 117:4, pp. 1193–229.

Goldfajn, et al. 'Brazil's Financial System: Resilience to Shocks, no Currency Substitution, but Struggling to Promote Growth' (Central Bank of Brazil Working Paper 75, June 2003, p. 5).

Goré, F., 'The Administrative Autonomy of Creditors and French Legislation on Bankruptcy', *American Journal of Comparative Law*, 17:1 (1969), pp. 5–23.

Granger, C.W.J., 'Investing Causal Relations by Econometric Models and Cross Spectral Methods', Econometrica 37, (1969), pp. 424–38.

Greene D., 'Measures that Matter, The Path of Intangible Value', Your Brand & the Bottom Line Conference, The Ernst & Young Center For Business Innovation, 25 February 1999.

Größl, I., 'The Poor Pay More': Another Case of Discrimination in the consumer Credit Market? *Homo Oeconomicus*, 22:3 (2005), pp. 381–400.

Guiso, et al. (eds). *Household Portfolios*. (Cambridge, MA: MIT Press, 2002).

Guyot, Y., and A. Raffalovitch, *Dictionnaire du Commerce, de l'Industrie et de la Banque, Tome II* (Paris : Guillaumin et Cie, 1901).

Habermas, J., *Moralbewusstsein und kommunikatives Handeln* (Frankfurt: A. M., 1983).

Hagel, J., Effizienz und Gerechtigkeit. Ein Beitrag zur Diskussion der ethischen Aspekte in der neoklassischen Wohlfahrtstheorie (Baden-Baden: Nomos Verlagsgesellschaft, 1993).

Hall and D. Soskice (eds), *Varieties of Capitalism: The Institutional Foundations of Comparative Advantage*. (Oxford: Oxford University Press, 2001).

Hall, 'The Discursive Demolition of the Asian Development Model', *International Studies Quarterly*, 47:1 (2003), pp. 71–99.

Hampel Report, *The Final Report* (London: The Committee on Corporate Governance and Gee professional Publishing, 1998).

Hampton, M. P., and J. Christensen. 'Offshore Pariahs? Small Island Economies, Tax Havens, and the Re-configuration of Global Finance', *World Development*, 30:9, pp. 1657–73.

Han, S., *On the Economics of Discrimination in Credit Markets* (Washington, DC: Federal Reserve Board, 2001).

Hautcoeur and N. Levratto 'Faillite', in A. Stanziani (ed.), *Dictionnaire du Droit/Economie* (Paris: LGDJ, 2007).

Hendry, J., P. Sanderson, R. Baker and J. Roberts, 'Responsible Ownership, Shareholder Value and the New Shareholder Activism', *ESRC, Centre for Business Research, University of Cambridge*, Working Paper, 297 (2004).

Hill, C. and T. M. Jones, 'Stakeholder-Agency Theory', *Journal of Management Studies*, 29 (1992), pp. 134–54.

Honohan, P., and P. R. Lane, 'Divergent inflation rates in EMU', *Economic Policy*, 37 (October 2003), pp. 357–94;

Hungarian Ministry of Finance, *Convergence Programme* (CP) (Budapest: Hungarian Ministry of Finance, various dates).

Hungarian Ministry of Finance, *Pre-Accession Economic Programme* (PEP) (Budapest: Hungarian Ministry of Finance, various dates).

IASC, 1989, *Framework for the preparation and presentation of financial statements*.

Imhoff E., 2003, 'Accounting quality, auditing, and corporate governance', *Accounting horizons*, supplement, pp. 117–28.

Jackson, G. and S. Vitols. 'Between financial commitment, market liquidity and corporate governance: occupational pensions in Britain, Germany, Japan and the USA', in B. Ebbinghaus and P. Manow (eds), *Comparing Welfare Capitalism* (London: Routledge, 2001).

Jackson, T. H., *The Logic and Limits of Bankruptcy Law* (Cambridge, MA: Harvard University Press, 1986).

James, H., *The End of Globalization: Lessons from the Great Depression* (Cambridge, MA: Harvard University Press, 2001).

Jarmuzek, M., L. Orlowki and A. Radziwill, 'Monetary Policy Transparency in Inflation Targeting Countries: the Czech Republic, Hungary and Poland', *Studies and Analyses*, 281 (Warsaw: CASE, 2004).

Johnson, C., *MITI and the Japanese Miracle: The Growth of Industrial Policy, 1925–1975* (Stanford, CA: Stanford University Press, 1982).

Jonas, J., and F. Mishkin, 'Inflation Targeting in Transition Countries: Experience and Prospects', in B. Bernanke and M. Woodford (eds), *The Inflation-Targeting Debate*, National

Bureau of Economic Research Studies in Business Cycles, (Chicago: University of Chicago Press, 2004), pp. 353–413.

Kauffman, J., 'Le secret bancaire en droit luxembourgeois. Actualité et perspectives', in *Droit bancaire et financier au Grand-Duché de Luxembourg* (Bruxelles, 1994).

Kirat, T., 'Introduction Générale', in T. Kirat (ed), *Les mondes du droit de la responsabilité : regards sur le droit en action* (Paris : LGDJ, 2003).

König, M. and A. Wespe, *L'histoire d'une banque extraordinaire : L'Alternative* (Zürich: Banque Alternative BAS, 2005).

Kumar, A., *Access to financial services in Brazil* (Washington, DC: World Bank, 2005).

Kydland, F., and E. Prescott, 'Rules Rather than Discretion: The Inconsistency of Optimal Plans', *Journal of Political Economy*, 85:3 (1977), pp. 473–91.

La Porta, R., F. Lopez-de-Silanes, A. Shleifer and R. W. Vishny 'Law and Finance', *Journal of Political Economy*, 106:6 (1998), pp. 1113–55.

Lajili K., and D. Zéghal, 'A Content Analysis of Risk Management Disclosures in Canadian Annual Reports', *Canadian Journal of Administrative Sciences*, 22:2 (2005), pp. 124–42.

Lainné, M. A. F., *Commentaire Analytique de la Loi du 8 Juin 1838 sur les Faillites et Banqueroutes* (Corbeil: Imprimerie de Crété, 1839).

Lazonick W., and M. O'Sullivan, *Corporate Governance and Sustainable Prosperity* (Basingstoke: Palgrave Macmillan, 2001).

Lele and M. M. Siems, *Shareholder Protection: a Leximetric Approach* (Working Paper 2006).

Lhabitant, F. S., 'Les indices de hedge funds doivent-ils être éligibles ou non aux fonds grand public?', *Les cahiers scientifiques*, 2 (September 2006)

—, Assessing market risk for hedge funds and hedge fund portfolios, *Journal of Risk Finance* (Spring 2001).

Locré, J-G., *La Législation Civile et Commerciale de la France: tome 19, Code de commerce* (Paris: Treuttel et Würtz, 1827–32).

Lyziak, T., J. Mackiewicz and E. Stanislawska, 'Central Bank Transparency and Credibility: The Case of Poland 1998–2004', *European Journal of Political Economy*, 23:1(2007), pp. 67–87.

Mallin C.A., 'The Voting Framework: a Comparative Study of Voting Behaviour of Institutional Investors in the US and in the UK', *Corporate Governance: an International Review*, 4:2 (April 1996), pp.107–22.

Malkiel, B. G. and A. Saha, 'HFs: Risk and Return', *Financial Analysts Journal*, 61:6 (2005).

Mangot M., 2005, *Psychologie de l'investisseur et des marches financiers*, Dunod.

Marco, L., *La Montée des Faillites en France, 19e–20e siècles* (Paris: L'Harmattanm, 1992).

Maréchal, C., *Meurtres à l'ombre de la qualité* (Paris: INSEP, 2002).

Mascret, H-F., *Dictionnaire des Faillites, 1848–1913* (Paris: Chez l'auteur, 1863).

Matalik, I., and M. Slavik, 'Fiscal Issues and Central Bank Policy in the Czech Republic', *BIS Papers*, 'Fiscal issues and central banking in emerging economies', 20 (Basel: BIS, 2003), pp. 122–30.

Matousek, R., and A. Taci, 'Direct Inflation Targeting and Nominal Convergence: The Czech Case', *Open Economies Review*, 14:3 (2003), pp. 269–83.

Mavrinac S., and T. Siesfeld, 'Measures that Matter: an Exploratory Investigation of Investor's Information Needs and Value Priorities ', *Actes du colloque 'Measuring Intangible Investment '*, OCDE (December 1998).Minow N., Monks R. A. G, *Corporate Governance*, 2nd edn (Oxford: Blackwell, 2001).

McQuerry, 'Managed Care for Brazilian Banks'. *Federal Reserve Bank of Atlanta Review*, 86:2 (2001), pp. 27–44.

Mena, J. M. M., and E. L. Errázuriz. 'The Chilean BancoEstado: Inclusive Finance, Expanding Borders' in K. Mettenheim and M.A.T. Lins (eds). *Government Banking: New Perspectives on Sustainable Development and Social Inclusion from Europe and South America.* (São Paulo: Konrad Adenauer Foundation Press, 2008), pp. 135–54.

Michel, G., 'Faillites', in L. Say and J. Chailley (eds), *Nouveau Dictionnaire d'Economie Politique* (A-H. Paris: Guillaumin et Cie 1900),

Milan, B., and C. Poutet. 'L'activité des Juridictions Commerciales en 2005' (Paris: Infostat Justice, 2006), p. 91.

Milgrom, P. R., D. C. North and B.R. Weingast, 'The Role of Institutions in the. Revival of Trade', *Economics and Politics*, 2:1 (1990), pp. 1–23.

Minsky, H. P., 'A Theory of Systemic Fragility', in E. Altman and A. Samaets, *Financial Crisis-Institutions and markets in a Fragil Environment* (New York: Wiley, 1977)

—, *Can it Happen Again?: Essays on Instability and Finance* (Armonk, NY: M. E. Sharpe, 1982).

—, *Stabilizing an Unstable Economy*, (New Haven, CT and London: Yale University Press, 1986).

MNB, *Annual Report* (Budapest: Magyar Nemzeti Bank, various years).

Monks, R. A. G., *The New Global Investors: How Shareholders Can Unlock Sustainable Prosperity Worldwide* (Oxford: Capstone Publishing, 2001).

Montgomery K. E., 'Survey of Institutional Shareholders', *Corporate Governance Review*, 5 (1992).

—, *Market Shift – the Role of Institutional Investors in Corporate Governance.*

Morin F., *Le modèle français de détention et de gestion du capital*, Lecture at the Ministre de l'Économie, des Finances et de l'Industrie, Les éditions de Bercy.

NBP, *Annual Report* (Warsaw: Narodowy Bank Polski, various years).

Nelson (ed.), *A Precarious Balance: Democracy and Economic Reforms in Latin America*, (Washington, DC: Overseas Development Council, 1994).

Neri, 'Miséria, Desigualdade e Políticas de Renda: O Real do Lula' (Rio de Janeiro: Centro de Política Social, FGV, 2008).

Noël, T., 'La Pratique du Droit de la Faillite dans le Ressort de la Cour d'Appel de Rennes au XIXe siècle – Les Prémices du Droit Economique' (Doctoral Thesis University of Rennes I, 2003).

O'Barr W. M., and J. M. Conley, *Fortune and Folly: the Wealth and Power of Institutional Investing* (Howewood, IL: Business One Irvin, 1992).

OECD, *Economic Survey of Hungary* (Paris: OCDE, 2004).

Orlean, A., *Le pouvoir de la finance* (Paris: Odile Jacob, 1999).

Parnaudeau, M., 'Natural Interest Rate and European Business Cycles: An Austrian Approach', *Economie Appliquee*, 40:2 (June 2007) pp. 5–28.

—, 'European Business Fluctuations in the Austrian Framework', *Quarterly Journal of Austrian Economics*, 11:2 (August 2008), pp. 94–105.

Pastré, O., 'Industrie bancaire : les espoirs des Davids face aux Goliaths ', *Revue d'Economie Financière*, 61 (2001), pp.53–62.

Peterson, R. L., 'An Investigation of Sex Discrimination in Commercial Banks' Direct Consumer Lending', *Bell Journal of Economics*, 12:2 (1981), pp. 547–61.

Phelps, E. S., 'The Statistical Theory of Racism and Sexism', *American Economic Review* 62:4 (1972), pp. 659–61.

Pinheiro, A. C. 'Uma Agenda Pós-Liberal de Desenvolvimento para o Brasil', IPEA Discussion Paper, 989 (October 2003).

Pochet, C., 'Traitement Légal de la Défaillance et Gouvernance : une Comparaison Internationale', *Revue Internationale de Droit Economique*, 4 (2001), pp. 465–88.

Polish Ministry of Finance, *Convergence Programme* (CP) (Warsaw: Polish Ministry of Finance, various dates).

Polish Ministry of Finance, *Pre-Accession Economic Programme* (PEP) (Warsaw: Polish Ministry of Finance, 2002).

Pons, *Cols blancs et mains sales* (Paris: Odile Jacob, 2006).

Rajan, R., and L. Zingales. 'Banks and Markets: The Changing Character of European Finance' (NBER Working Paper 9595, March 2003).

Rasmussen N. and Van Den Burg I., 'Capital Funds: A Critical Analysis', Draft Report, PSE, *European Parliament* (March 2007).

Recasens, G., 'Aléa Moral, Financement par Dette Bancaire et Clémence de la Loi sur les Défaillances d'Entreprises', *Finance*, 22:1 (2001), pp. 64–86.

—, 'Faut-il Adopter un Système Pro-Créanciers de Défaillances ? Une Revue de la Littérature', *Finance, Contrôle, Stratégie*, 6:1 (2003), pp. 119–53.

Rogoff, K., 'The Optimal Degree of Commitment to an Intermediate Monetary Target', *Quarterly Journal of Economics*, 100:4 (1985), pp. 1169–89.

Rothschild, K. W., *Ethik und Wirtschaftstheorie* (Tübingen: Verlag JCB, 1992).

Saleilles, R., 'Préface', in F. Gény (ed.), *Méthode d'Interprétation et Sources en Droit Privé Positif-Essai Critique* (Paris: Bibliothèque de jurisprudence civile contemporaine, 1899).

Samuels, D., 'Fiscal Straightjacket: The Political Economy of Macroeconomic Reform in Brazil, 1995–2002', *Journal of Latin American Studies*, 35 (2003), pp. 1–25.

Santella, P., *Le Droit des Faillites d'un Point de Vue Historique. Communication, Faculté de Droit de l'Université catholique de Louvain et Centre Jean Renauld. Louvain-la-Neuve* (2002).

Sgard, J., *The Liberalization of Bankruptcy Law in Europe* (Working paper, CEPII, 2005).

Sharpe W. and L. Tint, 'Liabilities : a new approach', *Journal of Portfolio Management* (Winter 1990), pp. 5–10.

Shiller, J., *The Subprime Solution. How Today's Global Financial Crisis Happened, and What to Do about it* (Princeton, NJ and Oxford: Princeton University Press, 2008).

Shleifer, A., and S. W. Vishny, 'Liquidation Values and Debt Capacity: a Market Equilibrium Approach', *Journal of Finance* (1992), 57:4, pp. 1343–66.

Siems, M. M., 'Numerical Comparative Law: Do We Need Statistical Evidence in Order to Reduce Complexity', *Cardozo Journal of International and Comparative Law*, 13 (2005), pp. 521–40.

Smith, R. C., and I. Walter, *Global Banking* (Oxford: Oxford University Press, 2003).

Social Investing Forum, ed. , *2003 Report on Socially Responsible Investing Trends in the United States*, (Washington, SIF Foundation, 2003).

Soinne, B., *Traité des Procédures Collectives* (Paris: LGDJ, 1995).

Solomon, J., *Corporate Governance and Accountability* (London: Wiley, 2007).

Stallings, B., and R. Studart. *Finance for Development* (Washington, DC: Brookings Institution, 2006).

Stapeldon, G. P., 'Exercise of Voting rights by Institutional Investors in the UK', *Corporate Governance: an International Review*, 3 (1995), pp. 144–55.

Stodder, J. 'Reciprocal Exchange Networks: Implications for Macroeconomic Stability', Working Paper, (Albuquerque, August 2000, available on line at www.appropriate-economics. org/materials/reciprocal_exchange_networks.pdf).

Studer, T., *Wir and the Swiss National Economy*, trans. P. H. Beard (Basel: Wir Bank, 1998).

Sylla, R., 'The Role of Banks', in R. Sylla and G. Toniolo (eds). *Patterns of European Industrialization in the 19th Century* (London: Routledge, 1991).

Taddjedine, Y., 1996, *Décisions financières, risques, politique prudentielle, mémoire mineur de DEA* (Paris: Université Paris X, 1996).

Tartarin, R., 'La Théorie des Droits de Propriété : vers un Historicisme Libéral?', in W. Andreff, A. Cot, R. Frydman, L. Gillard, F. Michon, R. Tartarin (eds), *L'économie-Fiction* (Paris: François Maspéro, 1982).

Thompson T. A., and G. F. Davis, 'The Politics of Corporate Control and the Future of Shareholders' Activism in the United States', *Corporate Governance*, 3:3 (1997).

Tripier, L., *Les Codes Français Collationnés sur les Editions Officielles* (Paris: Librairie de Jurisprudence de Cotillon, 1902).

Ulrich, P., *Transformation der ökonomischen Vernunft. Fortschrittsperspektiven der modernen Industriegesellschaft* (Stuttgart, Wien, 3. Aufl.: Haupt Verlag, 1993).

—, Integrative Wirtschaftsethik. Grundlagen einer lebensdienlichen Ökonomie, (Stuttgart, Wien: Haupt Verlag, 1997).

Vitols, S., 'Modernizing Capital: Financial Regulation and Long-Term Finance in the Post-war U.S. and Germany'. (Ph.D. Dissertation, Department of Sociology, University of Wisconsin, Madison, WI, 1996).

Von Hayek, F.A., 'Toward a Free Market Monetary System', *Journal of Libertarian Studies,* 3:1, (1979), pp.1–8.

Wagner, R., *Unternehmensführung, Ethik und Umwelt* (Wiesbaden, 1999).

Wermers R., 'Mutual Fund herding and the impact on Stock prices', *Journal of Finance*, 54, (1999), pp. 581–622.

White, M. J., 'The Cost of Corporate Bankruptcy : a U.S.-European Comparison', in J. S. Bhandari. (ed.), *Bankruptcy: Economic and Legal Perspectives* (Cambridge: Cambridge University Press, 1994).

Whitehead, L., and L. Sola (eds), *Statecrafting Monetary Authority: Democracy and Financial Order in Brazil*, (Oxford: University of Oxford Center for Brazilian Studies, 2006).

Woo, J. E., *Race to the Swift: State and Finance in Korean Industrialization.* (New York: Columbia University Press, 1991).

Woo-Cumings, M. (ed), *The Developmental State.* (Ithaca, NY: Cornell University Press, 1999).

Yinger, J., 'Evidence on Discrimination in Consumer Markets', *Journal of Economic Perspectives'* 12:2 (1998), pp. 23–40.

Zysman, J., *Governments, Markets and Growth: Financial Systems and the Politics of Industrial Change* (Oxford: Robertson, 1983).

INDEX

Note: page numbers in *italics* refer to figures or tables.